Dissident Discipleship

Published by Brazos Press
a division of Baker Publishing Group
P.O. Box 6287, Grand Rapids, MI 49516-6287
www.brazospress.com

Printed in the United States of America

Library of Congress Cataloging-in-Publication Data
Augsburger, David W.
    Dissident discipleship : a spirituality of self-surrender, love of God, and love of neighbor / David Augsburger.
        p.   cm.
    Includes bibliographical references.
    ISBN 1-58743-180-7 (pbk.)
    ISBN 978-1-58743-180-7 (pbk.)
    1. Spirituality—Anabaptists. 2. Spiritual life—Anabaptists. 3. Spiritual life—Christianity. 4. God—Worship and love. 5. Love—Religious aspects—Christianity. 6. Self-acceptance—Religious aspects—Christianity. I. Title.
    BX4931.3.A94 2006
    248.4'843—dc22   2005031102

Scripture marked KJV is taken from the King James Version of the Bible.

Scripture marked NASB is taken from the NEW AMERICAN STANDARD BIBLE®. Copyright © The Lockman Foundation 1960, 1962, 1963, 1968, 1971, 1972, 1973, 1975, 1977, 1995. Used by permission.

Scripture marked NEB is taken from *The New English Bible.* Copyright © 1961, 1970, 1989 by The Delegates of Oxford University Press and The Syndics of the Cambridge University Press. Reprinted by permission.

Scripture marked NIV is taken from the HOLY BIBLE, NEW INTERNATIONAL VERSION®. NIV®. Copyright © 1973, 1978, 1984 by International Bible Society. Used by permission of Zondervan. All rights reserved.

Scripture marked NKJV is taken from the New King James Version. Copyright © 1979, 1980, 1982 by Thomas Nelson, Inc. Used by permission. All rights reserved.

Scripture marked NRSV is taken from the New Revised Standard Version of the Bible, copyright 1989 by the Division of Christian Education of the National Council of the Churches of Christ in the USA. Used by permission.

Scripture marked RSV is taken from the Revised Standard Version of the Bible, copyright 1946, 1952, 1971 by the Division of Christian Education of the National Council of the Churches of Christ in the USA. Used by permission.

Dissident Discipleship

A Spirituality of Self-Surrender,
Love of God, and Love of Neighbor

David Augsburger

BrazosPress
Grand Rapids, Michigan

Contents

Introduction   7

1. The Practice of—***Radical Attachment***   23
   "Not believing in Jesus, but believing Jesus and believing what Jesus believed." (Core Christology)

2. The Practice of—***Stubborn Loyalty***   57
   "True community: where the person you like least always is; if that person dies or disappears, a worse takes the place." (Solidarity in Community)

3. The Practice of—***Tenacious Serenity***   85
   "Let go, let come, let be, let God; Get up, get going, get to it." (Willing Obedience)

4. The Practice of—***Habitual Humility***   99
   "Humility claimed is pride renamed." (Unpretentious Personhood)

5. The Practice of—***Resolute Nonviolence***   125
   "Because my life is in God's hands, I will never take my enemy's life into my hands." (The Way of the Cross)

6. The Practice of—***Concrete Service***   147
   "The best service ever seen, goes unseen, the best servants are, at their best, secrets." (Concern for Others)

7. The Practice of—***Authentic Witness***   171
   "Preach the gospel at all times; if necessary, use words." (Faithful Presence)

8. The Practice of—***Subversive Spirituality***   189
   "My nationality? Christian. My discipleship? Dissident. My spirituality? Subversive." (Dissident Discipleship)

Appendix One: Anabaptists Core Convictions   213
Appendix Two: The Politics of Jesus   217
Appendix Three: The Sermon on the Mount for
    Peditation   221
Appendix Four: The Jesus Prayer for Peditation   229
Appendix Five: Anabaptist Order of Communion   231
Appendix Six: The Discipleship Prayer   233
Bibliography   237

Introduction

This is a book about spirituality, not your ordinary garden variety, but the stubborn, persistent, radical spirituality appearing in unusual people across the last two thousand years who combined three strands—love for God, others, and self—in a unique way. This three-dimensional kind of discipleship that I call a tripolar spirituality links discovering self, seeking God, and valuing people into a seamless unity.

Spirituality, the real stuff of genuine spirituality, invariably boils down to some kind of the practice or apprenticeship in living that we call discipleship. We enter it by following a path, joining a quest, learning a new dimension, finding co-travelers, claiming a living tradition, accepting a guide, choosing a mentor. (Even a private, individualistic style of spiritual quest does the same—it follows a path of autonomous spiritual experience modeled by other such private persons, seeking a personal sense of wonder, awe, or reverence for life.)

Whatever sort of spirituality one is attracted to and eventually opts for, it takes a certain shape in its disciples. For example, take the spirituality that I discuss in this book.

It is about *discovering* a clear sense of self, a firm link to God, a sensitivity to others.

7

It is about *choosing*, not inheriting. It is a personal choice, voluntary, individual.

It is about *doing*, not high intentions. It is a set of practices for living out faith.

It is about *loving*, not civility. People matter. All people matter.

It is about *linking*, not individualism. It is a quest for real community.

It is about *serving*, not self-care. It is something you offer, concretely, caringly.

It is about *being*, not having. It is discovering authenticity and simplicity.

It is about *risking*, not withdrawal. It is constructive, courageous, bold.

It is about *reconciling*, not coexisting. It is open to healing and growth.

It is about *suffering*, not injuring. It is resolutely nonviolent and constructive.

This path of spirituality has appeared in various forms across two thousand years. It is a path worn bare by a particular line of spiritual people—a long thin line of spiritual dissidents that insistently reaches back to Jesus as mentor–originator–file leader for their a-bit-over-the-edge discipleship. People on this path are folks like Dietrich Bonhoeffer, Mother Teresa, St. Francis of Assisi, Thomas à Kempis, Gandhi, Tolstoy, Hans Denck, Michael Sattler, Menno Simons, Martin Luther King Jr., Desmond Tutu.

Some *groups* have pursued this path, like the community of people called Mennonites (or Anabaptists), and the best elements of Anabaptist spirituality have been taken and adapted by dozens of other groups that have often done them better. However, in this book we will draw on Anabaptism—the alternative to traditional, mainstream Catholic and Protestant spiritualities—that broke out in the sixteenth century as a revolutionary movement to recover a bare-bones discipleship to Jesus. This was a jolt in an era when there was little choice—the nation-state registered your religion and defined your spiritual path at birth. There was little freedom in living—worth was defined by birth, status, wealth, land ownership. There were limitations on loving—the powers declared who mattered and who didn't.

This is revolutionary stuff in the twenty-first century as well when spiritual passivity, collective helplessness, a sense of religious futility, and exhaustion with the disciplines of traditional spirituality have turned so many away from formal religion, church, doctrine, and theology. The Anabaptist alternative that continues in the Mennonite, Amish, and Brethren groups flows outside their boundaries and appears in Catholic, Protestant, and more particularly in charismatic and Pentecostal forms of spirituality. It is a cluster of practices of dissident discipleship, not a set of disciplines. It is an attitude of subversive spirituality, a stubborn set of commitments, a radical obedience to the Sermon on the Mount. It is a set of practices that return one to seeking a new attachment to Jesus. It is a constructive force when it crops up among Christians of many different heritages, histories, and traditions, and when it appears among those who recognize none. This is the spirituality we will be exploring in the following pages.

We call these practices spirituality because this is the word most frequently used to take the place of, or to fill the gaps between, terms like *religion*, *personal religious experience*, *reverence for life*, *unity with nature*, and *awareness of core humanity*. Various studies have listed over a hundred meanings for *spirituality* and have concluded that it is both one of our fuzziest concepts and one of the most appealing.

Spirituality has essentially replaced *religion* (which is deemed too public), displaced *faith* (too transcendent), nudged out *personal religion* (too narrow), and become preferable to *invisible religion* (too elusive). In popular usage it now refers to a privatized, individualized, nonrelational reverence for one's "unique humanness," "universal core," or "essential humanity."

The word *spirituality*, when used without a modifier, is a "glow word" that can be attached to persons, places, and things with a positive effect. It has become comfortingly vague and is usefully vacant, allowing people to insert and then extract meanings virtually at will. "The quest for the true essential meaning of spirituality is a fool's errand," Lucy Bregman has concluded after studying the uses of the concept over the last two decades. "As definitions of spirituality proliferated, these have enabled this one term to do double, indeed triple duty. . . . It is in the self-interest of many persons who like the term to keep it as loosely defined as possible; its meanings keep slipping and it can be relied on to fill gaps vacated by older terms, while at the same time pull in other meanings from other contexts" (Bregman 2004, 157).

In much contemporary usage, spirituality is a path of self-discovery. It is the secret of releasing and unfolding a deeper, wider, richer, gentler growing self. It promises, "You can be the you you long to be." In historic orthodox Christianity, spirituality is a path that leads beyond personal discovery to an encounter with a transcendent being, God. It promises, "You can come to know the God who knows you." As Rodney Clapp defines it, "Orthodox Christian Spirituality is participation and formation in the life of the church that is created and sustained by the Holy Spirit. . . . The *spirit*-uality of Christian spirituality draws its life and definition precisely from the Holy *Spirit* who is a person or a member of the Trinity" (Clapp 2004, 15).

From the first century until now, there has been a third way, a spirituality that unites three, not two strands—discovery of your true self, being discovered by the true God, and truly loving others who are the face of God to you. The three are inseparable. This way's promise: "You become you, God alone is God, we become we."

In this book there are many adjectives attached to the word *spirituality*. I write of lived spirituality, along with practiced, communal, relational, subversive, dissident, revolutionary, concrete, and thick spirituality; but the most frequently used designations are monopolar, bipolar, and tripolar spirituality. *Monopolar* refers to the discovery of an unfolding self, *bipolar* to the dual discoveries of depth of self and the height of the transcendent God, and *tripolar* to the inward, upward, and outward movements of the soul—or in other terms, the journey into the human soul, the quest for communion with the Divine, and the commitment to love and serve the neighbor.

The emerging vision of spirituality in the twenty-first century is largely monopolar and exclusively subjective. It is centered in the spiritual nature of the person, in the person's essential humanity and core humanness. This monopolar dimension is universal to all humans and necessary to their humanity.

Visiting the religious community of Findhorn, in northern Scotland, is a spiritual experience. Findhorn is one of the world's most creative experiments in gathering diverse people to construct a spiritually grounded community that seeks to live out its values "of planetary service, co-creation with nature and attunement to the divinity within all beings." They have no formal creed or doctrines except, as one leader said, perhaps tongue in cheek, "don't debate religion, don't smoke indoors, don't pick the flowers." The people work together in an ecologically responsible, mutually caring search to develop new ways of living infused with spiritual values expressed in almost exclusively monopolar spiritual language.

Monopolar spirituality, by definition, is the inner, subjective encounter with one's own inner universal self, with essential humanness that is reverent toward the uniqueness of the spiritual core that is universally present in all human beings. When respected, honored, expressed clearly, and realized more completely, it blossoms into the private inner experience of sacredness without sacred place, ritual, or tradition—of religiousness without formal religion. In fulfilling our unique humanness, we express our spiritual nature by becoming who we can truly and ought existentially to be and become. In its most individual forms, monopolar spirituality becomes a designer spirituality that each of us composes of themes and harmonies that are most consonant with our personality and preferences. As a shift from the purely mechanistic or largely utilitarian forms of secular value orientations, this is a welcome development of openness and creativity. All those interested in the advancement of spirituality in our world will welcome it as a new mood of exploration and emerging reverence. However, as it becomes more elusive of definition and inclusive of fantasy, superstition, and the magical, monopolar spirituality becomes a matter of mystics spelunking into their personal depths rather than an encounter with what is other. "Contemporary religious jargon so frequently refers to 'getting in touch with one's self.' These words replace what another age meant by 'seeking the face of God,' because we have lost confidence that anything beyond the self exists or can be trusted" (Palmer 1977, 10).

Monopolar spirituality is:

spiritual self-discovery,

spiritual oneness with nature, and

spiritual sensitivity to humankind.

Bipolar spirituality, by definition, is both an inner, subjective experience of coming to know one's true self and an objective experience of existence before God. It is the spirituality of a subjective, reflective life lived before the Transcendent, a life in search of and in compliance with the Divine. It questions whether one can know oneself apart from knowing God or can truly meet God as Other without humble knowledge of one's soul. It recognizes the need for self-knowledge and inner discovery, but sees them as inextricably linked to the divine presence and the moral demands it makes upon us. The inner pole of the soul is called to new life by meeting the divine Other; the self can now stand above the self as it participates in a transcendent pole. This new vision of who I am before a God who knows me as I am and accepts me in spite of what I am is a brush with a truth that is greater than my personal truth and leads to a transforming moment of grace that breaks through my narcissism. Spirituality in both Catholic and Protestant traditions has been and largely continues to be bipolar, possessing both a subjective and an objective side. It seeks to know a God who is truly there. It seeks through this relationship with the Divine to understand and to claim authentic freedom for the inner self.

As a professor at an evangelical seminary, I find that bipolar spirituality is the norm among my students and is assumed as a given in all faculty discussions and curricular planning. It is the standard understanding of mainstream Protestant Christianity, especially in the Reformed tradition. When people are challenged, they quickly affirm the third pole, but it is not assumed in discussion that arises naturally and directly from the basic assumptions.

Bipolar spirituality is:

discovery of, openness to, and participation in the Spirit;

neither self as spirit, nature as spirit, nor humanity as spirit;

but God as Spirit who calls us, God as Savior who redeems us, God as Origin who knows us, God as Presence whom we worship.

Tripolar spirituality, by definition, possesses three dimensions: it is inwardly directed, upwardly compliant, and outwardly committed. The spirituality of personal transformation (the inner journey), the experience of divine encounter (the God-ward journey) and the relation of integrity and solidarity with the neighbor (the co-human journey with friend and enemy, with neighbor and persecutor) cannot be divided. Tripolar spirituality sees all three as interdependent. No single one of these is fully valid apart from the other two; no single one can be truly experienced without the other two; no two can be extracted as primary or as actually present without all three. I come to know myself not alone, but in the company of fellow travelers; I come to know others not merely in collusion, but in shared commitment to the One who brings us together justly and safely in the triumphant surrender of ultimate trust. Inseparable, indivisible, the three poles of tripolar spirituality each define and determine the authenticity of the other parts.

For a decade I taught at an Anabaptist seminary. In any conversation about the nature of spirituality, people automatically and unselfconsciously assumed it to be tripolar. All three dynamics were included without question or exception.

Tripolar spirituality is the breakthrough in which:

love of God transcends and transforms love of self,

love of God and love of neighbor become one,

love of neighbor and love of self become one, and

submission to God and solidarity with neighbor are indivisible.

Spirituality as a monopolar in-search is an inviting quest, an open-ended question that appeals to persons who are habituated to a consumer culture and, having tried the wide range of other searches available, find the soul still empty and unfulfilled. Spirituality becomes the quest for wholeness, for a depth dimension that leads to a full and sensitive life.

Monopolar spirituality, crucial as it is in the first steps of opening the soul, and sensitive as it may be to an appreciation of an elusive, universal human essence, still remains attached to a single pole of experience.

Bipolar spirituality unites self and God and provides a referent outside the self. By defining spirituality as the tension between individual solitude and union with the Divine, it stimulates critique, reveals our finitude and brokenness as persons, and offers a divine vision to challenge human blindness. Crucial as these two poles are, the bipolar quest fails to situate the self in community and in vital, necessary relationships. When push comes to shove, it is ultimately about the individual and the singular relationship to God.

Tripolar spirituality, with its radical commitment to God-above-and-beyond-all yet God-for-us, and its daily practice of God-with-us-and-between-us-all, appreciates the neighbor in Christian love no matter the crises of threat and violence or the call of the nation-state to contradict the will of God on earth. Persons who find love of God inseparable from love of others discover that tripolar spirituality leads through love of God to love of neighbor (who stands in for God in our daily encounters) and ultimately to becoming a loved and loving self.

"To know one's true self and to know God" is the commonly quoted summary of St. Augustine's definition of the goal of spiritual life. In this dictum the father of bipolar spirituality has extracted two aspects as primary. When he makes reference to a third, he sees it as a desirable consequence to be sought whenever and wherever it is possible in the exigencies of each person's life situation and under the inevitable demands of society and the direction of the nation-state. If one must take up arms in self-defense or in military allegiance, bipolar spirituality presumes that though taking the neighbor's life into one's hands is a tragic event, it does not invalidate the spirituality of the one who does it in the name of God and country. In tripolar spirituality one pole cannot be split off without destroying the other two. In destroying my enemy, I destroy the integrity of my own soul. In taking my enemy's life into my hands, I do it (Jesus gave his own word on this) to Christ. When there is no selfward search, one becomes cut off from the spirituality of an open receptive soul by ignoring and betraying one's own being. When there is no God-ward longing, one becomes cut off from the divine transcendence of God-with-us by ignoring and betraying the call and claims of God upon one's life. When there is no equal reverence for the neighbor, one becomes cut off from (and in extremity, one cuts down) both God and neighbor by failing to see the neighbor as imaging God and failing to see the presence of God in the in-between.

Figure 1 shows the continuum of spirituality: first from monopolar spirituality through a spirituality of the mirrored self and on to a bipolar journey that links inner self-discovery with an encounter with the Divine; then making movement toward the other, initially as a service that springs from gratitude but has its survival limits, and finally culminating in radical commitment to live out love of God and neighbor in imitation of Christ.

Figure 1

Monopolar, Bipolar, and Tripolar Spirituality

1	1.5	2	2.5	3
Monopolar Spirituality	Mirror of Self: "My Own God."	Bipolar Spirituality	Benevolent Self that Serves God	Tripolar Spirituality
Spirituality of in-search and self discovery.	Spirituality of wish-fulfillment and projection.	Spirituality of God-encounter, God as Other.	Spirituality of gratitude, service, and neighbor love.	Spirituality of radical agape and enemy love.
I am a church of one, of me.	My god and I fulfill my life.	I know true self as I know God.	As I love God, I care for others.	I love God only as I love enemy.

Monopolar spirituality is professed by a friend who affirms, "My god is nature, the high Sierras my temple, the high I feel when hiking or climbing the only sacrament I need. I am never happier with myself than when by myself." Mirror-of-self spirituality is at least suggested by Deputy Undersecretary of Defense William Boykin, who concluded that Allah is not a "real god" and told Christian congregations how he was strengthened in his battle with a Muslim warlord in Somalia by his conviction that "my God was bigger than his." Bipolar spirituality is offered in the proclamation of a gospel that promises personal salvation through assent to basic spiritual laws, but is not an entrance to discipleship and a new relationship with the neighbor. Benevolent-self spirituality is the best of mainstream Christianity, Judaism, and Islam as one seeks to love God and to serve others in response to God's love. Tripolar spirituality is seen in many groups and places. In Christianity, it is the soul of Anabaptism, and it is practiced in Benedictine and Franciscan orders, the Catholic worker movement, and groups that practice radical discipleship in many denominations. In Judaism, Martin Buber's thought has influenced virtually all other religious groups to recover the irreducible value of a single life. In Islam, Sufism is a voice for unconditional love of God and other.

If, as in figure 1, we may call the three primary types 1, 2, and 3, then we may observe that since Christianity became Christendom in its union with the nation-state under Constantine in the fourth century (see chapter 5), Christian spirituality has largely varied between 1.5 and 2.5 on the continuum. The position at 1.5 relates the self to a mirroring god who reflects the individual hopes, understandings, and often pretensions of the self. The mirroring god may indeed be an extension of the self as one prays to a being created in one's own image. Type 2 recognizes a God who is Other and who makes divine demands that shape our lives. The benevolent-self position at 2.5 sees neighbor love as a desirable response of gratitude but not as essential to lived spirituality. When one reaches toward type 3 in theology and practice, tripolar spirituality brings all three aspects into a single unified field where God, self, and other all illumine, reflect, and express each other.

At 1.5 a warrior-saint may worship a god who goes along to war to destroy the enemy, or a prosperity religionist may offer a god who rewards the greed of the believer (if the greedy believer will help satisfy the preacher of prosperity's own greed). At 2 a believer may select texts that support a crusader spirituality and, while loving God, justify dominance, violence, and war. At 2.5 a philanthropist may aid the neighbor with generous gifts of well-earned or sometimes ill-gotten gain, or a just-war theorist may struggle with the dilemmas of war, striving to sort out primary and secondary allegiances while supporting the agenda of one state against that of another. All of these positions have been advanced as pathways of spirituality, and their travelers have quested for spiritual comfort and authority even when dealing in death or exploiting the poor.

As I write, I am recalling an obituary in this morning's *Los Angeles Times* that laments the death of one of the last surviving chaplains from the U.S. landing at Omaha Beach on D-Day during World War II. He is quoted as saying that as chaplain he was there "as a man of God, to lead men closer to God and to help with the morale, the families and loved ones, and to face up to the fact that they were called upon to kill people. War is one of those necessary evils in a world where nations are led by evil men" (Thurber 2004). In bipolar spirituality, the love of God enables us to face the difficult task of destroying stranger, enemy, and neighbor as part of our religious duty.

Tripolar spirituality is not a desirable consequence or an optional third way; it is not an extra or additive dimension. Rather, it is a radical alternative to both monopolar and bipolar spirituality. When love for God and neighbor are interdependent and inseparable, a pivotal redirection results, and an acute deviation from social norms ensues. Committing oneself to tripolar spirituality is making a painful decision to depart from cultural mandates and to risk countercultural actions motivated by a new agenda that becomes the prime factor revolutionizing one's life. In seeing the image of God in the other, we are opening ourselves to the One who is imaged. In turning to each other, we are turning to God, as Buber so often concluded.

The indivisible unity of the three poles is central to Jesus's teaching and is most explicit in his instructions on forgiving and being forgiven. The prayer at the center of the Sermon on the Mount, commonly called the Lord's Prayer, inseparably links forgiving and being forgiven. The prayer our Lord prayed from the cross (Luke 23:34) confirms that he lived as though—as well as taught that—forgiving and being forgiven are inextricably interwoven

(Matt. 6:12, 14; 18:34–35). Matthew is clear that "while God takes the initiative in forgiveness, the full and lasting experience of God's forgiveness is conditional on human forgiveness. The Matthean emphasis on human responsibility to forgive has long been neglected or misinterpreted in much Christian theological interpretation. And this has affected Christian practice. Matthew declares that Christians cannot receive the benefits of forgiveness without expressing these benefits in relationship to others" (Pokrifka-Joe 2001, 171–72).

Monopolar spirituality expresses itself in a forgiveness that accepts the other, tolerates differences, and enables the forgiver to claim closure—in order to set the self free, escape being held hostage, put the injury behind. Bipolar spirituality offers a forgiveness of obedience to divine command, a pardon that is unilateral and without condition, a release that asks for nothing from the other in superior benevolence. Tripolar spirituality gives a forgiveness that reaches out to the other, offers and awaits signs of genuine repentance, works to restore the relationship in an appropriate level of moral community. It recognizes that the goal of forgiveness is not one's personal relief or private release, but the hope of regaining the other as sister or brother (Matt. 18:15).

Advocates of this fully tripolar spirituality appear in the Pentateuch, Prophets, and Psalms, and they stretch from Mary the mother of Jesus, as expressed in her subversive psalm we call the Magnificat (Luke 1:46–55); to Jesus, its greatest teacher, model, and initiator; to Paul, Peter, James, and John who were clear articulators; and on to the early church fathers, such as Origen and Tertullian. Disciples practicing tripolar spirituality are scattered throughout the Middle Ages, and this form of spirituality breaks out stubbornly in St. Francis of Assisi, the Waldensians, and members of the larger movement of the left wing of the Reformation known as Anabaptists, in the sixteenth century.

Tripolar spirituality exists in many traditions and in a variety of forms among minority subgroups within the wider traditions of Judaism, Jainism, and Islam as well as within Orthodox, Catholic, and Protestant Christianity. Henri Nouwen and Thomas Merton offer two of the most widely known Catholic perspectives that embrace the unity of all three poles. Nouwen, for example, saw spirituality as linking three movements—reaching out to our inner-most self, reaching out to our fellow human beings, and reaching out to God. These three relationships teach us serene solitude, open hospitality, and authentic prayer (Nouwen 1996, xix). Jainism as a distinct religion within the tradition of Hinduism, and Sufism as a movement within Islam have adherents who unite reverence for the other, submission to the divine, and unfolding of the deeper nature of the soul into a coherent spirituality of tripolar concern. In Judaism there are those who embrace the threefold vision of inner devotion, obedience to the God of the Torah, and a life of good deeds that results in reverence and concern for every human life and teaches a shalom of radical peacemaking.

One of the longest-surviving countercultural Christian groups, the Anabaptists, have sought to live out a tripolar spirituality grounded in a restitution of the radical teachings of Jesus and his followers. The seriousness with which they have practiced this three-dimensional covenanting with God is evident in their communion liturgy, which asks for a threefold pledge of loyalty and radical willingness to suffer for the sake of God and neighbor as the full meaning of remembering Christ's death (see Appendix 5 for the liturgy). There are few streams of spirituality with the unique commitment to practicing all three aspects of this sort of obedience to the way of Jesus with the stubborn staying power necessary for sustaining community, but followers within many traditions have sought such faithfulness to Jesus.

Tripolar spirituality is neither the invention nor the property of any one Christian group. It is found not only in those groups calling themselves Anabaptist—it's not just for peace churches anymore—it is a widespread movement appearing in Protestant and Catholic streams of Christianity where the practice of dis-cipleship, the necessity of community, the radical attachment to the Jesus of the Sermon on the Mount, the life of service, and the commitment to sacrificial nonviolence are prized as central to spiritual life.

Rather than constructing a thin description that paints with a wide brush the common traits of all tripolar paths to spirituality, I will return frequently to a thick description of one community's flawed attempts to live out such a path over the past five hundred years. As Rodney Clapp writes about traditions of spirituality, "A lot of pyrite has gotten thrown in with the genuine gold, plenty of dingy coal with the bright diamonds, but we can have or accept none of the treasure they bore without shouldering the entire load. (Also, only time will tell how much trash our own generations are adding to the load, and how little gold)" (Clapp 2004, 14).

The Anabaptist form of tripolar spirituality is not the ordinary quest spirituality of individual discipline and discovery, but a communal spirituality of disciples (followers) following a cluster of practices, practices that are lived out in the relationships of community, where believers share in the rewarding struggles of faithful dialogue, discernment, and mutual discovery. Emerging churches around the world, renewal groups in historic confessions, creative experiments in the practice of discipleship, and parachurch groups that are training persons in the practices of discipleship, service, life in community, and authentic witness very often look to the Anabaptist movement for their inspiration and guidance. Whenever there is a fresh return to a spirituality of the imitation of Christ, there is usually a recognition of these roots in the sixteenth century, of those who sought to move the Reformation toward a spirituality of following Jesus daily in life. Such spirituality, in the Anabaptist tradition, is lived out in a distinctive cluster of traits or practices expressed in daily life, in work and in play—all experienced as worship. These seven are radical attachment, stubborn loyalty, tenacious serenity, habitual humility, resolute nonviolence, concrete service, and authentic witness.*

These seven practices, far from being unique to the radical wing of the Reformation, are shared by many other groups, some of which carry out one or several of them more faithfully and courageously than do Anabaptists. Dietrich Bonhoeffer, for example, in *The Cost of Discipleship*, maps radical allegiance to Jesus Christ at a depth perhaps no one else has done in centuries. But the simple, uncluttered, Jesus-focused, stubbornly loyal, humorously hum-

---

*In the German language that early Anabaptists spoke and wrote, these seven were called *nachfolge Christi* or *Juengerschaft*, *Gemeinshaft*, *Gelassenheit*, *Demut*, *Friedens-fertigkeit*, *Dienst am Naechsten*, and *Zeugnis or Beisein*.

ble, peacefully noncoercive, steadfastly serene, actively serving, and naturally sharing sort of spirituality of daily life that results from this particular cluster of traits is distinctively different from Catholic sacramentalism and the search for the holy, Protestant perfectionism and yieldedness to the sovereign God, charismatic piety and the rush of emotional enthusiasm, Holiness pursuit of goodness and entire sanctification, and Evangelical conversionism and triumphalism.

This is a spirituality of action on behalf of the neighbor, not just reflection on the desirability of being neighborly, of involvement in a committed life of relationships, not withdrawal and solitude. It is a spirituality of the feet, the knees, the hands, and the spine as well as the heart and the head, in contrast to spiritualities that are centered in contemplation, imagination, intuition, reflection, and meditation. Practices are a form of visible, not invisible spirituality, of action as embodied love and truth, worked out in everyday life "with a proper sense of awe and responsibility" (Phil. 2:12 Phillips).

In tripolar spirituality, we come to know Christ through participation in the practices of discipleship that express love of others and result in practices of inner depth. These three-dimensional practices of everyday spirituality are worked out in many different ways, but there is a common pattern, a familiar pathway with the guideposts that we will follow, chapter by chapter, as we trace the walk of the disciple in following Christ in daily life.

Hans Denck, an early Anabaptist theologian, leader, and martyr, wrote: "No one can know Christ truly except by following Him daily in life; And none can follow Him faithfully except those who truly know Him" (in Bauman 1991, 2). The strange name with which God identified himself to Abraham, often translated as "I am that I am," or "I will be what I will be," is better translated as "You will come to know me only as you follow me" (McClendon 1986, 182).

What is true of the Father is also true of the Son. We know him on the way. True spirituality is a spirituality of the road. We know him by following as we make the road by walking it, discover the way in obedient imitation, and participation in his life with us.

I come to know myself truly as a spiritual being by knowing God. I come to know who I truly am by being known by God. I come to know others by seeing in them the reflected image of God, the Other. I come to know this Other when meeting God in others, sister, brother, neighbor, stranger, friend, or enemy.

1

The Practice of—
Radical Attachment

"Do you believe the story of Jesus?
Do you believe in Jesus?
Do you believe Jesus?
Do you believe what Jesus believed?"

Radical attachment to Jesus is not believing something about Jesus (a pietistic experience), or believing in Jesus (a conversionist experience), but believing Jesus (in discipleship) and believing what Jesus believed (in imitation). So, as he believed, love of God, love of neighbor, and becoming one's true self are three indivisible sides of the primary spiritual triangle.

Core Christology

I am digging in the cactus garden that fronts our home when a voice calls me back from my concentration on plants and rocks.

"I've been watching the progress of the dry creek bed you are constructing. It's art replicating nature," says my neighbor from across the street.

"Thank you, Mrs. Guthrie," I reply. "I'm doing my best to imitate a desert stream, and being on sabbatical gives me time to add a few rocks or cacti each day when I take a break from writing."

"I spent my life in education, but never received a sabbatical. Fourth grade, Baldy View Elementary, Upland."

"Baldy View? I had two girls, Deb and Judy, at Baldy View in the early seventies, but probably not in the fourth grade."

"So many children come and go," she says. "Wouldn't that be a surprise if one of them was in my class thirty years ago."

A week later, I'm again on my knees in the rocks, and she interrupts my digging.

"I've something to show you," she says, and holds out a school picture of smiling fourth graders: "There, third row, see?" She is pointing to my little golden-haired daughter.

"She wrote me when you moved back east, to Virginia, I believe. I remember her well. She hid novels in her desk, books for grown-ups, and read at every possible moment."

"Yes, *Lord of the Rings*, instead of California history," I say as my memories flood back of the extremely bright little girl and her fondness for a special teacher whose name was as familiar as Frodo's.

I look at her wide-eyed: "You're not Mrs. Guthrie," I say. "You're THE MRS. GUTHRIE."

Which Jesus?

One can be familiar with the Jesus story, be an admirer of Jesus as a uniquely self-aware yet selfless person, know a great deal about the historical Jesus, be taught a helpful perspective on who Jesus is from the practice of a religious faith, and love Jesus in an experience of personal piety, yet fail to enter the encounter of discipleship in which one recognizes Jesus not as the popular, the mythical, the devotional, or the civilly religionist, but as the one who said "come and die." Only when one encounters Jesus as

Jesus will one feel the rush of surprise. "You're not Jesus Christ. You're JESUS THE CHRIST."

The images of Jesus absorbed from the pictures of popular culture; learned from the beliefs of parents, family, and church; collected from the distorted profiles of popular dramas; extracted from the reductionistic characterizations of denominational emphases; created from unconscious need for an archetype of perfection; woven from the projections of infantile need for an idealized image—all these prompt one to ask, Which Jesus are you quoting? Which Jesus do you cite as authority? Which Jesus is focal in your spiritual journey?

> Most churchfolk in American Christendom, especially those of a white, bourgeois background, have for generations, in both Sunday School and Sanctuary, been furnished with an impression of Jesus as a person who went briefly about teaching love and doing good deeds: gentle Jesus, pure Jesus, meek Jesus, pastoral Jesus, honest Jesus, fragrant Jesus, passive Jesus, peaceful Jesus, healing Jesus, celibate Jesus, clean Jesus, virtuous Jesus, innocuous Jesus. (Stringfellow 1976, 6)

If we speak of a radical attachment to Jesus as the original pathway to Christian spirituality, there must be clarity at the outset about where these roots are going and to whom this attachment is growing. In this study of a spirituality of radical Jesus attachment, I will be looking at rootedness into the Jesus of the Gospels. In the midst of all the characterizations, novelizations, cinematic portrayals, simplified caricatures, and pious reductions that surround us, those who take this path will be invited to return to the original narratives and seek the Jesus who walks through the accounts given us by Matthew, Mark, and Luke and appears in the theological portrait by John, to penetrate deeply into these texts as the proper ground for putting down roots.

Radical (from the root) and attachment (rooted and grounded in attached solidarity) are metaphors for those essential spiritual rhizomes of discipleship that link the believer to the originator of Christian faith and practice. The source of these metaphors is in Paul's Colossian letter, where we read: "Therefore, since Jesus was delivered to you as Christ and Lord, live your lives in union with him. Be rooted in him; be built in him; be consolidated in the faith you were taught" (Col. 2:6–7 NEB). And in the Ephesian letter the identical metaphor of central taproots is employed to describe not individual experience but the shared life of a community of persons with radical rootstock. "With deep roots and firm foundations, may you be strong to grasp, with all God's people, what is the breadth and length and height and depth of the love of Christ, and to know it, though it is beyond knowledge. So may you attain to fullness of being, the fullness of God himself" (Eph. 3:17–19 NEB).

German theologian Jürgen Moltmann, astounded and scandalized that American Christians took his book *Theology of Hope* to be a message of optimism about progress and prosperity, wrote a second book, *The Crucified God*, as a rebuttal that called for radical commitment. As he describes the resistance of the cross to all its interpreters and false interpreters, he writes:

> To be radical, of course, means to seize a matter at its roots. Radical Christian faith can only mean committing oneself without reserve to the "crucified God." This is dangerous. It does not promise the confirmation of one's own conceptions, hopes and good intentions. It promises first of all the pain of repentance and fundamental change. It offers no recipe for success. But brings a confrontation with the truth. It is not positive and constructive, but is in the first instance critical and destructive. It does not bring man into a better harmony with himself and his environment, but into contradiction with himself and his environment. It makes him "homeless" and "rootless," and liberates him in following Christ who was homeless and rootless. "The religion of the cross," if faith on this basis can ever be so called, does not elevate and edify in the usual sense, but scandalizes; and most of all it scandalizes one's "co-religionists" in one's own circle. . . . It alienates alienated men, who have come to terms with alienation. (Moltmann 1973, 39)

Participating as the Soul of Imitating

Authentic spirituality, which I am calling tripolar spirituality to clearly identify it as fully three dimensional, is self transforming,

God encountering, and other embracing. It accepts no substitute for actual participation.

Participation is something we do, just as imitation is something we become. Participating is the soul of all active imitation of Christ. Radical attachment, in tripolar spirituality, is observable. It is visible connectedness with Christ and with others lived out in identifiable, recordable, measurable relationships. Our actual daily relationships form this threefold participation. We are connected to Christ, to others, to the world we inhabit. We participate in Christ's life by reflecting him to our world, and through this we are participants in the lives of others who reflect him, so we join with them to participate in all of life as fellow participant disciples. We are not observers, not spectators, not admirers, not onlookers, not conceptualizers, but participants. Participation is the central theological framework of all careful thought about spirituality "because any alternative configuration perforce reserves a territory independent of God . . . leading only to nihilism (though in different guises). *Participation*, however, refuses any reserve territory" (Milbank 1999, 3). I no longer have private territory apart from God. There is no place to hide, nowhere to go that is not available to God's participation in my existence, and I am invited to participate as a disciple in God's life in the world. The ideal of discipleship as participation through the imitation of Christ is a recurring theme, reemerging wherever the practice of following Jesus in life is given priority. Anabaptist theologian-martyr Hans Denck put it tersely: "One who claims to belong to Christ must follow the path taken by Christ" (quoted in Bauman 1991, 50).

Beginning with the explicit teaching of the epistles, appearing in the selection of stories and the depiction of Jesus in the Gospels, and repeated in the writings of the apostolic fathers, the line of imitation runs through a rich stream of writers on spirituality, from St. Paul, through such as Irenaeus (c. 130–200) and the desert fathers (second to fourth centuries), to Augustine (354–430) and his opponent Pelagius (c. 354–415). "The gist of religion is imitation of him who is worshiped," Augustine wrote ("Religionis summa imitari quem colis," *City of God*, 8.17). Francis of Assisi (1182–1226), radical advocate of renewal, sought "to follow the footsteps of Christ in repetition"—"*repetitor Christi*," Leonardo Boff

calls him. The theme continues in the work of Francis's disciple
and biographer Bonaventura (1221–1274), Meister Eckhart (c.
1260–1327), John Tauler (1300–1361), Henry Suso (1295–1366),
and the Rhineland Friends of God, who produced the *Theological
Germanica*; Jan van Ruysbroeck (1293–1381) and his disciple Gerard Groot (1340–1384), who founded the Brethren of the Common Life, out of which came Thomas à Kempis (1380–1471);
Julian of Norwich (1342–1416), Teresa of Ávila (1515–1582), Igna-
tius of Loyola (1491–1556), Hans Denck (c. 1496–1527), Michael
Sattler (died 1527), Menno Simons (1496–1561), and Balthasar
Hubmaier (died 1528); and Jacob Boehme (1575–1624), William
Law (1686–1761), Charles de Foucauld (1858–1916), Friedrich
Schleiermacher (1768–1834), Søren Kierkegaard (1813–1855),
and Dietrich Bonhoeffer (1906–1945).

"Which is it?" Kierkegaard asked:

> Is God's meaning, in Christianity, simply to humble us through the
> model (putting before us the ideal) and to console us with "Grace,"
> but between God and humanity there is no relationship, that we
> must express our thankfulness like a dog to a man, so that the
> adoration becomes more and more true, and more pleasing to God
> as it becomes less and less possible for us that we could be like the
> model? Is that the meaning of Christianity? Or is it the very reverse,
> that God's will is to express that he desires to be in relations with
> us, and therefore desires the thanks and the adoration which is in
> Spirit and truth: imitation. The latter is certainly the meaning of
> Christianity. But the former is a cunning invention of us men in
> order to escape from real relation to God. (Kierkegaard 1938/1951,
> 474 [Item 1272])

What Would Jesus Do?

Imitation is the primary way we go about forming identity. Initially we identify with significant persons, then we internalize these
identifications into a new configuration of images, loyalties, and
commitments that define who we are. Imitation then matures to
voluntary participation, but the correspondence of the internalized
model to the external example remains as an enduring relationship

that continues to guide the added layers of the personality. In spirituality, as Kierkegaard so pointedly said, the gratitude, admiration, and adoration of identification with the other is in actuality lived out in imitation. So in its simplest form, discipleship is expressed by asking, "What would Jesus do?"

"What would Jesus do?" is the phrase inspired by Charles M. Sheldon over a century ago in his 1896 novel, *In His Steps*, which tells the story of a transforming moment in a pastor's life that evoked a sweeping renewal of faith in a dormant church. The widespread contemporary use of this concept (WWJD) among pietistic groups inspires a courageous imitation of Christ in personal life—often an individual pursuit of whatever image of Jesus the follower may possess. In asking "What would Jesus do?" and "What would Jesus not do?" the disciple links her ethical or relational decisions to particular teachings or actions recalled from the life of Christ. When ready examples do not spring to mind or parallel situations are hard to find, serious reflection leads the spiritual traveler to a more basic question: "What did Jesus do?"

"What did Jesus do?" is a question only answered by return to the synoptic Gospels to reexplore the actual relational, intentional, ethical, political, and missional behavior of Jesus. It takes the follower deeper into the actual life of Jesus as model, claims this story as mentor-story for life decisions, affirms the story as the revelation of ultimate goodness, and judges all human values (the good that we value and prize) by enduring virtues (the good with intrinsic value in and of itself). The disciple seeks to understand what Jesus did and how he went about responding to human need, and to follow his example as the most direct way of living by grace and truth. Inevitably this moves the disciple to develop theological constructions to explore the subsequent question: "What would Jesus have me do?"

"What would Jesus have me do?" This is the question of theology (theology is faith seeking understanding in an actual situation) that introduces new formulations—theological, ethical, and political—into the simple equations of imitation. Theology translates the model, values, and virtues of the one imitated into affirmations, propositions, and logical schemas for reflection and action. As faith seeks understanding of a particular cultural

and historical moment, it struggles to work out a coherent set of understandings that inevitably rank, select, sacralize, and enact clusters of principles appropriate to the thought of a particular culture, era, and social location. What Jesus embodied and lived in the ancient Near East is reformulated in the language and metaphors of a contemporary culture. In the process, Jesus inevitably gets translated, usually adjusted, often adapted, and sometimes co-opted to fit the more acceptable, to face the "hard realities," and bless what we consider necessary and inescapable. Such theologies about Christ may, and in fact often do, lead us away from simply seeking an understanding of "following after Christ" in wholehearted and loving imitation. It is the commitment to imitation that calls the disciple to look for the presence of Jesus in the present situation and ask, "What is Jesus doing here and now among us?"

"What is Jesus doing here and now among us?" With this question we move from the "there and then" of history and the "what and how" of theology to the "here and now" of the actual presence of Jesus. We can embrace Jesus as an experiential model with existential impact, as a historical mentor-story with textual authority, or as a theological Christ figure with rational conceptual coherence. Or we can encounter him as a contemporary presence in a believing community—that is, an imitating, participating community. Participation is a communal awareness of Christ in our midst; it is a liturgical recognition and celebration of his presence; it is a mystical moment of awe that an Other is undeniably here; it is an ethical experience of discerning together God's intentions for us; it is an encounter with a Third who walks with any two disciples as living presence; it is a deep, settled conviction that we are invited to continue his work in faithful extension of his way of being; it is discovering that we can be fully human as we follow him yet that we can imitate and participate in the Divine; it is revisualizing every encounter with human need as an opportunity to serve Christ himself; it is asking in such moments the question he taught us to ask: "What do I do with Jesus?"

"What do I do with Jesus?" transforms the meeting with a needy or needed neighbor; it offers the privilege of reaching out

and touching Jesus in those we encounter in daily life. Instead of seeing such meetings as irritations in our important schedules, we see them as divine interruptions. Instead of being preoccupied with ourselves as followers—asking "Am I an accurate reflection of Jesus the model, an adequate imitation of Jesus the example?"—we shift our focus to concern for the other. Then we ask the first question that St. Paul stammered out when he realized he was in the presence of Jesus: "What do you want me to do?" (Acts 9:6, author's paraphrase).

"Jesus, what do you want me to do?" is the question that marks the first step of discipleship: "Perhaps God has something for me to do with this life of mine."

"Inasmuch as you did it to one of the least of these My brethren, you did it to me" Jesus says to the righteous in his description of final judgment. In this account the unrighteous ask, "When did we see You hungry or thirsty or a stranger or naked or sick or in prison, and did not minister to You?" To which the Master replies, "inasmuch as you did not do it to one of the least of these, you did not do it to Me" (Matt. 25:40, 44–45 NKJV). Every act of service, of sharing, of offering care to somebody in need is an act of service to the One represented, the One who identified himself with the sufferer.

At the Sojourners Neighborhood Center, twenty blocks from the White House, the volunteers who will be serving on the food line for homeless people join hands for prayer. Mrs. Mary Glover, a sixty-year-old African-American woman prays, "Lord, we know that you'll be comin' through this line today. So help us to treat you well" (Wallis 1994, 51).

What I do or do not do to someone in need, I do or do not do to Jesus. The disciples' question is not, "What would Jesus do?" The question is "What do I do with Jesus?" It is Jesus I meet in the abused, in the needed, in the angry, in the enemy. As Mother Teresa said as we walked among pallets of dying men, "This is suffering Jesus, and this . . . is vomiting Jesus . . . and this is dying Jesus." When the unlovely other can be seen as the embodiment of Christ, the pinched face of suffering recognized as the face of Christ, then every other becomes the Other. This is where the second and third poles of spirituality become one.

The "As-So" Model of Spirituality

Immanuel Kant the philosopher wrote that if *is* is the copula of understanding, joining subject and predicate, then *as* can be called the copula of the imagination. *As* connects something not well-known to something better known (Spohn 2000, 61). *As, just as, likewise,* and the *"as-so"* couplets offer analogies for the analogical imagination by which we envision practices, visualize virtues, and see ethics in lived situations that can be replicated in our lives in transforming ways. Understanding these analogies—the *as-so* comparisons—teaches us to spot the rhyme so our lives will come not to repeat Christ's life but to rhyme with it.

> Christian practices have what we may call an "as-so" structure (or correspondence structure): as God has received us in Christ, so we too are to receive our fellow human beings. True, the way in which Christ's life is exemplary has to be carefully specified. Above all, the important difference between Christ and other human beings should counter both the temptation to supplant Christ and the presumption that human beings can simply "repeat" Christ's work. But in an appropriately qualified way, in relation to the practice of hospitality as well as in relation to all other practices, we must say: As Christ, so we. (Volf and Bass 2002, 250)

As your father is compassionate, so you must be compassionate; as you have been forgiven, so you must forgive. These are characteristic phrases with the structure explicit or implicit all throughout the teachings of Jesus, concluding with "As the Father sent me, so I send you" (John 20:21 NEB). In the prayer Jesus taught to his disciples, the central copula is as in heaven, so on earth (Matt. 6:10).

St. Paul picks up this same *as-so* paradigm to exhort us to practice obedient and faithful imitation in mirroring the call, model, and example given to us.

> As God has called each, so let each walk (1 Cor. 7:17).
> As Christ was raised from the dead, so we might also live anew (Rom. 6:4).

As Christ accepted us, so we should accept one another (Rom. 15:7).

As you received Christ Jesus as Lord, so walk in him (Col. 2:6).

As God in Christ has forgiven us, so we should forgive one another (Eph. 4:32).

As we have worn the likeness of the man made of dust, so we shall wear the likeness of the heavenly man (1 Cor. 15:49).

The *as-so* analogy may also be implicit, as in Romans 6:4, 6, and 11. The analogy is clearly *"As* Christ is dead to sin and alive to God, *so* likewise you are dead to sin and alive to God." The *indicative*—what Christ has done for us—is followed by the *implicative* of a moral, relational, mimetic call. The already/not yet tension of "God has acted/now you act in response" or "sin is destroyed/but not yet eliminated" is sustained as the *as-so* indicative-imperative. The model is lifted up for us; the practice is commended to us. The paradigm is set forth in person, story, and practice; the pursuit of it is defined for our participation.

The model is imitated, the practice is the participative realization. Thus we speak of imitation/participation as the *as-so* character of discipled practice. Jesus intended that as he lived, so would his disciples. E. J. Tinsley's argument—"If the life of the Lord is an imitation of the Father, the life of the disciple is an imitation of Christ"—is a clear *as-so* couplet. The disciple lives out the story of the One who lived out God's story by deliberately walking in his way. As Jesus lived in imitation of the Father, so our life as disciples is to imitate him (Tinsley 1960, 100–101).

"There is no general concept of living like Jesus in the New Testament," John Howard Yoder notes. When Paul argues for celibacy or for a widow not remarrying, he does not appeal to Jesus's example; when he explains at length his own employment as an artisan (1 Cor. 9), he does not refer to Jesus's work as a carpenter. When speaking of his mission and teaching style, there is no reference to the formation of a circle of disciples for training, no imitation of prayer, parabolic communication, association with villagers, preferences for desert places or mountains. The imitation is clearly focused on "the concrete social meaning of the cross in its relation to enmity and power. Servanthood replaces dominion, forgiveness absorbs hostility. Thus—and only thus—are we bound by New Testament thought to 'be like Jesus'" (Yoder 1972, 131).

The *As-So* Couplet as Correspondence

Jesus's initial summons to this participative life of correspondent imitation was a simple "Follow me." The way of the disciple is the imitation of the Master, "It is enough for a disciple that he be like his teacher," Jesus said (Matt. 10:25 NKJV). "The disciple is not above his master; but everyone, when his training is complete, will reach his master's level" (Luke 6:40 NEB). In Mark, for example, Jesus sees two fishers and says, "follow Me, and I will make you become fishers of men" (1:17 NKJV); to a tax collector he simply says, "follow me" (2:14 NEB); to the multitude, "If anyone would come after me, he must deny himself and take up his cross and follow me" (8:34 NIV); to the rich young ruler, "One thing you lack: go, sell everything you have, and give to the poor, and you will have riches in heaven; and come, follow me" (10:21 NEB). The blind man who could see again "followed him on the road" (10:52 NEB).

"Correspondence/participation" comes from two traditions, the following after and learning from of *discipleship*, and the structuring and patterning of one's life after a model of *imitation*. The concept of correspondence as imitation exists throughout the Hebrew scriptures, from the creation account where humans image their Creator, through the holiness codes, to the prophets, and emerges most clearly in the Christian scriptures.

John Howard Yoder has outlined this succinctly, with appropriate textual citations for the correspondence between disciple and Master (Yoder 1972, 115–27):

1. The life of the disciple or participant corresponds to the love of God: sharing the divine nature is the definition of Christian existence (1 John 1:5–7; 3:13). Forgiving as God has forgiven you is the practice of that love (Eph. 4:32; Col. 3:13), a love

that has no limits since we are to love indiscriminately as God does (Luke 6:32–36).

2. The life of the disciple or participant corresponds to the life of Christ: being in Christ is the definition of Christian existence (1 John 2:6).This requires having died with Christ and sharing his risen life (Rom. 6:6–11; 8:11)—loving as Christ loved, giving himself (John 13:34; 15:12); serving others as he served (John 13:1–17; 2 Cor. 5:14; 8:7–9); and subordination in revolutionary relationships (Col. 3:18–4:1).

3. The life of the disciple or participant corresponds to the death of Christ: suffering with Christ is the definition of apostolic existence (Phil. 3:10–11; 2 Cor. 4:10). This is voluntarily sharing in the divine condescension of Jesus (Phil. 2:3–14), which includes a willingness to give your life as he did (Eph. 5:1–2); embracing suffering servanthood in place of dominion (Mark 10:42–44); accepting innocent suffering without complaint as he did (1 Peter 2:20–21); being willing to suffer with or like Christ the hostility of the world, as a bearer of the kingdom cause (Luke 14:27–33); recognizing that death is liberation from the power of sin (1 Peter 4:1–2); realizing that death is the fate of the prophets and that Jesus, whom we follow, was already following them (Luke 24:19–20; Acts 2:36); and proclaiming that death is victory (Col. 2:15; 1 Cor. 1:22–24).

The way begins in renunciation (Mark 8:34; Luke 14:33) and proceeds in obedience (Mark 3:35; Luke 6:46), in walking humbly (Mark 10:42–45), in service (Mark 9:35; Luke 22:27), and in the acceptance of suffering, persecution, and abuse (Mark 10:39, Matt. 5:39) like the suffering servant of Isaiah (50:6, 8; 53:1–12). The very pervasive theme, perhaps the most widespread, is participation or correspondence, in which the believer's behavior or attitude is said to "correspond to" or reflect or "partake of" the same quality or nature as that of the Lord (Yoder 1972, 113).

In the Christian scriptures, identifying with Christ, conformity with his life, participation in the divine nature, sharing in Christ's risen life, being in Christ and letting Christ be in us all express this correspondence between model and follower. Imitation is the spiritual modus operandi of the disciple's existence. The imitative life of the Christian does not injure her individuality or creativity. Through the work of the Holy Spirit the relationship between the historical paradigm of the Lord's life and the life of the Christian imitator is active and reciprocal. The Lord who shaped the form of his historical ministry shapes the form of his followers through the personal and creative work of the Holy Spirit (Tinsley 1960, 178–79).

Imitation: Practicing the Life

Discipleship is always more than imitation (mimesis); never-theless, imitation is at the heart of discipleship. The New Testament treatment of the idea of imitating Christ—indeed, the selection of incidents from the life of Christ for recording in the Gospels (Dodd 1958, 85)—all offer this motif for thought and this discipline for practice to the disciple.

"Be imitators of me, just as I also am of Christ," Paul told the Corinthians (1 Cor. 11:1 NASB), and he repeated the invitation throughout this first letter (1 Cor. 4:11–16; 10:31–11:1). To the Thessalonians he wrote that he and his companions "give you in our conduct an example to imitate" (1 Thess. 3:9 RSV; note also 1:6–7; 2:14). He instructed the Ephesians, "Therefore be imitators of God, as beloved children; and walk in love, just as Christ also loved you and gave Himself up for us" (Eph. 5:1 NASB). Imitation of God is clearly identified and embodied for us in Christ.

> The error comes in . . . when we set before ourselves the idea of God the Father, or of the Absolute, instead of Christ, as the object of imitation. . . . Mystics of all times would have done well to keep in their minds a very happy phrase which Irenaeus quotes from some unknown author: "He spoke well who said that the infinite *(immensum)* Father is measured *(mensuratum)* in the Son *(mensura enim Patris filius)*." It is to this measure, not to the immeasurable, that we are bidden to aspire. (Inge 1899, 193)

The call to imitation takes a variety of forms and recommends various patterns for living. For example, Christians are not to be motivated by what pleases themselves precisely because "Christ did not please himself" (Rom. 15:3 NIV); they are to be generous because of Jesus's example in that "though he was rich, yet for your sake He became poor, so that you through His poverty might become rich" (1 Cor. 8:9 NASB); they are to be humble and obedient because "he humbled himself and became obedient to the point of death" (Phil. 2:8 NRSV; see also 3:17–18 NRSV). The most expressive call to imitation is in the Christ hymn in the letter to the Philippians (Phil. 2:1–11), and the writer of the letter to the Hebrews makes multiple uses of the call (6:12; 12:1–3; 13:7).

The one explicit passage in which we are commanded to imitate Christ is in the exhortation to nonviolently offer gentle love in response to abuse:

> Because Christ suffered on your behalf, and thereby left you an example; it is for you to follow in his steps. He committed no sin, he was convicted of no falsehood; when he was abused he did not retort with abuse, when he suffered he uttered no threats, but committed his cause to the One who judges justly. In his own person he carried our sins to the gibbet, so that we might cease to live for sin and begin to live for righteousness. (1 Peter 2:21–24 NEB)

This call to mimetic behavior also comes through clearly in the many invitations to "follow," and frequently in explicit commands to replicate the pattern shown in Jesus or revealed of God. "Be compassionate as your Father is compassionate" (Luke 6:36 NEB). "Love one another as I have loved you" (John 13:34 NKJV).

When imitation is internalized within identity (Gal. 2:20), the one imitating looks to the present Christ—not to the model of the historical Jesus of the past but to the continuing activity of the Jesus Spirit experienced in the self. Imitation is the medium for the activity of this Spirit of Christ working within "until Christ is formed in you" (Gal. 4:19 NASB).

The fundamental conception in Pauline thought that unites believers to their Savior Jesus Christ is the "in Christ" stream of emphasis, so pervasive that entire epistolary discourses are shaped by it (Romans 6 and 8; Ephesians 1) (Swartley 2000, 238). Willard

Swartley notes the *co-* constructions in these passages. They carry the Greek prefix *sun-*, which means "with." We are co-buried, co-united, co-crucified; we have co-died and now we co-live, co-inherit, and co-suffer as we are co-glorified and co-formed into the Son-of-God image to become sisters and brothers with Christ (Rom. 8:29). "The life of Jesus' followers is profusely and consistently described as a relation between Jesus as *model* and his followers as *imitators-disciples* in self-giving love, service, and suffering" (Swartley 2000, 239).

Catholic ethicist William Spohn, in his rich study on character ethics, concludes that "imitation of Christ is the touchstone for Christian moral discernment in Paul. Exhortations to imitate Christ punctuate Paul's letters; the imitation of Christ is the ethical subtext of all of them" (Spohn 2000, 146).

Mimesis—Central to Humanness

Mimesis is central to all human behavior. The penchant to copy, in one's own style, the language, dress, manners, and images presented by the surrounding culture is an essential part of the process of achieving identity through making and then internalizing identifications. Copying behavior is the major life task not only of young children; youth are also either busy copying others' behavior or urgently searching for models they might copy. In the ongoing process of imitating, we claim the human characteristics of those about us, and we may also incorporate less-than-human elements of character. In his chapter titled "Imitating Jesus in a Time of Imitations," Michael Warren writes:

> Intentional religious practice . . . needs a stance if it is to avoid being sucked into the vortex of commercial orchestration culture and if it is to contest that culture. Someone could rightly say, "We already have a stance, the gospel." But that answer begs the question. Which gospel are we talking about, the Reverend Jerome Fallbadly's, or Ignacio Ellacuría and Oscar Romero's?

He goes on the describe the gospel he hears preached:

... a version of religious Reaganomics: "Are you religiously better off—filled with more religious comfort—now than you were four years ago?" . . . "Move ahead; move up; have more." Or the self-enhancement ads: "You are the best; have the best." Their religious form is: "You are good, and God's love makes you a better you. There's nothing to worry about. Pray and put everything in God's hands." Or the genre of "pamper yourself" ads: "God wants you to be happy, to feel better about yourself." In other words, get more of the religious capital or get more of the religious goods, and you'll be more secure. These are the "Be-Happy Attitudes," and they emanate not only from the Crystal Cathedral, but from a variety of religious edifices. . . . These are not stances that question the dominant culture; instead they embody it. (Warren 1992, 254)

The imitation of Christ commits the believer to obedience to both the message and the "method" of Jesus. The incarnation is seen as the way God would have his truth taught, and this same manner must be reflected in any presentation of the gospel of the incarnation. The form of the gospel is part of its content (Tinsley 1960, 180).

Sorting Out Attachment

Eccentric ethicist and Anabaptist prophet Clarence Bauman was fond of asking students rapidly, in speech made almost indecipherable by Parkinson's disease, "Do you believe something *about* Jesus—do you believe in Jesus—do you believe Jesus—or do you believe what Jesus believed?" He would wait with rapt attention to see what kind of belief or understanding of belief the student would offer. Then he would gently suggest that "Correct belief *about* Jesus, important as it is, or pietistic experience of believing *in* Jesus, meaningful as it may be, only *point* one toward discipleship. Becoming a disciple requires actually believing the Master and slowly coming to believe what the Master believed."

Christian spirituality breaks open into such an actual encounter with Jesus, meets Jesus again as at first sight when one takes the risky and demanding step of "believing Jesus." An even more difficult step is to "believe what Jesus believed." Then one makes an attachment to this Jesus as a vivid presence, an actual co-traveler in life. The question "What would Jesus do?" is no longer a sentimental piety with simplistic answers, but an attachment that results in following practices that mirror the radical values of this most unique of all people, most insightful of all teachers, most subversive of all prophets, most compassionate of all human beings, most courageous of all activists, most inspiring of all models, most intriguing of all mysteries.

We may explore these questions by asking ourselves, "What is discipleship?" If we listen closely to our first answers—dropping nuance or explanation—we can learn a great deal about our attachment. We may answer: "It is primarily a matter of true faith, of learning correct doctrine. The secret is knowing and holding right beliefs *about Jesus.*" Or, "It is actually a matter of religious experience, of taking Jesus into your heart by public confession of faith and perhaps joining a church. The secret is believing *in Jesus.*" Or, "It is a matter of practice, of following the practices of Jesus in imitation of his character, courage, and compassion. The secret is *believing Jesus.*" Or, "It is a matter radical attachment; of following Jesus as a model of service to both God and the neighbor; of taking him as a radical example of rejecting dominance, violence, or coercion; of investing your life in him by living out the reign of God on earth. The secret is seeking to *believe what Jesus believed.*"

Following Jesus as his disciples does not call for obliterating our mimetic desires; on the contrary, it demands that they be redirected, reoriented, and refashioned away from selfish, acquisitive, and violent forms of mimesis to patterns of imitation that are forgiving, other-regarding, peaceable, loving, and marked by humble service. Indeed, embarking on the way of Jesus, being made part of the life of Christ through incorporation into his body, the church, is precisely to have our mimetic desires so ordered, disciplined, shaped, reformed, and reeducated that we become what we have already been made; namely, a new creation (2 Cor. 5:17) (Fodor 2000, 247).

Attachment—"Jesus-Attachment"

Attachment is the word used to define authentic relational bonding. It requires two physically present persons connecting in emotional relational depth, loyalty, and continuity. So how do we speak of attachment to a historic personality who is met in meditation and prayer, but not physically present? This is a key element in Anabaptist spirituality. A classic Platonic spirituality describes this attachment in terms of spiritualized interior claims of touching the invisible, feeling the ineffable, communicating with a silent inner presence through mystic envisioning and encounter. There are such moments of being touched by the beyond and moved by the transcendent that are central to all spiritual experience, but in Anabaptism the attachment is to actual persons who, as fellow believers, become the physical presence of Jesus. To name this concretely, the attachment includes:

1. Historical location. The first three Gospels—Matthew, Mark, and Luke—provide a historical location for attachment to a larger overarching story that situates us spiritually. So we are simultaneously attached to two social locations—attached to the day-to-day situation where we live each day (a geographic place with culture, social context, and a world of relationships) *and* attached to a second location in history (the circle of disciples surrounding the Teacher, who provides ultimate values and reason for being).

2. Identity formation. The identity formed is that of a disciple. Standing in the historic biblical location, encountering the Jesus who calls us to follow, entering the circle of discipleship with fellow disciples defines who we are and becomes the primary identification point for the construction of a spiritual identity. The encounter with the Jesus who comes to us saying "Turn, follow, learn of me" is the place of spiritual identity formation and reformation.

3. Relational attachment. The circle of fellow disciples is essential. This is actual, tangible, observable social attachment, truly human sister-brother bonding with relational attachment to other disciples who are not just co-travelers but are the presence, the face of Jesus in the actual body of Christ, which is a human, vulnerable, broken community seeking to be faithful.

4. Community formation. The community seeking to be faithful sees itself as a circle around Jesus. Attachment to Jesus
is attachment to others in the circle of disciples. Just as one
cannot be human alone, one cannot be a Jesus-attached
disciple alone. Catholic and Protestant spiritualities that
are individual, private, and vertical in metaphor aim toward
personal growth and spiritual maturity and may include the
individual imitation of Christ in life, but "Jesus-attachment"
is not real, not actual, not tangible, not existent unless one
bonds with this circular presence in participation.

5. Participation in solidarity. Through participation in the ongoing life of Jesus in his body the church, disciples meet
and recognize Christ, who is present within, between, and
among them. Since each disciple is the actual face of Christ
to another, they recognize Christ within them; since two disciples know that in their meeting they encounter an invisible
third, they realize that Christ is present between them; since
gathered disciples know that the Presence who connects
them, corrects their connection, and collects them into the
larger unity is Christ among them, then all who say "Jesus
is Master; Jesus is Lord" become sisters and brothers.

This description of discipleship as actual attachment (biblical
location, identity formation, relational bonding, and community
formation through participation in the life of Jesus) does not make
spirituality an individual quest, a private adventure of the soul. This
is connection to others—very human, conflicted, broken, fallible
others. But we gather to connect because that is the place where
Jesus is, where we find him as we find each other, and ultimately
as we find our true selves.

Spirituality as attachment is not a concept unique to Anabaptist
spirituality. It is commonly used in bipolar spiritualities as well,
where the concept of attachment offers a primary metaphor. In
tripolar spirituality it is considered not as metaphor but as actuality, not as spiritual concept but as social reality. When our
attachment to Christ cannot be split off from our attachments to
a community of co-travelers, the actual interface of persons connected in stubborn loyalty are ties that bind, bonds that unite.

Personal story, personality in relationships, and personhood in community share a spiritual rootedness in location, identity formation, relational depth, and communal belonging that has real names and familiar faces. To understand the nuances of attachment processes, it is helpful to explore its first and foundational levels in early childhood.

Attachment as Attunement to Another

Attachment theory, which is grounded in the study of mother-child relationships during the first two years of a child's life, defines three distinct processes at work in early childhood: attunement, misattunement, and reattunement. The mother and child form a crucial bond as the mother attunes herself to the child's inner affects, particularly during the first year. Loving gaze, facial warmth, and nonverbal sounds of joy, excitement, pleasure, and security nourish the bond and minimize distress, aloneness, and fears of abandonment. The child's feelings are mirrored, amplified, resonated. (This is now thought to develop pathways in the brain that produce pleasure hormones, which trigger euphoria, joy, and the capacity for trusting the experience of emotional oneness with another. These pathways endure and shape the style of life [Schore 1994, 142].)

Misattunement between mother and child emerges in the early second year. The primary caregiver misattunes as a means of correction and induction of negative affect (shame and humiliation), and this threatens a disruption of the attachment bond that will disorganize the relationship. Disgust, absence of gleam and warmth, and negative facial signs induce anxiety and shame. This develops brain pathways that produce stress hormones. The neural circuitry expands to help the child manage and reduce stressful states.

Reattunement reestablishes the primary bond, reconnects the two in a return to joy. The relationship has gone from positive to negative and returned to positive feeling tones.

The idea of attachment can be helpfully used to explore the conflicts experienced in one's perceptions and feelings toward God. All religious belief and behavior can be construed as an experience of attachment and the creation of a deep emotional bond. When the primary focus of religious experience is relationship with God, the attachment mirrors the person's parental bond. Parental availability is one of several factors influencing the development of one's image of God. Was the parent consistently available and responsive, and thus is the bond secure? Or was the parent distant and inaccessible and so experienced as avoidant? Or was the parent vacillating, alternately available and unavailable, inconsistently reliable so that the child experiences the parent as ambivalent? As a result, is God experienced as available, avoidant, or ambivalent? Can the person attune, and reattune after having misattuned? (Kilpatrick 1998, 961).

Walter Brueggemann, drawing on the work of Paul Ricoeur, has described a parallel sequence of orientation, disorientation, and reorientation as a dominant theme of the book of Psalms. He drew a parallel with the mother-child relationship:

> The God who evokes and responds to lament is neither omnipotent in any conventional sense nor surrounded by docile reactors. Rather, this God is like a mother who dreams with this infant, that the infant may someday grow into a responsible, mature covenant-partner who can enter into serious communion and conversation. (1995, 104)

Theologian Jürgen Moltmann, writing of the face of God, tells of the bonding dynamic in these metaphors:

> When a mother takes her child in her arms and loves it, we see her eyes shining. . . . Radiant eyes bring joy. . . . The soul "radiates" from them. We can imagine all this and more when we think of God's "shining face" and await the light of the Holy Spirit from that source. Assurance of life and new energies for living awaken in us when God looks at us with the shining eyes of his joy. (1997, 13)

The monopolar spiritual experience grows into a bipolar experience as the spiritual self attaches to the divine and is warmed by the radiated grace. Although this relationship is an extension of the bonding achieved from the first significant others, it is the breakthrough to a transcendent grace that enables one to embrace the persons met in life with that same attaching love.

Imitation or Justification—Which Way?

Theological criticism of imitation themes has focused on several problems: (1) Does imitation make it difficult to draw clear boundaries between Christ and the Christian, or are such distinctions blurred? (2) Does it imply that disciples continue Christ's incomplete or unfinished work as they devote themselves to the same reconciliation process as their Lord (2 Cor. 5:14–21)? (3) Does the language of imitation reduce Jesus to the status of exemplar rather than the utterly unique? (4) Does imitation shift the focus of discipleship from gratitude for God's prior agency and exclusive action in grace to the moral action that participates, and perhaps works out the whole of salvation through some part of human initiative or will?

Martin Luther, for example, sharply rejected the idea of the imitation of Christ (*imitatio Christi*) as a human route to salvation by good works, not by faith alone. Justification is by faith alone, he maintained, and any effort to imitate Christ invites a works righteousness to steal in through a side door and thus invalidates God's grace and its unique and exclusive agency in salvation. Luther preferred to speak of conformity to Christ in Christian vocation, but not in radical imitation. "It is not imitation that makes sons," he said, "but sonship that makes imitators." The neat distinction between following and imitation became a dominant motif in Lutheran theology. When Dietrich Bonhoeffer wrote of discipleship, the accent fell less on sharing the Master's way or nature, and more on the unquestioning willingness to obey—it's a different shade of meaning (Yoder 1972, 113n).

Although at certain moments Bonhoeffer moved beyond his tradition, and with studied carefulness of word choice almost, but not quite, spoke of imitation, he described the Christian experience as "a formation in his likeness, as *conformation* with the unique form of him who was made man, was crucified, and rose again. This is not achieved by dint of efforts 'to become like

Jesus,' which is the way we usually interpret it. It is achieved
only when the form of Jesus Christ itself works upon us in such
a manner that it moulds our form in its own likeness (Gal. 4:19)"
(Bonhoeffer 1955, 80).

This conformation without imitation, in which the believer
does not seek to become like Jesus but awaits an act of grace that
molds us to his likeness, humbly places the emphasis on Christ
appearing in us as an act of grace rather than through human
effort. Yet it points toward active conformation, not the passivity of a nonresponsive clay pressed to conform to the potter's
mold. Bonhoeffer's concept of obedient discipleship is the choice
of radical Christian faithfulness. He came to this perspective on
following Christ from within a classical Lutheran tradition that
viewed it with caution, yet he asserted it unequivocally, without
any compromise with "reality."

> The disciple simply burns his boats and goes ahead. . . . The old life
> is left behind, and completely surrendered. The disciple is dragged
> out of his relative security into a life of absolute insecurity, from a
> life that is observable and calculable into a life where everything is
> unobservable and fortuitous, out of the realms of finite, and into
> the realm of infinite possibilities. . . . Discipleship means Jesus
> Christ, and him alone. It cannot consist of anything more than
> that. (Bonhoeffer 1963, 51)

Programmatically, Bonhoeffer notes, "'Follow me' are Jesus'
first and last words to Peter." Perhaps they are Christ's first and
last words to any and every disciple.

Martin Niemoeller, a Lutheran pastor who, like Bonhoeffer,
staunchly opposed Nazism, wrote: "When I was a school boy of
eight, . . . I saw something framed and under glass which was
embroidered in pearls—nothing but the question, 'What would
Jesus say?' I've never forgotten it—never. And that is the sum of
Christian ethics" (quoted in Wallis and Hollyday 1994, 275).

The contrast between admiration, veneration, and ritualistic
worship, on the one hand, and imitation, participation, and
the service of discipleship, on the other, was a crucial point
of difference in the Reformation. Peter Erb has brought the

argument into focus for us: "For medieval Catholics the model of grace was medicinal—each human being is sick unto death, and unless a physician comes, death will be inevitable" (Erb 2000, 95).

Christ the Physician comes to us bodily through the church, which is his body, and offers the medicine of grace. Grace is both his presence to us in the church and his acceptance of us in unconditional love. If the patient continues to take the medicine—the sacraments—regularly and follows the Physician's advice, then healing, change, and growth take place in the imitation of Christ.

For Protestants, on the other hand, the model was a forensic or legal one. Each individual has committed a crime and deserves the death penalty. The individual comes before God the Judge, who pronounces the believer free of the penalty. After the pronouncement the person is saved from death (justified before the law, *justis*), but remains as guilty (a sinner, *pecator*) of the crime as before the court appearance (in Luther's oft-repeated phrase, *simul Justus et peccator*) (Erb 2000, 95).

No change in character has occurred, and the person has not gained or attained justification; rather, justification has been granted freely and solely by grace. The person is always guilty and deserving of death, but out of gratitude may follow Christ—follow him, but not imitate him. Ephesians 2:8 (KJV), the *fide sola* text, "by grace are you saved through faith," was central to the Reformers. Catholics turned to Galatians 5:6 (RSV), the *fide charitate* formula, "faith working through love." Anabaptists, such as Michael Sattler in "On the Satisfaction of Christ," cite the Galatians rather than the Ephesians tradition. In their search for a middle way they contend that grace is not experienced apart from works. It comes to us as a presence that is received as a practice, not as something accounted to a passive recipient. Grace results in a newly awakened graciousness in the believer. To say yes to the grace of God is to say yes to neighbor and enemy. This is a formula not of "grace not works" or "grace from works" but of "grace that works its loving chemistry." It is evident or it is not present. There is no invisible grace; grace is visible or it is not viable.

From Practice to Presence

Following Jesus is a multidimensional, not step-by-step, process. The dimensions, following Jesus in practice, following him as a person, and him as presence, are to be pursued not separately or sequentially, but simultaneously.

When we follow Jesus in practice, we follow him in the whole range of activities he used to act faithfully (in the love of God and neighbor) in a way that confronted the social realities around him and redirected them toward the reign of God. When we follow Jesus as a person, we follow the more intimate dimension of who he is in spirit, in hope, in faith, in intimate relationship with God, in relationship with friends and disciples, in daily encounters, and in a radically changed attitude toward enemies. Nothing reveals a person more fully than the person's relation to those who are close and response to those who are opposed and closed. When we follow Jesus as presence, we have a relational, mystical, existential encounter with the Jesus who is the exemplar to our practice, the identity who shapes our identity formation, and the spirit-mentor who engages us in the daily dialogue of prayer and action.

> The indwelling Presence is a divine, not a human reality. The incarnation of divine sonship . . . manifested as "soul-spark" (Eckhart), *Seelengrund* (Tauler), "Inner Word" (Denck) or "Inward Light" (Quaker) represents in mystical consciousness . . . God's own immutable eternal Presence. (Bauman 1991, 46)

James McClendon contends that:

> presence is a particular Christian virtue that requires simply the quality of *being there for* and with the other. . . . Presence is being one's self for someone else; it is refusing the temptation to withdraw mentally and emotionally; but it is also on occasion putting our own body's weight and shape alongside the neighbor, the friend, the lover in need. (McClendon 1986, 106)

In describing authentic presence, McClendon contrasts it with "stage presence," the actor's simulacrum of reality, and "politician's" or "salesman's presence," that is, artificial assumption of a relationship not possessed. Both of these imitate the virtue of presence but without the depth that makes presence valid. The reverse of presence is nosiness, butting into another's life, or coexistence like that of an estranged couple at a table for two staring moodily past each other, bodily near but mentally distant.

Presence is the powerful confrontation of being there for or with the other, like Martin Luther King and his people confronting oppressors, Gandhi and his followers standing against the British in their call for justice, teams of Christian peacemakers living supportively with the abused in Guatemala, Nicaragua, Haiti, Palestinian villages in Israel, and other places of armed conflict. Each of us has stories of moments of authentic presence when another was there for us and with us in a time of loss, need, or danger.

Human presence is not the answer to the roll call, "Here." It is the deeply alive being-in-relationship-to-another that answers "Here I am" in availability and integrity. When I am in relationship to you with presence, then I am not withdrawn into or encumbered by myself. Some people are capable of authentic presence, but others are not. As Gabriel Marcel, the philosopher of presence, writes: "Though it is hard to describe in intelligible terms, there are some people who reveal themselves as 'present'—that is to say, at our disposal" (Marcel 1949b, 25).

Marcel notes that presence is most visible in the way persons attend to each other—in how they listen or refuse to listen to truly hear the other's deeper message.

> There is a way of listening which is a way of giving, and another way of listening which is a way of refusing, of refusing oneself; the material gift, the visible action, do not necessarily witness to presence. We must not speak of proof in this connection; the word would be out of place. Presence is something which reveals itself in a look, a smile, an intonation or a handshake. (Marcel 1949b, 26)

To not attend in presence is to be absent. In absence one flees to the past in memory, or projects into the future in fantasy without inviting the other to come along.

Attachment to the Jesus of the Gospels

Attachment to Jesus, we must first clarify, is neither admiration (though Jesus fully deserves admiration) nor adulation (although that may result from attachment), nor assimilation into a culture and lifestyle (although that is inevitable). Attachment is actual encounter with the Jesus of the Gospels and engagement with his utterly radical claims on us and on creation. To state this in concise propositions:

- To be a Christian is to be absolutely convinced that Jesus is the Christ and that Christ is the Lord of creation.
- To acknowledge that Christ is Lord is to admit that human life can be understood only in terms of Christ's intentions for creation.
- To understand human life in terms of Christ's intentions for creation is to perceive that Jesus's activity for the world is totally pervaded by nonviolent agape love and by renunciation of power, of justice for oneself, and of purpose-driven effectiveness.
- To participate in Christ's activity is to shoulder the weight of restoring love toward offenders, of forgiving the guilty, of responding nonresistantly when attacked, of acting on behalf of justice for others in loving, nonviolent ways.
- To follow Jesus is to willingly accept his way of unlimited love (agape), to accept the call to self-renunciation (the cross), to accept self-relinquishment through giving up sin and its defenses (the way of discipleship), and to accept inner self-transformation in repentance and a new life (resurrection) (Yoder 1972, 55–58).

This is the soul of radical attachment spirituality. It meets the Jesus of the Gospels and allows him to address us with his simple call, "Follow me."

Imitation as Lived Agape

Imitation of Christ is, at heart and center, imitation of Christ-like love, the love we call *agape*. My favorite definition of *agape*, compiled from many sources, is: a radical commitment to the welfare of the other that sees the other with an equal regard in spite of the other's response; that seeks to be understanding without need to understand or to be understood; that risks, cares, gives, and shares with no need for reciprocity, no need to be respected, no need to be appreciated, no need to be thanked, and no need to enjoy the process.

Agape love is love of neighbor given because the neighbor is also a creature, a precious creation of God. It is uncalculated, impartial, unmerited, disinterested goodwill given to each as a precious person. Agape love is a nonconditional acceptance (God loves unconditionally; we love nonconditionally). Agape love is at first imitative love, then participative love as Christ is formed within the lover. Jesus's love has distinctive characteristics:

1. Jesus, in agape, demonstrated a reverence for persons in his recognition of their worth and of their mystery as fellow humans, and in a sense of receptive awe in response to the image of God in broken humanity.
2. Jesus, in agape, saw the inner purpose of another and called it to be realized and fulfilled. He cared for this inner potential in persons by attending, observing, listening, inviting, and caring with grace and confronting with truth.
3. Jesus, in agape, gave himself to others with sensitivity to the particular person, clarity about the particular situation, and accuracy about the particular needs manifested.
4. Jesus, in agape, loved each person for that person's own sake and for God's sake, not for his own sake, and he bid the other to grow even if the other grew to be against him or made choices that grieved him.
5. Jesus, in agape, loved with a willingness to be hurt by enmity yet stay connected, to be vulnerable to enemies rather than be safe. He remained willing to forgive even in extremity, open to a future friend or foe even when dying.

6. Jesus, in agape, became fully his own person, using all his gifts and strengths, venturing courageously and acting prophetically while knowing that in doing this he courted the disapproval of those he loved most, those whose opinions mattered most in his community, those whose influence was feared most in his society, those who could hurt him most deeply.

7. Jesus, in agape, identified so completely with others he embodied love, enfleshed compassion, and expressed this positive regard for others as an equal regard—not as a benevolently superior, compulsively sacrificial, obediently virtuous vertical regard of condescending, magnanimous grace, but as a truly identified equal regard of the fellow sufferer, fellow traveler, fellow human.

How do you experience the presence of Jesus in this practice of agape?

Not as a direct physical presence—a sense that another person is actually in the room with you. (Although there may be moments when you sense the presence of someone actually in between in conversations with another or in conversations with God.)

Not as a sound—an actual voice, not even as a still, small voice or a tiny whispering sound or a hint of a soft breeze. (Although there are moments when words from another touch a deep place in your soul and you know that God has just spoken.)

Not as a something physical apart from other people. (Although in hindsight you know that you were not alone.)

Jesus himself told us where to experience his presence. We meet him in serving those whom he once called "the least of these my brothers."

"For I was hungry and you fed me," Jesus said. It was he.

"For I was thirsty and you gave me drink," Jesus said. It was he.

"For I was a stranger and you welcomed me," Jesus said. It was he.

"For I was naked and you clothed me," Jesus said. It was he.

"For I was sick and you cared for me," Jesus said. It was he.

"For I was in prison and you came to me," Jesus said. It was he.

So he is there. It is he.

On the Other Hand

The other side of all this talk of radical attachment is worth noting. What if your tradition focuses much more on God as Heavenly Father or Heavenly Parent, or on the presence of God in the Holy Spirit? Is this Jesus fixation a bit out of balance? Why take as a mentor, in a postmodern age, a prophet from premodern times? If attaching to Jesus is in actuality attaching to the circle of followers around Jesus, doesn't this detract from one's autonomy as an individual? And doesn't radical devotion smack of extremism? Is anything really worth being radical and extreme about or isn't wisdom more often found in the middle, on the median? What if the imitation of Christ is seeking to imitate the inimitable? How do you imitate One who imitated no one? By refusing to imitate and by being one's true self? Or is one's true self found in the imitation of the One who reveals what our humanity can truly be?

The shadow side of a spirituality of radical attachment to Jesus is a constant sense of frustration as co-opted Jesus figures multiply in the culture. One must constantly say, "but not the popular cultural icon Jesus, not the 'God bless America,' 'America, love it or leave it,' or 'Jesus Saves' bumper-sticker Jesus, not the sweet Jesus of romantic piety that is the permissive deity of easy religiosity, not the ritual Jesus of crucifix and WWJD insignia, neither the cleanly scrubbed and assimilated Jesus of Hollywood nor the bloody, masochistic Jesus of *The Passion*." It is the Jesus of the Gospels, the Jesus of the Sermon on the Mount, the Jesus who calls us to leave all and follow, the Jesus of a visible circle of gathered disciples who are seeking to continue his work by doing it in his way in self-forgetful honoring of his name.

In spite of the difficulties, one can attach radically, from the roots to the tiniest shoots letting life grow from him. Daniel Berrigan,

a Catholic disciple whose dissidence has marked his life and the
life of our generation, has written as his credo:

> I can only tell you what I believe: I believe:
> I cannot be saved by foreign policies.
> I cannot be saved by the sexual revolution.
> I cannot be saved by the gross national product.
> I cannot be saved by nuclear deterrents.
> I cannot be saved by aldermen, priests, artists,
>   plumbers, city planners, social engineers,
>   nor by the Vatican,
>   nor by the World Buddhist Association,
>   nor by Hitler, nor by Joan of Arc,
>   nor by angels and archangels,
>   nor by powers and dominions.
> I can be saved only by Jesus Christ.
>
> Daniel Berrigan (in Wallis 1976, 26)

For Meditation

From the *Ausbund*, the Anabaptist hymnbook of the martyrs,
1564:

You Have Called Us, Heavenly Father

You have called us, Heavenly Father,
You have bid us join your reign.
Jesus walked this way before us,
He endured the cross and pain.
If we follow, joy or sorrow
We shall not have lived in vain.

You have promised, if we follow
In the footsteps of your Son,
We will find him ever present
And we never walk alone.
Christ beside us, Christ to guide us;
Your way, Lord, shall be our own.

Jesus, you are our example,
You we daily imitate;

Your life is our guide and model
You reveal love incarnate.
God we name you, Lord we claim you,
The sole king we celebrate.

Ausbund, 1564, Hymn 55, stz 1, 2, and following stanzas
Sing to tune of "Let All Mortal Flesh Keep Silence"

2

The Practice of–Stubborn Loyalty

"We might define true community as that place where the person you least want to live with always lives."

Parker Palmer (1977, 20)

"True community exists when the person you dislike most dies or moves away and someone worse takes that place."

Quaker proverb

Stubborn loyalty to the community of the Spirit is joining the circle around Jesus as the primary social location where we learn to act toward all others as, in reality, we act toward Jesus.

Solidarity in Community

"Yes, I ran that horse and buggy off the road," the man said. "I'd run all the Amish out of the county if I could."

The angry man, a neighbor to my oldest brother in Holmes County, Ohio, is one of the last of a large, historic Lutheran community that settled these beautiful rolling hills in the 1800s. Now they have virtually all moved to the city, and Amish families have claimed their farmlands.

Like his parents, the neighbor tells scornful stories about the Amish and jokes about how his Lutheran forebears drowned the Anabaptists in the sixteenth century. He makes light of their simple lives, horse-drawn buggies, and old style of dress. His hassling of Amish people on the road or at the store is a facet of community life.

On a humid day last summer an electrical storm broke out. The air crackled, and the neighbor's barn burst into flames and burned to ashes.

By the time the ash heap had cooled, he had begun to hear word of his neighbors' plans. Amish people from all around gathered to begin clearing the rubble, drawing up plans, cutting timbers, and scheduling a barn raising.

When the day came for the event, the neighbor's previously off-limits barnyard was swarming with men in straw hats and barn-door denims. By evening, the great framework was complete, the roof was sheeted, and the siding was going up.

And the neighbor stood in the driveway, shaking his head wordlessly, tears running lines down his face. The barn stood fresh against the sky, and long tables of food and drink—homemade bread, noodles, chicken, date pudding, and rivers of lemonade—welcomed him into the circle of tired celebrants.

—ɯ—

At a Kansas university in the 1970s, five sophomore guys climbed down a manhole and went exploring beneath city streets. As they went, they closed valves, pulled breaker switches, and rerouted water and power. The city awoke to scrambled services. The police followed the abundant clues and the five young men were picked up.

Dean of Students Walter Friesen went with them to the station. There he persuaded the chief of police to remand them into his custody, promising that they would return with an appropriate recommendation of resolution. Then he sat down with the young men.

"What went wrong last night?" he asked.

"We got caught," one replied.

"No, no, no," he answered. "What went wrong?"

"We were trespassing, we broke the law," said another.

"No, no, no," Walt interjected. "Come on now, what really went wrong?"

"We got the college into trouble with the town?" ventured a third.

"You can do better than this. You are university students. What went wrong?"

So the question-and-answer dialogue went on and on until finally one said, "We betrayed the community—the university community's trust in us and the city community's safety and security."

"Now you're getting at the heart of it," Walt replied. "You endangered the whole community. So what do you suggest you might do for the community? How can you restore trust?"

At the end of another hour the young men had volunteered two hundred hours of community service and written an apology to all involved, as well as agreeing to meet face to face to discuss any damages done to anyone by their underground lark. Then they went to meet the police officers, seeing them no longer as enemies, but as representatives of community.

"Education," says Walt, an Anabaptist and now a Mennonite minister, "is learning to live in that interdependence we call community."

—∿—

"Tell them respectfully that it is none of their business what kind of home you purchase," a faculty colleague said heatedly.

I was moving from a mainline Protestant seminary to join the faculty of Associated Mennonite Seminaries, and my new colleagues in the Mennonite community had asked for a conversation on what kind of home we planned to build or purchase. As a community of practiced faith, they had covenanted as a faculty to live simply, to purchase lower- to middle-class homes, and to have a flat salary scale with equal distribution in order to express solidarity with pastors, missionaries, and church leaders around the world who do not share American affluence.

"It's none of their business what you invest. I've researched my home carefully and bought where appreciation is highest, where I will get maximum returns when I sell my home. Remember, the three key words: location, location, and location," the dean of my old school advised.

"But it's different in the Mennonite community," I tried to explain. "Here in metropolitan Chicago we are an association of individuals. There in the Mennonite community, they have a sense of peoplehood, a practice of mutual accountability, a solidarity in values and behavior."

"That's all fine in spirituality, but not in buying a home," another interjected.

"What kind of spirituality is it if it doesn't affect lifestyle or standard of living?" I asked.

"Obviously that's biblical," he replied. "But we don't live in first-century Palestine."

"And so much for living by biblical values!" another said.

We all shook our heads at the irony and returned to the work of training people to be mainstream Protestant pastors of individual disciples.

—w—

A Rabbinic Tale: The Cost of Community

Long ago in a distant land, a prince dreamed of creating more than a geographical or political kingdom. He dreamed of establishing a community in which all persons were committed to each other in loyalty and equality, where every person sought the welfare of the neighbor even at a cost to the self. So the prince called a great meeting of all the heads of clans, all the wise and trusted people of the land, and dared to tell his dream. Each chieftain and his clan were invited to join in the foundation of a new society.

As part of the community's inauguration, each was requested to search his cellar for the best wine produced from his ancestral vines. These treasured bottles would be uncorked, poured into a great communal vat, and blended, as the true community it represented, into a common vintage.

"How can I mix my exquisite wine with that of my neighbors?" asked one of the winegrowers invited to this covenanting. I would sacrifice the unique variety of grape, the special climate of the year, the sweetness of a late harvest, the indefinable magic of bouquet, and I would violate my art as a winemaker. Impossible! Give up my distinct variety? Lose my separate self? I will not be adulterated in such a common cup."

So he corked a bottle of tap water, affixed his most beautiful label to the bottle, and at the time of the ritual poured the water ceremoniously into the vat. When the covenanting was solemnized, all filled their glasses for the communal draft, the toast that would seal commitment to community. As the cups touched their lips, all knew the truth. It was not wine. It was water. No one had been willing to pay the cost of community.

Community as Loyalty

Christian community is a web of stubbornly loyal relationships knotted together into a living network of persons. We recognize authentic community by the visible strands of commitment and concern that enable people to live jointly, corporately, and cooperatively together.

And this resilient web of stubborn loyalties is spirituality.

Recognizing that Christian community is not just webbed from one believer to another but is held firm by a central strand resolutely attached to Jesus Christ, it is no surprise that members listen to each other attentively, expecting to sometimes hear his voice as another speaks, and look to each other knowing that now and again they may see his face in the other.

And this stubborn attentiveness is spirituality.

Recognizing that community is a group in which free conversation occurs, the stubbornly loyal participants risk openness in revealing their struggles and vulnerability in accepting help, and they find that others are sensitive and responsive to their self-disclosure.

And this stubborn vulnerability is spirituality.

Recognizing that community is a place where one can feel freely and speak frankly about deep inmost feelings, the stubbornly loyal participants plunge into sharing what is precious and deeply valued.

And this stubborn inwardness opened outward is spirituality.

Recognizing that community is a setting for dealing clearly with unity and discord, positive attachments and negative repulsions, concord and conflict, stubbornly faithful participants seek a unity that accepts and integrates discord, not a unity without or excluding discord.

And this stubborn openness to difference is spirituality.

Recognizing that community is a natural therapeutic context that fosters maturation, healing, and growth for its members, stubbornly loyal participants band together to provide stabilizing connections and correctives and to offer support when personalities fragment or boundaries break down. One need not go it alone or live only by support purchased by the hour. Community is available to help bind up what is broken.

And this stubborn support and confrontation for growth is spirituality.

Recognizing that community is a place where both good friends and predictable frustrators are present, needed, valued, respected, incorporated, and indeed learned from in genuine dialogue, stubbornly inclusive participants do not give up on the irritating or withdraw into the conforming, but rather welcome both.

And this stubborn inclusiveness of enemy and friend is spirituality.

In the stubbornly loyal community, we look on diversity not as our enemy, but as a cause for gratitude. "People are talented and untalented, simple and difficult, devout and less devout, sociable and loners. Does not the untalented person have a position to assume just as well as the talented person, the difficult person just as well as the simple one?" (Bonhoeffer 1952, 93). The weak need the strong for support; the strong need the weak for balance and guidance. We dare exclude neither from community, or community dies; both must be included in mutual service and ministry.

Monopolar spirituality tends to connect persons as fellow humans on the basis of those shared experiences that create a community of similarity. Its best advocates promote a community of diversity where all humanity stands equal, and they often teach the solidarity of all humankind. "Nothing human is foreign to me"; "The more truly personal is the most universal"; "Every pathology seen in the human race is present, in seed, within each human member." The community experience is grounded in the wisdom of the individual to experience and express this solidarity and humanity for all living, but with an elusive universal as its ground and offering its inner power.

Bipolar spirituality links the depths of personal discovery of the uniqueness of each member with the height of open receptivity toward the transcendent—toward God, who validates and prizes each. It gathers a worshiping community, a mutual-encouragement community, and a community of outreach in witness, social concern, and service. The two directions of spirituality are measured in two dimensions—the height of the person's aspirations coupled with the depth of inner reverence. Or to say it another way, the reach toward transcendence and the sense of the holy are balanced with the recognition of the holy also present in the mundane, the routine, the common stuff of life.

Tripolar spirituality realizes that love of God and love of neighbor become one when united in shared life together. It embraces all humankind—friend and enemy alike, while seeking to model this love in the creation of actual, local, visible communities where the three dimensions of spirituality become one reality. In a tripolar community, each person's individuality is affirmed (you can be truly you), yet joint participation is achieved (we can be truly we) because at the center we together recognize that God is present (we gather around him). Community is the setting where solitude is protected yet solidarity becomes real. Such a union of person and group is an expression of spirituality when it is attuned to its center, God, and attached to the neighbor. In tripolar spirituality we affirm the following:

Spirituality is not free-floating; it has a location, and that location is community.

Spirituality is not a private inner temple; it is a place of meeting where we can safely share our private souls, and that meeting place is community.

Spirituality is not a retreat where we learn the art of being alone or solitary; it withdraws for the moment in order to engage more deeply, genuinely, stubbornly, and that engagement is in and with community.

Spirituality is not a comfort zone that is primarily concerned about new happiness, peace of mind, or resolution of inner conflict and guilt, although all of these are connected to the experience of God's presence; it is concerned "with the new network of communal relationship and the perception that the presence of God makes possible for each spiritual person" (McIntosh 1998, 7). That "perception" is the ability to see other community members with new eyes.

Contemporary spirituality has become an individual quest that must be pursued outside community. No longer is each necessary to the other. But spirituality is what one does with aloneness. (Aloneness is being solitary, utterly individual.) Community is what you do with your loneliness. (Loneliness is a sense of missing or failed relationships.) These two have little relationship in much Christian practice. In actuality, individual spirituality is only one part of personhood, one half of the alternating rhythm of human wholeness. The other half is community. If we cannot be truly human alone—if we need the sacred relationship with a significant other—then is it possible that one is not truly growing in spirituality without co-travelers?

Christian spirituality is not, as popularly believed, a matter of individual salvation leading to a life of individual self-realization and pointing toward individual growth and perfection. It is not the private encounter of the soul with its own personal deity. It is a public encounter with a God who meets us in community. "We expect a theophany of which we know nothing but the place, and the place is called community," Martin Buber testified (in Palmer 1977, 4).

The natural habitat of any true disciple of Jesus is community. Those who seek to know Christ know that he is most truly known in community. This is the original description of Christian spirituality. It is what is truly interesting and distinctive about Jesus's disciples:

> To describe the original Christians as persons of spirituality who believe in God is true enough, but it is neither interesting nor truly accurate. What is interesting is that they thought that their belief in God as they had encountered him in Jesus required the formation of a community distinct from the world exactly because of the kind of God he was. (Hauerwas 1992, 34)

Misunderstanding Community

The great hunger for community, experienced both by persons and by social groups, is increased by several misconceptions that are basic beliefs of contemporary culture. Expectations become demands, and these demands are self-defeating. The most prominent and enduring of the common myths about community are not difficult to name. The first three were articulated by Parker Palmer in 1977, in a commentary on community as accurate as any in the twenty-first century.

1. Community is a creature comfort, a consumer item; it is one more luxury that can be bought in retreats or seminars, purchased with small town property, obtained by paying membership dues at a country club or fitness spa, or even by joining a church.
    Community is not a commodity; it emerges from common struggle for integrity, shared commitment to justice, joint covenants to work for wholeness and mutual respect. It is created when we step forward to serve, to right wrongs, to heal hurts.
2. Community is a utopia of easy access to others, of unconditional social acceptance that happens when we find the right people; a panacea for our fears and anxieties if we can

afford to live in a gated community, enjoy a vacation in a timeshare that offers a paradise of fun, or join a club that promises fellowship and the agreement and acceptance of those with similar values and lifestyle.

Community is a collision of egos, a furnace for welding steel-hard opinions, a crucible for melting the hard ores of self-interest into common goals. It offers the pain of not getting our own way, the promise of finding a third way together.

3. Community is the fulfillment of our individual goals, an extension of our egos, an expansion of our hopes of finding people just like ourselves, a confirmation of our cherished but partial view of reality.

In true community we do not choose our companions, we receive them as gift; we cannot sort, select, and assemble our kind of people, they come to us by grace. Likeness eliminates challenge; uniformity reduces growth; sameness frustrates creativity.

4. Community is achieved by the pursuit or the creation of an extended family of loving people who provide the nurturance and support our family of origin failed to supply.

Community is not a supra-familial network that fulfills our dreams of familial perfection of solidarity or supportive parental permissiveness; it is a network of fallible individuals and flawed families seeking together to learn how to work through the various issues they carry with them (Palmer 1977, 18–20).

All these are dreams of a community of similarity that guarantees our survival, satisfaction, safety, and security. These dreams are deep misunderstandings of what community is truly about. It is not difficult to fall in love with such dreams; what is difficult is to genuinely love the real community that God has given us in the people that surround us. Bonhoeffer, in his unforgettable warning, nailed this truth into our memory walls:

Anyone who loves a dream of community more than the Christian community itself [warts and all] becomes a destroyer of the latter even though the devotion to the former is faultless and the intentions may be ever so honest, earnest and sacrificial. (Bonhoeffer 1952, 27)

Communal Spirituality

Dissident disciples, in the communal practice of spirituality, stick together in a stubborn loyalty of community. This is not just any community. Not a community of consumption that gathers in a mall or at an auction; not a community of leisure in a health, fitness, or sports club; not a community of expression in an arts, drama, or literature group; not a geographic community of location, location, location. Not a community of contemporary megachurch worship-entertainment; not the temporary community of an exciting sports, music, or political event. This is a unique sort of community that presses the word back to its origin, *koinonia* (the loving fellowship of co-disciples).

This community of disciples is connected by two powerful attachments—attachment to Jesus, the living center of the group, and attachment to fellow disciples. This circle around Jesus is a circle connected in solidarity. It is around Jesus, who is the convener, the center. Here spirituality is lived out in relationships, in right relationships that endure suffering with stubborn hope.

In communal spirituality, community, not the private closet, is the location—the community of the Spirit—where we experience God-with-us. Community is a circle of faith, active in love, serving in obedience to God (Dyck 1996, 23).

In communal spirituality, ethics is the preamble to, the preparation for, the initial impulse of all authentic spirituality. One asks, "Am I in right relationships?" before any act of giving (Matt. 5:23–24); "Am I at peace with fellow humanity?" before one takes the bread and wine of communion (1 Cor. 11:27–29); "Am I willing to forgive my brother?" before asking forgiveness for the self (Matt. 6:12, 14–15).

In communal spirituality, justice as well as harmony are essentials. No one dare overlook domination and oppression, injustice and injury, exploitation and abuse; they are central concerns. The stories of the suffering Servant's life of self-giving, of the dying Redeemer's self-sacrifice that exposes evil, of the innocent Victim who endures the pain of the cross all serve to define the characteristics of true spirituality.

In communal spirituality, *transformation* is not just a word; it is the essential element. The *anastatic* (walking in the way of the resurrection) is the final goal. *Anastatic*, Greek for "to stand up again, to be risen or raised from the dead, to be brought to life," is from the noun *anastasis*, which means "rising, awakening, uprising, or resurrection." Resurrectionists are those who live out of "the sphere of the *anastatic*, an ethic, a life-style, a discipleship informed by Easter" (McClendon 1986, 142).

The *"anastatic* experience" is an embracing of a holiness, a sanctification that joins in "an indictment of evil in all its forms—personal, social, communal, political," and results in a living out of the new covenant in community (Dyck 1996, 23). This experience embraces not only a vital hope in the final resurrection and a certain faith of hearing the call of the One who will summon us to life in his presence, but also a belief that our present experience of the presence of God is a foretaste here and now, as well as a guarantee, of our ultimate resurrection.

A Community of Love

The highest word for love in the Christian scriptures is not *agape*. Ever since the publication of C. S. Lewis's classic study *The Four Loves* in 1960, it has been common to speak of these four Greek words: *sorge* (care), *eros* (desire), *philia* (friendship), and *agape* (benevolence) as the accepted spectrum of positive attachment to others. Agape, as disinterested, compassionate, benevolent love, is defended as unquestionably superior to all other forms in its potential for selfless, altruistic care for the other. Over the centuries, the definitions of each of these words has gradually become more individualistic, more unilateral, more arranged along a spectrum from superior to inferior. In contrast to current usage, in the New Testament all four of these words refer to a shared, participative love, to love in mutual relationship.

Love in the high New Testament sense, whether named *agape* or *philia*, is a deeply communal word. It designates a relationship in which the separation of "I" and "Thou" is overcome in a sense of "We" (De Wolf 1971, 107).

But in the Christian scriptures, the highest word, the most virtuous form of love, is not agape, but koinonia, the mutual, reciprocal, committed, and celebrative love of intimate relationship, authentic community, and responsive fellowship. For disciples in the circle around Jesus, the experience of koinonia was the communal expression of loving relationship among fellow followers of the way. "The way of Jesus" was the way of neighbor love, which included enemy love as well as friendship love lived out in solidarity. The solidarity of koinonia is not just a peak experience of "fellow-feeling"; it has continuity, a stubborn loyalty that endures. In this profound fellowship of life lived in relationship, the individual self is surrendered and then regained transformed, yielded in its individualism but rediscovered with rich individuality.

To live in koinonia is to rely on a web of relationships of loving, caring community. When this community is centered in Jesus Christ, it takes on the unique character of the One who was willing to suffer the ultimate human injustice, abuse, and social scorn without yielding to fear or betraying the way of redemptive love. To have koinonia with the suffering of Christ means to identify with his movement (the church) and to suffer the consequences of loyal engagement in his mission (Kraus 1979, 39–40).

Such participation, or koinonia, in Christ's life, death, and resurrection is what is called discipleship. This loving participation in profoundly connected relationship—*koinonia*—is what St. Paul identified as the inner focal point of his discipleship in Philippians 3:10–11. In the preceding verses (Phil. 3:7–10), Paul traced and explained his experience of discipleship, clearly patterning his story, point by point, after his earlier description of Christ's solidarity with us (Phil. 2:5–11). This set of parallel patterns set forth in mimesis reveals the inner working of the imitation of Christ, not facile duplication but authentic and integrated participation, an embodiment in the life of another, an incorporation of the experience of another in actual lived life—struggle, suffering, and all.

In the most profound benediction he penned, in 2 Corinthians 13:14, Paul set *koinonia* as the final word, the capstone of our experience of God. "The grace *(charis)* of the Lord Jesus Christ, and the love *(agape)* of God, and fellowship *(koinonia)* in the Holy Spirit, be with you all" (NEB). In the fellowship (koinonia) with God around Christ, we participate here and now in the kin-dom of God. The kin-dom of heaven is not only an extrahistorical lure that draws us into the future in faith, it is a reality here, now, within the conflicts of history. The kin-dom of God grows among people as they join together in viewing one another in a radically new perspective—seeing each other as God sees us in grace—and then treating each other accordingly. Within this new kin-dom, followers of Christ participate in the social construction of an alternate reality. In place of the vengeful, violent reality based on retaliation and retribution, they construct a world by the words and actions of forgiveness, restoration, and reconciliation.

The kingdom (kin-dom) of heaven is a present reality that grows among us amid all the contradictions of the political and social order. But believers are called to live in discipleship that sees all those about them as God sees them; acts toward them with compassion as Christ acts; risks suffering, reconciliation, and forgiveness in the way of the cross; and creates a community of both faith and practice that seeks to embody this way of life.

The community of faith and practice that lives in this present kin-dom of God lives out the actions of inclusive love, speaking the words of grace and forgiveness to create a social reality of unconditional acceptance. Simultaneously it is a community of judgment that is not judgmental, of discernment that is not exclusionary, of direction that is not authoritarian.

False and True Community

In false community, the group is always superior to the individual, the safety and security of the institution more important than that of the member, so a few casualties are expected; necessary injuries are tolerated for the greater good. In true community, the person and the group have an equal claim on truth, integrity, and compassion. Neither is sacrificed for the advantage of the other (Palmer 1977, 16).

In false community, the group ultimately relies on power rather than love in dealing with hard decisions. It is inevitably power-conscious, manipulating and being manipulated in vertical control patterns. In true community, the whole remains person-conscious, renegotiating all its power functions and constantly returning to horizontal interaction patterns as its home key even though it plays in a leadership key for brief passages to accomplish short-term goals. It knows its long-term goal is in the horizontal circle around distributive justice that transforms power for the good of all and each.

In false community, the ongoing process of co-existence tends to homogenize, to slough off unwieldy variation and exclude the eccentric so that the community becomes solidly uniform and gradually more exclusive. In true community, the process welcomes diversity, stubbornly violating social, ethnic, or racial lines to renew relationships with those who differ and with the stranger or the newcomer (Palmer 1977, 17).

In false communities, some finite attribute like race, religion, or political ideology is elevated to ultimacy, and the system turns idolatrous. At its worst the community confuses its power with the power of God and eventually that power is used to decide questions of life and death (Palmer 1977, 17). In true community, the chosen part does not get mistaken for the whole because the group is voluntary, the process is voluntary, and membership is a choice. No one has absolute power—power belongs finally to God—and God stands in judgment of all our choices, all our communal values, so no one knows, speaks, or acts out absolutes.

In true community, *the person is protected.* Indeed, a solitary person may take a lonely stand in witnessing to a particular truth. *Dissent is welcomed.* In fact, the safe sharing of both agreement and disagreement is one of the first signs of authentic respect. *Identity is ascribed.* In collective identity, the community offers a place to belong, a place to stand, a place to slowly form one's individual identity. *Ethics are discerned.* Here, in a community that recognizes, honors, and upholds virtues, we are most free to examine our shortcomings and commit ourselves to integrity.

Freedom is protected. In a setting where there are limits, we are most free to explore the unlimited; in a context where there is commitment, we are most free to press our deeply held values and jointly practiced virtues to higher and more complete ends. *Interdependence is experienced.* When we realize that to be human is to be interdependent, our inescapable need for communication, commitment, and solidarity with others is fulfilled in our trusting and trustworthy relationships. *Stories become significant.* Our narratives find a meaningful place in a larger narrative. Each member's personal story assumes meaning because it is an authentic part of the community's story; it is caught up in the narrative of a people that surrounds and supports. Humans are *Homo narrans*, story creatures and creators (Buber 1965; Arnett 1986).

Community is formed by the slow, deliberate invitation to trust, to belong, to finally join together in common purpose. This process is not accelerated by coercion, facilitated by persuasion, achieved by seduction. It is created through invitation. The participant catches a vision of tasks and goals above and beyond the participant's own narcissism.

Communities are replaced in consumer societies by social groupings that are better called lifestyle enclaves. In their landmark study *Habits of the Heart*, Robert Bellah and his associates wrote of this radical shift. Although the term *community* is widely and loosely used, often in connection with lifestyles, what is actually experienced is not community (an inclusive whole of differing people committed to interdependence in both public and private life and honoring each other's callings), but a lifestyle enclave. These enclaves are segmented, and they celebrate the narcissism of similarity. They involve only a segment of each individual—usually leisure and consumption—and a segment of society that includes only those who share the lifestyle of a particular kind of consumer at leisure. The lifestyle enclave becomes the appropriate form of collective support for individualists in a radically individualized society. Individualism requires finding others who can reflect and confirm one's selfhood and thus validate identity and one's private life (Bellah et al. 1985, 84). In critique of this self-centered social narcissism, Bellah writes:

We find ourselves not independently of other people and institutions but through them. We never get to the bottom of ourselves on our own. We discover who we are face to face and side by side with others in work, love and learning. We are not simply ends in ourselves, either as individuals or as a society. We are parts of a larger whole that we can neither forget nor imagine in our own image without paying a high price. If we are not to have a self that hangs in the void, slowly twisting in the wind, these are issues that we cannot ignore. (Bellah et al. 1985, 84)

A Community of Virtues

Community is where one learns virtues, not where one chooses values. Values are selected out of the tendencies of personality, chosen out of individual inclination, pursued by personal preference. Virtues are intrinsically good; they form the structure of what is good, what is right, and what is worth the investment of a life. Values are good because I prize and choose them. Virtues are chosen because they are good. Community is where we learn what is worth choosing.

Virtues are practices, practices formed by community, modeled in community, and taught by community, that express what is good, right, and worthy.

Virtues are habits, and what we do habitually, naturally, without pretense reveals our character.

Virtues are those qualities and skills that link together to form the structures of character; "they are characteristic of a person." "A virtue is an acquired human quality the possession and exercise of which tends to enable us to achieve those goals which are internal to practices and the lack of which effectively prevent us from achieving any such goal" (MacIntyre 1981, 191).

Virtues and character do not make any sense unless there is a story to tell. That is, unless a person lives by some unity of conviction or vision there is no stuff for a story. . . . Another important fact of life is that character formation happens in relationships with other people. A fundamental truth is that character first of all is given to us before it can be shaped by us. (Huebner and Schroeder 1993, 177)

We find ourselves and form a self in community. The community has a story that creates and sustains it. We are invited to join and participate in this story.

Theologian Harry Huebner describes a community as a people with a shared identity and common virtues woven into a coherent story. The stories that define his composite "we" are from multiple sources—biblical stories, his Mennonite history, his family's personal history of threat and courage, persecution and conviction during the Russian revolution.

> These stories made me immensely proud. The message I got as a little boy on hearing them went something like this: "My people know what they believe and take their convictions to be ultimately true. They are not about to sacrifice their identity for an expedient end, won at the threat of death. Wow, this is who I am: these are my stories. I can (want to) participate in them by putting on the character that makes such stories mine!" Although I was not personally involved in any of them I experienced these stories as being about me. (Huebner and Schroeder 1993, 172)
>
> To call the church a community of virtues is to identify the habits of the church. The church is that body which out of habit tells the truth; which out of habit loves enemies, feeds the hungry, forgives sinners; which out of habit praises God for what we have received, . . . prays and worships. (Huebner and Schroeder 1993, 179)

As a community of virtues, the church works hard to create practices that embody its deepest beliefs, to define rules that guide its pursuit of those practices, to articulate principles that link rule and practice together, to act out these practices in daily life.

In a community of virtues, spirituality and morality are two sides of the same reality. They are inseparable from each other. The popular stereotype that one is personal, interior, and directed toward the transcendent; the other social, exterior, and directed to the surrounding world is wrong. Spirituality is both personal and social, both interior and exterior, both focused on the transcendent and focused on the present world. So is morality. We dare split neither. Each has both a God-ward and an other-ward aspect; Each has an inward and an outward vision. I meet God in my brother; I know God as I know and am known by my sister. I live morally as my character is formed by the story of God's call and gift, which is also the story of responsible life in community, where any act toward another is an act toward God. "Inasmuch as you did it to one of the least of these My brethren, you did it to Me," Jesus teaches (Matt. 25:40 NKJV).

The church is an alternative community—an alternative to human communities that live by coercion, competition, and collective self-interest. It seeks to be a community of disciples obeying the particular ways of God that are revealed in Jesus. It models neighbor love, transformative redemptive justice, inclusion of the stranger, servanthood to each other and beyond, creative love, forgiveness and reconciliation, and the humility to recognize and confess its own need for repentance and forgiveness.

Alternative communities that live as deeply rooted islands of commitment are necessary, as Alasdair MacIntyre reminds us, in the "new dark ages." We need small communities with a new and different Benedictine commitment to a moral tradition and cultivation of virtue in the context of friendship within and outside of the tradition (MacIntyre 1981, 263).

Nothing is real until it is embodied. The community of faith must be a community of deeds. It is in action that we see the conception. Only the racially integrated church has a basis for speaking about racial justice; only a church involved in prisoner rehabilitation and victim and offender reconciliation has a "moral right to speak—or to offer any good ideas—about prison conditions or parole regulations" (Yoder 1994, 22).

The link between spirituality and discipleship is largely a matter of slowly developing "a set of Christian instincts":

> Discipleship usually is not a grand calling or a spectacular act of martyrdom. Rather, it is a set of Christlike instincts and reflexive responses of love that gradually take shape in our lives over a period of years. We immerse ourselves in Scripture and in awareness of his presence. Then, when we have to respond quickly to a life

situation, we are more likely to act in a way that is a credit to our
Lord. (Kraybill 1989, 78)

To be in Christ, in the Spirit, in the Lord, in the body, in the
church, are interchangeable, essentially equivalent. So the evidences (the co-effects called the fruits) of the Spirit—the signs one
is living in the guiding energy of the sacred—are the marks of true
discipleship. These are the radical act of love for the neighbor; the
joyful delight in the way of Jesus; the stubborn commitment to be
reconciling and bridge building; the capacity to outlast, outsuffer,
outlove the enemy; the warmth of nonpossessive gentleness; the
passionate pursuit of justice as true goodness; the recklessness
to cast oneself and one's future trustingly upon God's ultimate
acceptance; the courage to live faithfully without self-defense,
self-protection, or self-survival as a final value; the discipline to
stay the course, hold true to the goal. Evidences, each of them;
fruits, all of them—fruits being the mature, nourishing results of
productive life, characteristics, every one of them, that reveal the
character of the disciple.

As John Milbank argues, for one to belong to the church means
one has become part of those practices of perfection that make us
capable of becoming friends with one another, friends with ourselves, and friends with God. This, then, constitutes the music of
creation. The music which the church has learned to sing through
this threefold friendship is a music for all of creation, and its calling is to outsing all competing songs (Milbank 1990, 424–30).

A Community of Health and Healing

The quality of community that surrounds a person is the most
significant factor in wholeness and well-being. Positive community invites growth to balanced personhood; negative community
meets only basic survival needs. The individual-in-community is
the proper unit of humanness. Creative, curative, sustaining community is a network of significant others knit together by a web of
covenants and contracts. Some of these are explicit commitments,
others are implicit; some are conscious and responsible, others

are unconscious and therefore mixed in our understanding and expectations. These covenants and contracts nourish health and may enable healing.

Community is the natural setting for healing, and in positive community, persons are sustained and guided, sometimes confronted and corrected, always accepted and prized. In negative community, injured persons may be bypassed; oppressed persons often become invisible.

> The ultimate therapy is to translate our private problems into corporate issues. In doing so we will discover that some of our private problems are too trivial to be dignified with public status, and they will fall away. But others, we will discover, are not private at all—they are common to our time. And as we see our own plight in the lives of our sisters and brothers we will begin to find health. Therapy involves identifying and building communities of concern. Only so can we heal ourselves. (Palmer 1977, 12)

The actual community surrounding a person is only one of the multiple communities necessary for this balance of well-being and growth. Each person maintains both an actual/local community and an individually created/widely scattered network of friendships composed of significant persons from many circles of involvement. Healthy personalities create and sustain these several communities, which balance and correct each other. When one community fails to support or intervene in aspects of one's life, another community supplies the missing aspects of presence and authenticity.

The "normal," healthy person creates and sustains a "normal" system of twenty to thirty people (twenty for introverts, thirty for extroverts) with high relational strength. About 50 percent of the people in this system are interrelated in a semi-open network of relationships. This rich human system allows for interaction with representatives of the various circles when appropriate to balance and interconnect the varied aspects of one's life. Thus one participates and contributes to multiple communities, such as a familial community of extended family; a friendship community of persons gathered in a lifetime of experience; a work commu-

nity of colaborers and colleagues; a church community of fellow
worshipers and disciples; a recreational community of people with
whom one enjoys leisure, art, sports, or other entertainments; a
guild community of fellow professionals or associates in one's
career or avocation; and other communities chosen out of the
richness of the one's interests.

Visualize this system as a daisy. Each group is a petal, and all
are connected at some point to the person and thus related to
each other. So healthy people have three or four truly significant
persons in their family of origin, two or three in the present
nuclear family, five or six constant and utterly reliable friends,
three or four persons at work they can count on no matter what,
three or four persons they look for at church to connect with in
genuine spiritual intimacy, three or four they join with in play
and recreation, and so forth. These make up the personal community of positive support, celebration, and active participation
that keeps them alive and flourishing as personalities and as
persons.

The "conflicted" person creates a much poorer system—we
sometimes call it a "neurotic" system—of only ten to twelve people
with mixed communication and often ambivalent relationships
with many of the groups. The system is more rigidly divided and
has little interrelationship between the various groupings. It may
actually depend on people who are emotionally distant, even persons who are dead. Visualize this system as a spider with very long
legs. The individual is the center, and each long spider leg reaches
to a separate and isolated relationship with some other person. The
individual is careful to keep the others separate and uninformed
about each other lest they compare notes and confront a common
reality. So the individual goes to one person for support (but does
not want the next to know of this), then proceeds to another for
contrasting needs (but keeps this dependency hidden from the
first), and so on. The spider system is a shadow of community;
because it lacks interconnectedness, it is not community in the
true sense, with accountability and answerability to a balanced
circle of co-travelers.

The deeply injured person sustains a "troubled" system of
only four to five people, with a low or negative connection to

each. It is often 90 to 100 percent interwoven as an enmeshed support system and is often made up of caretakers and enablers who surround the individual and, when together, speak of how to be helpful and supportive in light of the individual's brokenness or inability to cope daily. Visualize this system as a football huddle with the injured person in the middle pretending to play but seeking support and cover. This is an exclusive, binding, constrictive system that becomes crazy-making even as it offers help.

Mobility, career choices, occupational commitments, compulsive work habits, emotional cutoffs in relationships, and natural aging losses can all move a person from the normal to the neurotic or the deeply troubled system pattern. Clergy, for example, often report having experienced a normal system while in seminary, then moving to the neurotic and then to the deeply troubled system existence as they proceeded from one pastorate to another and failed to keep the multiple petals of their daisy of communities alive and well. Physicians complain of the difficulty of maintaining a healthy daisy of personal group commitments because of their schedules. Every profession has its demands that insulate; every calling can alienate and isolate.

The persons who make up our sustaining systems are not pictures in an album or names in an address book. They are real, living people who know us and are known in return. There are seven characteristics of the interpersonal relationships between individuals and those who are their truly significant others:

1. *Interaction and interface.* Whether face-to-face or by phone, letter, or email, the individual spends time with and expends energy on these people.
2. *Intensity and involvement.* The depth of thinking, feeling, and emoting time invested in the other persons shows intensity in the giver, involvement in the listener.
3. *Affirmation and acceptance.* The individual's recognition of the other person, the affirmation of the importance of this indispensable relationship, and the other's acceptance of the individual as a valued and important partner make this a truly positive connection.

4. *Instrumentality and material aid.* The relationship can be counted on for concrete assistance in times of need, for mutual aid on call.

5. *Mutuality and reciprocity.* Both the individual and the other return aid and assistance in a solid give-and-take of reciprocal exchange that lets the giving and receiving of help go in both directions.

6. *History and continuity.* Testing and growth occur over time as trust is reaffirmed and confidence matures.

7. *Depth and transcendence.* Over time the relationship deepens to the level of profound humanness, opens to the sharing of central commitments, and breaks through to respect and understanding of the other's relationship with God and orientation toward living out faith in daily life—indeed in this very relationship that the two share.

In every person's system, relationships will vary from high to low on the above elements. Higher ratings on all seven characteristics indicate strong, supportive, celebrative relationships that promote well-being.

Improvement of one's system—growing the daisy of interrelatedness and sweeping out the spider of dependency—is the path to spiritual as well as emotional growth. We help others grow by inviting them to create healthier systems and by maintaining a good balance with them in our own systems—neither clinging and invading with unhealthy closeness nor distancing and co-existing without genuine connectedness and mutual respect for their distinctness and dignity as persons.

The person-in-community, the self in tripolar relationship with God and neighbor, the disciple in solidarity with fellow disciples joins fully with those who travel the path from one-dimensional narcissism through two-dimensional religiosity to a full, three-dimensional spirituality of radical participation in the multiple richness of actual, local, creative personal communities. "We are formed by the lives which intersect with ours. The larger and richer our community, the larger and richer is the content of the self," Palmer writes (1977, 12). The way to selfhood, the way to personal emotional health, the way to fully dimensional spirituality, is the way of community.

On the Other Hand

There are so many questions that remain. Even after we have done our best to define the kind of community that can summon us to wholeness, there are still many questions that nag our consciousness. These can be actual probes for integrity, or they can be rhetorical items for reflection that do not function as real questions. Or they can nudge us to pay the spiritual costs of sustaining community—after all, real community does not come cheaply.

How can I learn a spirituality that nurtures human wholeness unless I commit myself to do all I can and contribute all I can to building a community where we together are seeking ways to practice the imitation of Christ? Or will I have to be content with a spirituality of desirable but finally optional virtues?

How can I find spiritual co-travelers who are willing to invest time, give attention, risk self-disclosing, and jointly covenant for a life of shared responsible discipleship? Or will I have to go it alone and learn that part of spirituality that is possible for a self that is seeking to transcend itself by itself?

How can I learn a spirituality of accountability to God the Other unless I have the opportunity to be accountable to significant others? How can I live a spirituality of accountability unless I participate in a community where my acts and their consequences are visible to all who are affected by them? Or will I have to settle for a spirituality that is answerable ultimately only to itself?

How can I learn a spirituality of humility and equality before God unless I live in a community where hierarchy is unnatural, where dominance is not rewarded, and where superiority is neither desirable nor inevitable? Or will I have to claim my place in a spirituality of entitlement if I am privileged, or of unentitlement if I am not?

How can I learn a spirituality of immediate and reflexive concern for the needs of others that seeks to do something about the unjust distribution of resources unless I contribute to a community where sharing is meaningful because we agree to consume less, waste less, do more with less? Or will I have to follow a spirituality that costs me little?

How can I learn a spirituality of dissident discipleship that takes risks in the imitation of Christ unless I join a community that offers support for maintaining a consistent and sensitive conscience? Or will I have to find a rationale for a spirituality that smoothes the contradictions and offers comfort for my unease before the call of Christ?

How can I learn a spirituality of deep reverence for the preciousness of persons unless I practice such honor of others in a community where we are persons, not roles, to each other? Or is the cost of all of this too high to consider in a world that allows self-realization and self-fulfillment as less demanding paths to a spirituality of personal self-actualization?

For Meditation

The following hymn is freely adapted and condensed from the twenty-five stanzas of Hymn 119 in the *Ausbund*, the 1564 hymnbook of Anabaptist martyrs. It offers a vision that suggests a sort of stubborn, Jesus-in-our-midst loyalty to the community of the Spirit.

> We gather, we sing from the heart,
> We celebrate Christ-unity;
> And in our midst Jesus takes part,
> Creating his community.
>> Together we sing out his life,
>> Together we sing out his grace.
>> Together we sing out his gift,
>> Together we sing out his peace.
>
> We gather, we sing out our fears,
> Confess them in humility;
> And as we meet Jesus appears
> And transforms our futility.
>> Together we reread his words
>> Together we recall his death,

Together we retell his works,
Together we rebreathe his breath.

We gather, we sing out our pain,
Our sadness our grief and our loss;
And as we meet Jesus again,
We yield to the way of the cross.
Together we search for his will,
Together we offer our prayer,
Together we surrender all,
Together we rest in his care.

3

The Practice of–
Tenacious Serenity

"If it be possible, let this cup pass
Nevertheless, not my will but thine"
And . . . "Get up, let us go forward."

A life never goes wrong because of turning aside on a false trail,
It goes wrong because the main trail is false (Yalom 1989, 227).

Serene tenacity is the quality of yielded fortitude, of surrendered steadfastness that stays the course, commits the soul, and relinquishes the self to what is truly good, what is ultimately prized, what is the will of God.

Willing Obedience

On the night of April 15, 1912, Annie Funk found a seat in one of the last lifeboats about to be lowered from the sinking Titanic, but as the

85

command "Lower away!" was being shouted, she saw a mother with children in the throng left behind on the deck. She did not hesitate to call out, to summon them to the boat, to give up her place and then watch them swing over the side to safety as the Titanic began to break apart and slip into the North Atlantic depths.

"It was just like Annie to do something like that," Annie's friends in the Butter Valley, north of Philadelphia, all said.

When she had left Berks County in 1906 to travel to India as a teacher and missionary in Janjgir, a friend had cautioned her about the dangers of an ocean voyage to the other side of the world. "I have no fear," she replied, "Our heavenly Father is as near to us on sea as on land."

Did she recall those words as the band reputedly played the hymn "Nearer My God to Thee" (Kraybill 1978/1990, 891)?

—⁂—

Michele Hershberger tells of going through a different kind of Gethsemane.

The phone rang in my new little office. The call was from my husband, Del. Someone had beat up Tara, our oldest daughter, at school. She was not badly hurt. It looked like a random act of violence. She was a new kid in an inner-city school. Maybe this was a freak incident.

But two days later, the same girl waited for Tara to get off the bus, threw her to the ground, and began kicking her in the head. Teachers stopped the girl as quickly as they could, but Tara was terribly shaken, and so were Del and I. I felt an overwhelming sense of hatred. Tara and her sister Erin did not want to go to school. They both had nightmares. This was a new community. We had moved from Oregon to Indiana only three weeks before and now this.

I sat in my seminary class on Christian peacemaking and heard people making connections between spirituality and love for the enemy. Finally in tears I told the class what had happened. I told them about my hatred, that I was not ready to do anything yet but hate this child I had never met. They put their arms around me, prayed for me, affirmed my honesty. Give it time, they said.

As my heart began to yield to reality, I knew I had to meet the girl who had beaten up Tara. I had to put a face to the name. How hard could it be? She's just a little girl, I thought.

"Have you ever considered volunteering to be this girl's mentor?" a friend asked. "We have this adult-selected child mentoring program at the school. Why not give it a try?" The logic was clear. "You have hateful feelings toward her that you will never get rid of unless you get to know her as a person."

I set up an appointment to meet her. I was nervous as I waited in the office. Then she walked in—a fifth-grade girl, almost my height and strong enough to take me down. She could not look me in the eyes. "Sondra, I'm Michele. I know you don't know me. I'm Tara's mom. I'm here because—well because I have some pretty hard feelings toward you for beating up Tara. But Jesus told me—do you know about Jesus? (She nodded her head.)—that I must love people, people I may really dislike. So that's why I'm here. I can't love you unless I learn to know you. Will you let me be your special friend, your mentor? We could see each other every week." There was a long silence. Then Sondra looked straight at me and said, "Yes."

That began our mentoring relationship and the slow building of a friendship with trust and genuine care for each other. Our relationship is rocky at times. Sometimes I want to give up. When I see only the failure, the hopelessness of a home life filled with physical abuse, neglect, and drugs, I'm scared. But we meet, we work together, we read together at school, we go to Dairy Queen, we welcome each other into our homes, and we conquer the fears inside us of each other's culture. I make peace with the fears for my own children; we learn to love. Sometimes I can glimpse God's greater good. God used that negative situation to transform me (condensed from Hershberger 1999, 154ff).

Essential Serenity and Tenacity

Serenity and tenacity go together. For Annie Funk, this unity of serenity and tenacity gave her the ability to not be overwhelmed by fear, to see the mother and children in the throng, to shout

"Stop the boat!" and give up the last seat rather than praying for them while leaving them behind. This unity of serenity and tenacity enabled Michele Hershberger to go beyond acceptance of her fears and release of her hate to the discovery of relationship. In both stories, the two sides of essential serenity and existential tenacity are inseparably united. The practice of self-surrender is not separated from stubborn commitment. A yielded will is a resolute will.

In the literature of sixteenth-century spirituality, there is a word for this indivisible quality of surrender and stubbornness: *Gelassenheit.* This word for an essential spiritual virtue has a long history. It is central to the work of Meister Eckhart in the thirteenth century, John Tauler and Gerard Groot of the Brethren of the Common Life in the fourteenth century, and Thomas à Kempis in the fifteenth. All prized *Gelassenheit.*

The word is not easy to translate; indeed, it has over fifteen acceptable definitions. In medieval devotion, this word for self-surrender was invariably passive. It referred to the soul's submission before God. But in the Radical Reformation of Anabaptism it came to mean both passive yieldedness and active unyieldedness. This union of self-surrender and radical obedience, uniquely Anabaptist, echoes the identification of martyrs with Gethsemane: the resistance ("If it is possible, let this cup pass me by" [Matt. 26:39 NEB]) and surrender ("yet not as I will, but as thou wilt" [Matt. 26:39 NEB]) with courageous consequence ("Enough! . . . Up, let us go forward!" [Mark 14:41–42 NEB]). Serenity with tenacity is the heart of Anabaptist spiritual devotion. It unites the passive "not my will but yours" with the active "Thy will be done on earth."

C. S. Lewis once wrote, "There are only two kinds of people in the end: those who say to God, 'Thy will be done,' and those to whom God says in the end, 'thy will be done'" (Lewis 1946, 72).

Essential Serenity

Serenity is the essential relinquishment of one's rights as sacred; it is the essential renunciation of one's claims to survival as divine right; it is the essential release from self-preoccupation that keeps one centered in the self. It is essential in both meanings of the word—essential as necessity, essential as essence. It is necessary to authentic spirituality, and it is the soul of genuine spirituality and therefore its essence.

Serenity is necessary to spirituality because human existence is by nature anxious. Anxiety is the primary characteristic of self-awareness. When it overwhelms us, the rush of life traps our center. We become hurried, captive souls, entangled in a web of routine involvements, preoccupied with the mundane, caught up in the anxiety of the business of life. Spirituality shifts our center to a higher vantage point, from which life can be seen with patience, work can be viewed as vocation, and the routine of daily tasks can be met as service. Spirituality offers the serenity necessary for us to step outside, stand over against, and rise above routine and let it become a fresh stimulus. The center of our soul has then been relocated above the tyranny of the trivial. Then we see all of life as significant within a larger purpose; it becomes a calling.

Serenity is essential to—that is, part of the essence of—deep spirituality. It springs from the soul of spirituality because it is the inner state of basic trust that is the primary connection to the transcendent, the peaceful sense of resting in the awareness of God. Serenity is a core calmness, a deep confidence running down to—or up from—the substrata where we make our most intimate contact with God. Faith reaches, with its longest, strongest root, down underneath all we have learned, underneath all that has been nurtured in our growth as persons, to connect our life to the streams of trust and serenity that flow along the inner watercourses in the bedrock of spiritual depths. So we can speak of this profound inner quiet of ultimate trust as essential serenity.

In essential serenity, one rests from having and relies on being; one embraces humanness, accepts limitations, admits pretenses, confesses finitude; one encounters the inevitability of mortality and surrenders the fantasy that death is for others, but not for the self; one confronts fallibility, frailty, and failure with little denial and does not flee into hyperactivity, distraction, or a dream world of alternate reality. In essential serenity, the backrooms of the soul that have never heard the whispers of divine love, never felt the attention of God's unconditional positive regard, never risked

opening to the light are touched, warmed, welcomed, prized. John
Claypool writes about discovering these depths:

> Between my ears, I knew all about grace and justification by faith
> and mercy and forgiveness, but to quote the great black preacher
> Howard Thurman, 'the other parts of me had not yet heard the
> word.' Grace was a concept to me at that time, not an event in which
> I participated to the depths of my being. (Claypool 1983, 55)

In serenity one can let go, let be, let come what may, and ultimately, let God. These four dimensions of freedom for the soul,
which I shall call let-go-ness, let-be-ness, let-come-ness, let-Thy-
will-be-done-ness, are successive acts of relinquishment and moments of discovery. In these discoveries, the soul makes radical
shifts from controlling and demanding to releasing the clenched
fist and welcoming serenity.

As I write, it is one week since I learned amid tears that my clos-
est brother has an inoperable and inexorable pancreatic tumor. He
will lose almost all that is precious to him in a matter of months.
In a terribly short time, I shall lose his friendship, the knowledge
that he is there. When we talk, his faith is fixed in God, his soul
yearns for a miracle, and our hearts are breaking. I go about my
classes, meetings, and (formerly) important work with newly naked
eyes. A voice in my soul constantly reminds me, "Someone I love
knows that he is dying." We all are, of course. One out of one dies.
But he knows. With this stunning rediscovery of the perfectly ob-
vious, I am sobered, silenced. I feel not the professional empathy
of my trained therapeutic self, but the pathos of an untrained co-
sufferer. The world stands still in moments of pain. I am counting
the months he has until this not yet known sorrow.

In the midst of this my daughter calls from Moscow. She is
pregnant. Her voice is radiant. My heart glows incandescently. I
laugh tears. I am incredulous before such happiness. *She's going
to have a baby.* Her first. Their first. Our first. I am counting the
months she will have until this not yet known joy.

Both of these events of waiting "until" require letting go. They
come in their own way, and although we do all we can to forestall
death and prepare for birth, we ultimately must also let them

come. Waiting for such ultimate events touches the deepest long-ing, yearning, caring, wanting, hoping center of the soul. There is a seismic response along the primary fault lines of personhood and personality. The heart becomes volcanic. Feelings well up like burning magma that can force themselves outward as we try to take control of the unknown, take away the threat, take charge of what is beyond our reach.

This eruption from the center, from the nexus of personhood, from the core, is the executive message from the true self, the core of our being. If our core is the hard nut of control and command, then the need to dominate, dictate, master, or play god will, in the context of evil events, rage against the bad news, or in the context of good events, attempt to usurp the joy or take charge of the good. Striving and stress will radiate from the center rather than serenity. When the center that is touched is the still turning point of our soul, essential serenity with its core of calm, then we will see with humility, feel with gratitude, and know with certainty that there is a God who is not the self, but an Other. If the core has this open, welcoming, receptive center, there is serenity.

Existential Tenacity

The other side of serenity is tenacity. The two are one. In yielded-ness, I surrender self-will, committing myself to live out a higher will, praying "Thy will be done."

This yieldedness of the will, in *Gelassenheit*, is not the *will-less* resignation characteristic of classic pietism—of the "Have Thine own way, Lord, have Thine own way. Thou art the potter, I am the clay; mold me and make me after Thy will, while I am waiting yielded and still" variety; nor is it the *willful* "sin boldly" freedom of Luther's trust in all-inclusive grace. It is the *willing* yieldedness of the stubbornly faithful yet incorrigibly nonconformist radi-cal disciple. This active yieldedness we are calling tenacity is the positive twist made most clearly by the early Anabaptist Hans Denck, who wrote of the serenity side, "There is no other way to blessedness than to lose one's self-will," and of the tenacity side, "If I run in the truth, then I run suffering-ly, then my running will not be in vain" (in Bauman 1991, 72, 87). The courage to run one's life course with every energy available is an utter surrender of the whole soul to the larger vision and in obedience to a call that is heard above all others.

Condemned Anabaptist leader Michael Sattler, just before he was burned at the stake in 1527, wrote to his congregation at Horb: "In this peril I completely surrendered myself unto the will of the Lord, and . . . prepared myself even for death for His testimony. [Yet] I thought it necessary to stir you up to follow after us in the divine warfare" (Van Braght 1660/1985).

A neither will-less nor willful, but willing commitment to seek, to serve, and to surrender to the will of God in life requires an existential tenacity and temerity that risks all, that is willing to die, that accepts the harsh penalty of martyrdom if necessary to hold true to the way of Jesus. This call to be willing, to even appear willful, summons us to pray the Lord's Prayer (actually the Disciple's Prayer) without glossing over the request, "Thy will be done on earth as it is in heaven." The willing disciple recognizes that these words express a radical political, economic, social, relational commitment of the heart, not just a personal, interior spiritual aspiration. We seek to will what God wills, dangerous and presumptive though that may be, and rigorously seek to match our vision of God's will to the clear way of Jesus.

The human will is not the essential villain of rebellious evil, which is bound by sin and must be finally, totally silenced. The will is capable of choice—we are each the sum total of all our choices—yet it has fallen from the health and wholeness of original creation. As early Anabaptist theologian Balthasar Hubmaier wrote, "the image or inbreathing of God is still in us all, although captive. As a live spark covered in cold ashes, it is still alive and will steam if heavenly water is poured on it" (Snyder 1995, 89). This was written by way of contrast to the Reformers' vision, where no free will—authentically free choice—is possible, so all salvation is by grace and we are justified by faith alone.

Luther, like his colleague and former benefactor Andreas Karlstadt, taught that sin is volitional—the choice of self-will—so that conquering evil is accomplished by incrementally yielding self-will. This passive stance he called *Gelassenheit*. Anabaptists instead saw the dual character of this "yielding-and-striving" as the core of spirituality in an "obedience of faith" that visibly conforms to Christ. This affirmed the medieval vision of spiritual resignation yet reformed it by pointing it resolutely toward the imitation of Christ (Snyder 1995, 26). We yield courageously, surrender stubbornly, relinquish resolutely.

> The early Anabaptists used the term Gelassenheit to convey the idea of yielding absolutely to God's will with a dedicated heart—forsaking all selfishness. They believed that Christ called them to abandon self-interest and follow his example of suffering, meekness, humility and service (Kraybill 1989, 25).

Gelassenheit, the German word for serenity, contentment, and a calm spirit, also has a deeper, more demanding meaning that has shaped Anabaptist spirituality. This core meaning is relinquishment, submission, resignation to the will of God, yielding to God and to others in God's family. It links together the virtues of humility: simplicity, austerity, obedience, submission, and solidarity. It contrasts sharply with the rugged individualism prized in modern culture, in which a lifestyle of individual fulfillment and achievement is the core value of a society of autonomous selves.

The goal of *Gelassenheit* is fulfillment in community, not self-actualization in isolation; it is a commitment to seek consensus through sacrifice, service, respect for others, and obedience to the collective will of the group. This is needed for all social order, but modern Western life sets only the boundaries that are necessary to protect the safety and security of society, allowing individual choice and self-determination to express a wide latitude. In the early Anabaptist community, a common cluster of prized virtues defined a range of acceptable practices—ways of showing modesty in how one acts, talks, dresses, walks. The person relinquished the use of force, the option of violent self-defense. The offended gave up the desire for revenge, the right to hate the oppressor or persecutor, the entitlement of insisting on one's own way. Giving up self-realization as an independent agent, letting go of the self-actualization that one could achieve by leaving church and family to "find oneself" apart from community are all a part of this relinquishment.

This basic attitude of the Anabaptists is richly illustrated in *The Martyrs' Mirror* of 1660, which tells the stories of people preparing for death, like Hans van Overdam, who wrote from his prison cell to the authorities of Gent in 1550:

> We would rather through the grace of God suffer our temporal bodies to be burned, drowned, racked, or tortured, as it may seem good to you, or be scourged, banished, or driven away, or robbed of our goods, than to show any obedience contrary to the word of God, and we will be patient therein, committing vengeance to God, for we know that He says vengeance belongeth to me, I will recompense. (Van Braght, 1660/1985)

As the Anabapists faced incarceration and execution, the primary biblical text that epitomized the concept of *Gelassenheit* was found in Revelation, in the story of the beast who persecutes the followers of the way of Jesus: "This is where the fortitude and faithfulness of God's people have their place" (Rev. 13:10, NEB). *Gelassenheit* combines these two qualities, patience and endurance, or better expressed, "fortitude and faithfulness," as the New English Bible translates the passage: "Whoever takes the sword to kill, by the sword he is bound to be killed. This is where the fortitude and faithfulness of God's people have their place" (13:10). And later John says, "This is where the fortitude of God's people has its place—in keeping God's commands and remaining loyal to Jesus" (14:12). This is serenity in the face of fire, stake, and sword; this is tenacity in spite of rack, thumbscrew, and drowning sack. The verse that follows was claimed as a guarantee sufficient to sustain *Gelassenheit* even through martyrdom:

> I heard a voice from heaven, saying, "Write this: 'Happy are the dead who die in the faith of Christ! Henceforth,' says the Spirit, 'they may rest from their labours; for they take with them the record of their deeds.'" (Rev. 14:13 NEB)

Serenity in Practice

Serenity finds courage in asking, "If it be possible, let this pain pass"; it finds peace in "Not my will but Thine" and tenacious endurance in resolving, "Enough, get up, get on with it." This is the tenacity of "Thy will be done on earth as it is in heaven."

Serenity refuses control but tenaciously welcomes and assumes responsibility. I cannot force my life or world, but I can respond with my whole soul to whatever life or the world may offer.

Serenity is beyond self-control. It is the discovery of self-patience, self-compassion, and self-understanding, which it extends equally to every other person.

Serenity is learning to differentiate between intentional and unintentional thoughts, and then, with tenacity, renewing one's mind intentionally with trust, confidence, hope, and joy.

Serenity is giving up on trying to get others to love you; it is giving love whether reciprocated or not. Serenity is giving up on expecting or demanding love from others and thinking of new ways to offer love even to those who seem unloving.

Serenity is giving up on a purpose-driven life, an outcome-oriented existence, a managerial attitude toward events, and personal power in encounters with others, and becoming someone who tenaciously prizes integrity and intimacy in relationships, loves collaboration and cooperation in community, and cares more about the welfare of the next generation than about the record of this one.

Serenity, the essence of our center, is not self-created, not learned, not given to us. It is there already. But we have closed it off. It must be opened again. Serenity opens as we let go of trying to become something and begin to savor being someone. Serenity is the courage to let go, to open, to be.

Serenity sustains us from within. Tenacity directs us outside ourselves. Both serenity and tenacity embrace the possible; they do not spend themselves yearning for the impossible.

Serenity is valuing what you have done in life more than reviewing and defending the record of what you have done; it is prizing what is good and right more than what appears to be good or is praised as right.

Serenity for a moment can release a lifetime of striving; calmness for a time can relieve years of turmoil; openness for a period can cleanse a long accumulation of debris.

Serenity is not the brother of ambition, the child of greed, the sister of competition, but it may be the father of service and the mother of surprising success.

Serenity may be found in accepting grace and accepting ourselves as a gift of grace; we are now what we always shall be, and it is enough. At other times serenity is claiming courage and risking what it is we shall become. It is not yet apparent what we shall be, but we do know that when Christ appears to us, we shall be like him (1 John 3:2).

"Like a River Glorious, Is God's Perfect Peace"

At the age of eighty Dr. Erland Waltner wrote:

> During the last decade of my life . . . I have sensed I am in transition on my experience of God. . . . For many years my time with God was something like a quick stop while driving on a long and sometimes rough road . . . a pit stop in the Indianapolis 500 when drivers stop to refuel, to check tires, to watch for possible trouble ahead before hurrying back to the fast lane as quickly as possible. I called mine a "spirituality of the road."
>
> Now I am beginning to see my relationship with God as being like a river which helps me get from here to there, to carry me along from day to day, from task to task, from one experience to the next. I am experiencing God as One who is not only daily present with me but One who is in motion, bearing me up, sustaining, renewing, enabling me.
>
> Spirituality of the river asks for a higher kind of trusting in God, a deeper kind of love, a profound hope to be carried on by this river. (Waltner in Koontz 1996, 83–84)

When we trust in God, relinquishing control, we discover a deeper kind of love as we relax in his grace, a profound hope as we come to peace with what is coming. The river of God's presence carries us and bears us up as, in serene tenacity, we flow from one moment to the next.

On The Other Hand

If the goal of life is not to be better, bigger, more perfect, more capable, more competitive, more admired, or more famous, then what is it? If the signs of God's blessing are not prosperity, sweeping success, wealth, megaspirituality, mega-acclaim, leadership in a megachurch, or being remembered in generations that follow, then what are they? Perhaps serenity is for the passive, tenacity for stubborn losers, and what counts is doing great things—for God, of course.

Or is the secret letting go? Is the path to change and growth found not in trying to be different from who we are, but in accepting who we truly are? Is the heart of spiritual discovery finally found in grace, received as a gift, and does it result in our seeking to be less, not more?

For Meditation

The following hymn text on relinquishment *(Gelassenheit)* is from Hymn 110 in the *Ausbund*, the 1564 hymnal of Anabaptist martyrs:

> Jesus our guide, stands by our side,
> To follow him is true life;
> Take up his cross, whatever loss,
> Home, husband, or child and wife.
> Answer his call, relinquish all,
> Offer him your servanthood
> Join with the poor in spirit for
> Theirs is the kingdom of God.
>
> Jesus our Lord gave us this word;
> Yield your heart, soul, strength and mind,
> Give up control, deny self-will

As was he, so be resigned.
Embrace his way without delay
In selfless relinquishment.
And poor in soul, at last find all
That gives eternal content.

4

The Practice of—Habitual Humility

"Humility claimed is pride renamed."
(If I admit I invented this proverb am I no longer humble?)

Habitual humility is the primary evidence, the undeniable sign of Christian discipleship. Humility is sincere concern for the good of others balanced with simple gratitude for the gift of one's self, shown in a genuine willingness to serve the neighbor and heard in the gentle laughter of self-effacing humor.

Unpretentious Personhood

"Someone paid my rent again. I've gone the last two times to pay, and it's already paid."

The man reporting on this strange turn of events had just lost his job and was struggling to keep food on the table. As a young pastor in the Shenandoah Valley of Virginia, I found myself caught

99

up in the mystery. Someone was repeatedly, anonymously, continuously doing good on the sly.

I would be calling on a poor neighbor downhill from the Mennonite church and the woman would confide, "I was just returning home and I saw that the truck had pulled in and was filling my tank with heating oil—I'd been out of oil for three days—and it's been so cold, goodness knows I needed it. 'I can't pay for this,' I told him. 'What do I do?' 'It's OK. It's already paid for,' he said."

Then two brothers got into a hassle over a couple-hundred-dollar loss from calves that died. In their anger, they stopped talking to each other. After a week of silent standoff that put the whole neighborhood on edge, each of them got an envelope in the mail with nothing but a couple of crisp hundred-dollar bills inside, and each thought the other had reached out, had gone the extra mile. They both apologized and things were healing between them when they found out that neither had sent the money. They laughed so hard tears ran. They named the stupidity and resentfulness and promised never to act like spoiled children again.

I had no right to play detective, knowing that the mysterious giver wanted anonymity. But then he slipped up. A great job fell out of the sky for a man who had been unemployed for months. Obviously someone had opened a door for him, and I was pretty sure who it was. Something in the last good deed gave the final clue.

One night the man I suspected as the invisible benefactor picked me up for a long drive across Rockingham County to attend a meeting. As we followed the winding and icy road through the hills, I casually told him about this amazing series of acts by an unknown Good Samaritan. He drove quietly, listening with interest, but gave no flicker of response. I added as an afterthought, "He tipped his hand this last time. I now know who he is, but I've decided never to tell."

"Sounds like you made the right decision," he said. When I glanced at him again a hint of smile flickered for a second. I suspected that he knew I knew that he knew I knew.

"But I could be wrong," I said, "and he may never be found out."

"Isn't that the way it should be?" he replied.

Jayber Crow, the town barber in Port William, a fictional town in Kentucky, is the hero of a wonderful novel by the farmer poet Wendell Berry. One morning in his barber shop, a father named Troy, whose son is in Vietnam, is talking about the people he hates who are protesting the Vietnam war. He not only hated them, he loved hearing himself say bad things about them. As the barber tells the story, Troy says:

> "They ought to round up every one of them sons of bitches and put them in front of the damned communists, and then whoever killed who, it would all be to the good."
>
> There was a little pause after that. Nobody wanted to try to top it. It was hard to do, but I quit cutting hair and looked at Troy. I said, "Love your enemies, bless them that curse you, do good to them that hate you."
>
> Troy jerked his head up and widened his eyes at me. "Where did you get that crap?"
>
> I said, "Jesus Christ."
>
> And Troy said, "Oh."
>
> It would have been a great moment in the history of Christianity, except that I did not love Troy. (Berry 2000, 287)

Humility as Antispirituality

There's something about this tripolar spirituality that reduces one's own part in the equation. In monopolar spirituality it's really about me, about my growth, fulfillment, and actualization as authentically human; in bipolar spirituality it's about the self before God and the discovery of who I am as a person with significance in the grand scheme of things. Too often it's about the self and a god of the self's own creation—"My god and I have a special thing going." In tripolar spirituality, I am of no more worth than any other; instead I must view the other as showing me the face of God. True, I image God in return, but in the reciprocity of seeing both myself and the other as equally loved and prized, there is more than a nudge toward humility. Indeed, there is a nudge toward humor, which is the root of all genuine humility. I must learn to take myself more lightly, even smiling deeply in my soul at the vanity of holy pretensions. Humility requires me to look askance at claims of sainthood so that thoughts of beatification and canonization serve as spiritual funny bones in the knees instead of the elbows. Humility is almost an antispirituality since it looks on the "superspirituality" of pious pretense with a crooked smile.

The laughter of unconscious humility bubbles up out of a sane evaluation of one's own abilities and achievements. Honest, selfless laughter is the effervescence of humility; it is carbonated simplicity. Laughter is the champagne of the Spirit.

Humor and Humility

"Laughing is our way to humility," Mennonite minister and satirist Ryan Ahlgrim has written, "Perhaps the way to puncture pride without wounding the personality is to laugh at ourselves. Humility is very tricky—it easily turns into another form of pride. But taking ourselves less seriously can keep our humility true" (Ahlgrim 1995, 2).

Humor steps back from seriousness to see the lighter side; it holds events at arm's length to see their irony. It is a perspective on life that allows us to discover, express, and appreciate the ludicrous, the absurd, the incongruous elements in ideas, situations, and happenings.

There are many kinds of laughter, and this leads to different theories of why we laugh. The superiority theory is the oldest—we laugh at evil, folly, and ignorance as we look down on the fool. The incongruity theory is less emotional, more rational—we laugh when things don't fit into the pattern or our expectations. The relief theory is more physical—we laugh to vent our nervous energy, anxiety, pent-up emotional drives of anger, jealousy, hate, aggression, and sexual desire. The pleasure theory is more inclusive—we laugh as the result of a pleasant psychological shift that triggers mirth (Morreall 1983, 4–38).

In a community that nourishes a habitual humility, seeing presumed superiority exposed, incongruous vanity deflated, and overcontrolled emotions relieved all contribute to pride's undoing and to humility's quiet return. Playful shifts in how we see things set us free to laugh together. Laughter is a cohesive force; it binds us together, it aids in reconciliation and the restoration of relationship. It is like eating a meal together. It pushes aside rivalry and quarreling, evokes friendship, smoothes interactions, and restores things to a more realistic valuation.

> We should find laughter performing, with mathematical regularity, one of its main functions. . . . We should see that vanity, though it is a natural product of social life, is an inconvenience to society, just as certain slight poisons, continually secreted by the human organism, would destroy it in the long run, if they were not neutralized by other secretions. Laughter is unceasingly doing work of this kind. In this respect, it might be said that the specific remedy of vanity is laughter and that the one failing that is essentially laughable is vanity. (Bergson 1911, 156)

Humor teaches us humility; humility inspires our humor. It helps us see ourselves for what we really are—a bit of dust, a flash of light that burns for a brief second; it nudges us to see life for what it truly is—the search for, not the possession of, truth. One can hold to truth with deep commitment and at the same time handle it with humor. Reverence and irreverence belong together like conviction and imagination, like mature respect and childlike impudence.

Humorous humility sees the foolishness of putting on airs, so it smiles at its own pretenses; it recognizes the pettiness of comparing ourselves to one another, so its tongue is always thrust into the cheek of pride; it knows its own selfish bias, so it persistently pokes fun at its own claims to virtue. It feels its constant inner tug toward self-preference that is insidiously opposed to concern for the other, so it shakes its head self-effacingly when speaking of goodness or stepping up to any moral high ground.

As Anabaptist John Howard Yoder would drolly say, "The world is made up of two kinds of people, the good and the bad, and it's always the good who take it upon themselves to decide which are which."

Because it is not a trait to be achieved but a state of honest self-recognition momentarily experienced, humility happens when self-elevation is leveled, when self-inflation is deflated, when self-appreciation spikes and then drops back to equality. All these are moments of embarrassment for the defensive, but moments of humor for the truly mature.

"Do you know how many true Christians there are in this church?" one judgmental deacon asked his pastor. "No, I don't," the pastor responded, "but I suspect it may be one fewer than you're thinking."

Faith and humor are closely related because both:

> deal with the incongruities of our existence. Humor is concerned with the immediate incongruities of life and faith with the ultimate ones. Laughter is our reaction to the immediate incongruities and those that do not affect us essentially. Faith is the only possible response to the ultimate incongruities of existence which threaten the very meaning of our life. (Niebuhr 1969, 15)

Humor has this intriguing paradoxical quality of putting things together that do not go together; it is called the principle of incongruity. It is the surprising, attention grabbing, often liberating juxtaposition of contradictory and therefore comic opposites—the real and the unreal, the normal and the not normal, the anticipated and the unexpected. Or it highlights and exposes the gap—or gulf—between the ideal and the actual, between intention and achievement, between desire and fulfillment. Often it turns on the eternal conflict between individual and institution, between male and female, between dreams and hard reality.

The comic vision is essentially a protest, so rather than being dour and gloomy persons, Protestants should be first-rate comedians. Unfortunately, they have been known more for their gravity than their levity. The comic perspective protests all finite claims to speak the infinite; it is genuinely prophetic, truly iconoclastic, ultimately humbling. The lofty become the lowly.

"Pride comes before disaster, and arrogance before a fall" (Prov. 16:18 NEB) the old Hebrew proverb warns in a collection of some of the wittiest and wisest words ever written. The humor of elevated pride tripping, of arrogance being toppled by overstepping itself, appeals to everyone except the one in midair.

Humor as Illumination

Humor can be visualized as light and dark—humor that illuminates or humor that paints things with tar. Dark humor is veiled or open aggression; it perpetuates prejudice; it denigrates persons or groups; it buttresses threatened hierarchies; it defends vaunted superiority; it is antihuman.

The secret of light humor is sudden illumination with surprising insight. It is the subtle deflation of whatever or whoever is inflated; it is the re-elevation of those who have been devalued; it is shock when arrogance is humbled; it is relief when pretense is punctured; it is amusement when false claims are exposed.

Light humor is, at its core, about humility. It smiles when pride is invalidated—whether in oneself or in another. It does not yield to aggression, animosity, or the urge to annihilate. It smiles ruefully when reminded of its own fallibility; it chuckles in self-recognition before another's inadequacies; it laughs aloud at the folly of the human situation. These three—the failings of self, the foibles of others, the foolishness of context and conventions—are all about humility.

A humble sense of humor shows us our own absurdities, reveals our own contradictions, as well as revealing the absurdities and contradictions of those around us. Humor will not keep us from all sin, but it is a significant deterrent. When we laugh at ourselves, the laughter is a kind of reverence, a kind of self-deprecation and truth appreciation that expresses acceptance and wonder. In practice, it is a type of confession, a means of contrition; indeed, an act of repentance.

Anabaptist songwriter Linda K. Williams wrote, "When Jesus said, 'love your enemies,' I think he probably meant don't kill them" (Williams 2002). The humor is light, though the time in which she wrote it—the threat of the Iraq war—was dark indeed. One bumper sticker with her words is worth a thousand thoughtless chants of "God bless America."

Laughter keeps the human spirit alive in the midst of deeply troubled times. It is a kind of subversive defiance against both the laws of nature and the laws of human governments. Laughter defies the law of entropy, the downward pull of gravity, and the inertia of evil. When hope should be extinguished, humor ignites the spark of faith. And most important, laughter unites us in solidarity with fellow strugglers, encouraging them to resistance and fortitude. The laughter of solidarity, of lament, of hoping in spite of the odds is, in its purest form, a cry to God, a voice of the soul, a prayer of spirit calling to Spirit.

African-American theologian James Cone tells of a slave who gave the perfect answer to his master and presumed owner, who had just said; "I dreamed I went to Nigger Heaven last night, and I saw there a lot of garbage, some torn-down houses, a few old broken down, rotten fences, the muddiest, sloppiest streets I ever saw, and a big bunch of ragged, dirty Negroes walking around."

"Umph, umph, Massa," the slave replied, "yah sho' musta et de same t'in Ah did las' night, 'cause Ah dreamed Ah went up ter de white man's paradise, an' de streets wuz all ob gol' and silvah, and dey was lots o' milk an' honey dere, an' putty pearly gates, but dey wuzn't uh soul in de whole place" (Cone 1975, 159–160).

In sixteenth-century Poland, a "fool society" named the Babinian Republic was created to celebrate the vanity of feudal powers. When any nonmember did something sufficiently foolish, that exemplar of stupidity or irony was invited to join and to assume an office appropriate to the faux pas committed. A new member could be consecrated an archbishop, for instance, for speaking publicly and authoritatively on matters about which he was totally ignorant, or promoted to a general in the army for maintaining that war was just and good for the society. The fool society grew with such rapidity that it soon included virtually every important official in both church and state. The king of Poland inquired whether the Babinian Republic had a rival emperor and was reassured that as long as he reigned, the society would not dream of electing another (Willeford 1969, 85–86).

Humor as Seriousness

What makes humor and humorous people humble? Humble humor takes life, death, faith, and human fallibility seriously—so seriously that it can laugh at our flawed and feeble efforts to transcend them. We laugh best—indeed, most deeply—in our struggles with those things we hold in utter reverence. We take ourselves, our work, our best efforts at justice and mercy so seriously that we can see their lighter side and feel the deep mirth of humble paradox and contradiction, and then explode in laughter.

Humor that does not take its subject seriously is mockery, derision, or cynicism that snidely victimizes or dehumanizes and can turn vicious and ugly. Humorous humility humanizes the laugher, the smile of the laughee, the wit of the laughter, and the wisdom of their laughing together as it recognizes our shared simplicity or stupidity.

Humor at the hostile and aggressive end of the spectrum may attack offensively or retaliate defensively. It may be actively confrontational or passively caustic; it may overwhelm or undermine. Cast as a joke, the most surgical judgment or the most subtle castigation can be used offensively while avoiding responsibility. ("Why did you take offense? How could you possibly have thought it was aimed at you?") Humor that dismisses another in a cynical or cavalier way ignores the real significance of the other. Glib, superficial exploitation of wit to devalue another blinds the self to the meaning of the person as a person. It is profoundly arrogant, choosing to stand over the other in scorn or contempt rather than to stand with the other in cohumanity.

The cutting humor of "the tall poppy syndrome," where anyone who stands above the crowd gets lopped off with the machete of wit, occurs in groups in which no one is allowed to excel. "It's the nail that sticks up that gets pounded," says the proverb. This prohibition against uncommon excellence is, in inverse strategy, as comparative as any other form of pride. It holds others down in a vain attempt to deny what is possible and withstand the inevitable.

Social, ethnic, class, cultural, or religious slurs give voice to such aggression, and when they are artful or clever, they assume a life of their own and pass from mouth to ear at high speed. An aggressive joke is a communicable disease with greater spreading power than a virus.

Critical humor is rarely associated with relational integrity or authentic spirituality; neither includes self-centered joking, prejudice-laden jesting, intergroup labeling, or stereotyping. The humor that enhances spirituality is the insightful truth-telling of irony that points out paradoxes of existence or contradictions between behavior and belief, first of the self, and with an element of grace when it includes others.

Early Anabaptists who were deeply committed to truthfulness—letting yes mean yes and no mean no—did not hesitate to point out the contradictions of destroying persons to save their souls, of killing to convert, of burning people at the stake to perhaps stave off their inevitable end in hellfire, of persecuting to promote the love of God and neighbor. Sharp satire crackles and surprisingly subtle irony sparkles in their repartee with the religious prosecutors and judges. The feigned compassion of the executioner as the wood was being piled around the stake did not go unnoticed by the ones being torched, and their prayers and songs have an uncanny accuracy in pointing out the incongruity and contradiction of "killing for salvation." Humorous humility, for those in desperate times, is the voice of faith, the courageous laughter of hope that breaks out of sadness and suffering. It is an irrepressible, radical, unreasonable hope that sustains our sanity in insane situations. Through humor, hope has the last word.

Humility as Balance

Humility is a fine balance—it is neither self-deprecating nor self-promoting. The humble person sees the self with equanimity, acts with unpretentious simplicity, assumes an essential equality of persons that makes it possible to flow with others, neither climbing above nor stooping below. The gyroscope of sane self-worth constantly rights and levels the soul in the ups and downs of relationships, the successes and failures of one's dreams, the give and take of commerce and community. Humility, when balanced, provides a fair and just way of perceiving one's place in the human family.

> Humility consists, roughly, in having oneself and one's accomplishments in perspective. On this view, to be humble is to understand

yourself and your moral entitlements sufficiently clearly that you are disposed not to exaggerate about these. (Richards 1992, 188)

There are no splendid human beings; none are so perfect, so balanced, so without fault that we must hold them totally in awe. There are those we admire, deeply respect, and seek to follow as guides, but each has a shadow side, all have areas of immaturity or incongruity.

Genuine humility is free of any pretense; it is not persuaded by exaggerated praise; it is not gratified by flattery or overestimation by others even when such positive evaluation is deserved and appropriate. Humility neither undervalues nor overvalues achievement or service rendered. Humility does not take the other more seriously than the self or the self less seriously than the other. It does not overlook evil done to any person, whether self or other. (However, if you took all the evil done in your community as seriously as though it had happened to you, then reading any newspaper would be insufferable—indeed, emotionally impossible.)

What is appropriate to true humility is a genuine respect for another's right to feel deep pain or outrage at being misused, just as you have the right to feel that way when similarly wronged. Believing that we are all of equal intrinsic worth, refusing to believe that one's own rights are greater than those of others, insisting that each person's dignity and worth deserve full respect is this point of view or perspective of balance that we are calling humility.

"Humorless people are almost always hopelessly condemned to immaturity. Or should we say that immature people are condemned to a humorless existence?" (Häring 1970, 75). In his wonderful insights on maturity and spirituality, Harry Abbott Williams writes in the book *Tensions*:

God, we believe, accepts us, accepts all [persons], unconditionally, warts and all. Laughter is the purest form of our response to God's acceptance of us. For when I laugh at myself I accept myself and when I laugh at other people in genuine mirth I accept them. Self-acceptance in laughter is the very opposite of self-satisfaction or pride. For in laughter I accept myself not because I'm some sort of super-person, but precisely because I'm not. There is everything funny about a person who thinks he is. In laughing at my own claims to importance or regard I receive myself in a sort of loving forgiveness which is an echo of God's forgiveness of me. In much conventional contrition there is a selfishness and pride which are scarcely hidden. In our desperate self-concern we blame ourselves for not being the super-persons we think we really are. But in laughter we sit light to ourselves. That is why laughter is the purest form of our response to God. (Williams 1982, 11)

Humility as Courage

Humility is not a word held in high regard, with its undertone of low self-esteem, powerlessness, subservience, and overready subjection to authority. But this modern conception of the word is a legacy of pagan Greek and Roman antiquity that stands in sharp contrast to both the Jewish and the early Christian traditions. In both of these, humility was seen as a characteristic of a people humiliated yet secure in their identity. They had arrived at a state in which they were no longer afraid of their condition, and they had lived with a vision of society that was not based on dominance and oppression. *Humility* was a term these people chose for themselves and used to express their solidarity (Wengst 1988, 35–36).

In the Greco-Roman world, humility designated a lowly social position, or subjugated citizens or slaves. "It was the lowly disposition of insignificant people" (Wengst 1988, 5), a state to be gladly left behind as one climbed upward in social mobility. The noble, high-minded, self-possessed individual was free from humility.

In the Hebrew scriptures, the writers speak from the perspective of those who have been downtrodden or humiliated and take the side of the oppressed. God is on the side of the humble. Psalm 37, for example, offers radical assurance to the oppressed that in spite of all appearances to the contrary, God is on their side, not that of the oppressors, that God supports the humble, hears their laments, and refuses the arrogance of the rich exploiting the poor. God stands against the violent, the oppressive; God promises their removal and the emergence of a people who are truly humble:

> Then I will remove from your midst your proudly exultant ones, and you shall no longer be haughty in my holy mountain. For I will leave in the midst of you a people humble and lowly. They shall seek refuge in the Name of The Lord, those who are left in Israel; they shall do no wrong and utter no lies, nor shall there be found in their mouth a deceitful tongue. (Zeph. 3:11–13 RSV)

Whether rich or poor, the people of God are to walk humbly, to express modesty (Prov. 15:33; 18:12; 22:4). After reviewing the Hebrew scriptures and associated writings, Klaus Wengst concludes:

> There is a completely new aspect in the understanding of humility when it does not describe a relationship between the lowly and the better-off, whether as subservience on the one side and modesty and gentleness on the other, but is to issue in mutuality. (Wengst 1988, 35)

The "humble" in the Jewish scriptures are "the impoverished and humiliated who deliberately accept their situation, set their hope on God, withdraw from the complex of violence and practice a different form of justice and righteousness from those who rule by force" (Wengst 1988, 39). In all these texts, humility in the prophets' vision is not a relationship between the lowly and the well off; it does not consist of subservience by the poor and modesty and generosity by the wealthy. True humility results in mutuality, in concern for the common welfare of each and all.

This same vision of humility, an inversion of values, is taught in Matthew 11:28–30 (NEB) in Jesus's call to the humble laborer, "come to me, all whose work is hard, whose load is heavy," and in his identification with them, "for I am gentle and humble-hearted." Those two Greek words, *prous* and *tapeinos*, bring to bear the long tradition of prophetic affirmation of the humble—those who accept conditions of poverty and social humiliation while claiming the justice of compassionate sharing with others and the righteousness of mutual respect that rejects all force and violence (Wengst 1988, 39).

Jesus, himself lowly and humble, calls others to join him as yokefellows—to walk and work in tandem with him—in a world that exploits the humble. He has taken the cause of those brought low; he is in solidarity with them. "To learn from him can only mean to learn solidarity" (Wengst 1988, 39). In that solidarity, there is relief for the heavily burdened and overworked; the exhausted can rest.

Four times, twice each in the Gospels of Matthew and Luke, Jesus teaches that those who humble themselves will be exalted and those who exalt themselves will be brought low (Matt. 18:4; 23:12; Luke 14:11; 18:14). The path of teaching on this downward movement throughout the Christian scriptures is clear and definitive. From Mary's Magnificat (Luke 1:46–55); to the exaltation of the lowly through the teaching and life of Jesus, with his subversive parables and his acceptance of unacceptable people; to the hymn of Philippians 2 and the many references to this principle by Paul (2 Cor. 10:1; 11:7; 12:7–11; Phil. 4:10–20; Rom. 12:16; and many more); to the letters of James (1:9–11; 2:5; 5:1–6, 10) and Peter (1 Peter 5:1–5), the location of discipleship is explicitly among the lowly.

Jesus's parables, subversive stories all, end with a twist. There is irony in their structure, satire in their plots, and humor in the quick bite of their conclusions. The ironic twist in the parabolic form follows a long tradition of Jewish prophetic storytelling. Nathan's pretension-shattering parable of the rich man with the great flocks of sheep fetching the poor man's pet lamb to feed his guests (2 Sam. 12:1–5); Jotham's tale of the trees and bushes choosing the prickly thorn as king (Judg. 9:7–20); and the greatest of parables, Jonah's story, with its sardonic jibe in the last lines (Jonah 4) set the pattern of humor that protects us from creating an idolatrous image of God. The ironic endings break up the mirrored image, and we discover that that image is only a word written on water, and thus does not violate the second commandment.

At the end of his classic study on the humor of Christ, Elton Trueblood concluded that we cannot know with certainty how much humor there is in Christ's teachings, but we can be sure that there is far more than is normally recognized. In any case, there are numerous passages in the recorded teachings that are practically incomprehensible when regarded as sober prose, but are luminous once we become liberated from the gratuitous assumption that Christ never joked (Trueblood 1964, 10).

What we sometimes call simple Jesus theologies make room for humble humor. Assembled from the human stories, the wisdom sayings, the compassionate acts, the biting parables, and the ultimate confrontation of Jesus and his contemporaries, they open the door to a rich storehouse of humor and comedy, of incongruence and irony, particularly in the synoptic Gospels. The parables, one discovers, are subversive, and each tweaks our worldview with an unsettling twist. The teachings, with their wide use of metaphor, simile, paradox, hyperbole, and comic aphorism can jolt the hearer to new awareness. In contrast, christological theologies with less human content and more stress on high deity have little, or at best a grudging, place for humor or comedy.

Humility as Wise Foolishness

Humorous humility was brilliantly introduced by the Renaissance scholar Erasmus (1466–1536), a major voice and influence preparing the way for the Protestant Reformation, who gave us the paradox of the wise fool. The illegitimate son of an obscure father, as a wise fool Erasmus came to be courted by scholars, princes, and popes, and he was quoted by Reformers Luther, Calvin, Zwingli, and Menno Simons.

Erasmus's book *The Praise of Folly* leveled the pretensions of the wise, powerful, and great to offer a new paradigm of self-acceptance and other-regard. Folly, the heroine and voice, argues that it is foolishness, not calculating reason, that makes possible everything we treasure most in life. She walks irreverently through the fortified walls of convention, leaps moats of feudal hierarchy as though blind to their impermeableness, ignorant of their existence. The delicate balance between what is absolute and what is absurd, serious and comic, eternal and ephemeral is maintained in the ironic voice of Folly as she satirically deflates the pretensions of the academy, the wisdom of the clergy, the authority of the princes. But her wit is equally applied to herself as she unhesitatingly names her own failings and frailties, not defending her weaknesses, but listing them among her strengths: "A normal reasonable man is expected to 'know better'" than to challenge convention, "but the fool is not expected to know anything, he is a difficult adversary, precisely because he is only a fool" (Erasmus 1518/1941, 15).

The "good judgment" of the wise is often the conventional wisdom of the closed-minded who know what is best and gladly impose it on others. The fool is willing to risk being ridiculous, to step outside of the socially accepted.

> There are two great obstacles to developing a knowledge of affairs—shame, which throws a smoke over the understanding, and fear, which once danger has been sighted, dissuades from going through with an exploit. Folly, with a grand gesture, frees us from both. (Erasmus 1518/1941, 16)

For Erasmus, it is folly above all else that enables us to live together and even to love each other. He concludes the long monologue by Dame Folly with a stunning paragraph rendered in Folly's voice.

> In sum, no society, no union in life, could be either pleasant or lasting with out me. A people does not for long tolerate its prince, or a master tolerate his servant, a handmaiden her mistress, a teacher his student, a friend his friend, a wife her husband, a landlord his tenant, a partner his partner, or a boarder his fellow-boarder, except as they mutually or by turns are mistaken, on occasion flatter, on occasion wisely wink, and otherwise soothe themselves with the sweetness of folly. (Erasmus 1518/1941, 28)

Erasmus himself foolishly reclaimed the original Greek text of the New Testament and made it available to scholars, thus starting the great chain of events that led to the Reformation; foolishly thought his own thoughts in an era of papal infallibility; and foolishly published his own questions in an age of prescribed answers. He daringly contrasted the traditional church with that of Christ and the apostles, referring to "these charlatan popes who encourage the disregard of Christ, who depict Him as a mercenary, who corrupt His teachings by forced interpretations, and who scandalize Him by their infamous lives" (Erasmus 1518/1941, 158).

"I do not refuse to be the whole world's fool," wrote Menno Simons, the Dutch Anabaptist, who often quoted his countryman

Erasmus. Menno described his own risky life as "humility, well-meant boldness and folly," concluding, "I know well that Christ and his apostles and the prophets promoted the same 'foolishness'" (Wenger 1956, 405).

In humorous humility, we come to accept the natural foolishness that is a part of the human condition and learn to enjoy it. We pass from being simple fools to, at times, becoming wise fools. We relinquish the idealized goals of what we should be and therefore must appear to be and embrace new goals that disavow the old dreams of triumph and the fearful fantasies of humiliation. We recognize that just as those who join in laughing at our errors, we have feet of clay, clay that sometimes reaches to the knee and hip. We all leave some muddy tracks in our passage through life, many revealing how flat-footed we actually are.

In humorous humility, one has learned not to take oneself too seriously or to respond defensively. Once one accepts the fact that life is laced with surprises and embarrassments, one relinquishes the demand to always be above shame. Unwarranted pride can produce unlimited quantities of shame; unbridled vanity can create immeasurable embarrassment. Humor is the appropriate answer to both. The wise fool has given up pretensions of fulfilling self-imposed expectations of complete competence and constant superiority. The wise fool who fumbles can shrug with self-accepting chagrin at being temporarily less than what might be expected; the wise fool who stumbles can smile at the faux pas.

Humility is being gentle with the fool who lives within me—

- the fool who pretends to know more than I actually do, to be more sure about things than anyone can be, to be optimistic about the impossible or pessimistic about the probable.
- the fool who talks too much when presence is all that is needed, or talks too little when comfort of kindness must be put into words.
- the fool who takes too many chances when it would be wiser to act with caution, or refuses to risk and dare when what is needed is foolhardy courage.

- the fool who wins when it costs too much, or loses when investing a little more could have made all the difference.
- the fool who makes promises and breaks them by forgetting how important they may be to the other.
- the fool who laughs easily at its own fallibility, forgetfulness, frailty, and sometimes woeful inadequacy.
- the fool who knows and understands its own foolhardy attempts to do the impossible, its foolish faith in others that may not prove justified, its nothing-but-a-fool attempts at realizing dreams, reaching great goals, stretching toward what is unlikely, yet necessary.

Humility as Simplicity

Traditionally, Anabaptist spirituality has seen an inseparable connection between humility and simplicity. The most visible exemplars of this are the Amish, who avoid luxuries, ornamentation, and modern conveniences, believing that humility requires such visible and practical simplicity. Such sacrifice of the unnecessary is seen as a sign of the yielded self (of *Gelassenheit*) and of a willingness to work for the common good (Kraybill 1989, 41). The pleasure-seeking person is preoccupied with self-fulfillment, with ambition that is the drive to do well for oneself. As Donald Kraybill writes insightfully:

> The size and number of mirrors in a society indicate the cultural importance attached to the self. Thus it is not surprising that the mirrors found in Amish houses are smaller and fewer than those found in modern ones. Whereas Moderns are preoccupied with "finding themselves," the Amish are engaged in "losing themselves." The Amish work just as hard at losing themselves as Moderns work at finding themselves. Either way it is hard work. Although uncomfortable to Moderns, who cherish the flowering of individuality, losing the self in Amish culture assumes a dignity because its ultimate redemption is the gift of community. (1989, 29)

Losing oneself is a process of blending into the solidarity of community rather then standing out and seeking to be recognized. A modest way of acting, talking, dressing, and even walking expresses this common life with others.

> Modern culture produces individualists whose prime objective is personal fulfillment. By contrast, the goal of Gelassenheit is a subdued, humble person who discovers fulfillment in the community. Amish who give up their selves to the community receive, in return, a durable and visible ethnic identity. (Kraybill 1989, 25)

The Amish deplore public recognition, although within relationships there is an open interchange of recognition and appreciation for personal contributions. Seeking or receiving public acclaim is akin to boasting, to asking strangers for praise, or an unknown society for its admiration.

An Amish minister was telling us about the hymnbook the *Ausbund*, the oldest collection of songs in continuous use since the sixteenth century. "Some people are now translating hymns into English for worship use," he said.

"I've done a bit of that," I said, "One of my translations has been printed in the last two Mennonite hymnals, and also it is used by many other groups."

"Possibly," he answered.

"No, actually," I replied, thinking he had misunderstood. He overlooked my response and went on with his description of the hymnbook. Only later did I realize that in his community, one does not tell of one's own accomplishments, even when it is public information. He was gently covering his embarrassment at my lack of embarrassment in reporting on my work.

This love of simplicity is a preference for an unobtrusive life. It is not a virtuous asceticism, but rather a communal modesty. It is not shyness, lack of self-confidence, or low self-esteem. Instead it is a refusal to exaggerate or even to defend the importance of what one has or has done. So the Amish do not put themselves forward. Jesus's teaching about choosing the lesser or less obtrusive place is practiced in life. Humility is seeing one's place in the wider world and not using the world's resources in such a self-serving way that it denies the needs of the world's poor or profits grossly from inequities of distribution. Humility is seeking a consistency between our empathy with others and our expectations of how our own needs will be respected. Humility is bent toward empathy for the suffering of strangers. Humility is not ignoring the suffering of the hungry, ill, imprisoned, and abused to such an extent that one fails to give to those in such extremity. Humility is a consistency between our compassion for others and the way we expect our own troubles to be treated. Humility is turned toward compassion with the suffering stranger (Richards 1992, 47).

Humility as a Spirituality of Imperfection

The German word for humility *(Demut)* is the Anabaptist designation for a spirituality of simplicity, imperfection, and understatement. As a piety of imperfection, not perfectionism, humility is grounded not in unworthiness, but in awareness of one's limitations; not in a striving for divinity, but in the full recognition of humanity.

German theologian Karl Barth, author of the many volumes collectively called *Church Dogmatics*, told of a dream he had of dying, arriving in heaven, and being questioned by St. Peter:

"Who are you?"—"My name is Karl Barth."

"What have you done?"—"I taught theology."

"What have you written?"—*"Church Dogmatics."*

"Can I see it?"—"Well, it's a whole shelf."

"Big isn't it?"—(proudly) "Ja!"

"Here is a little red wagon. Put it in. Now, pull it up the street." As Barth obediently pulls the little wagon, the angels line the street, and laugh!

True humility is as much different from self-abasement as it is from self-exaltation. Humility that devalues self is too easily self-absorbed. The denigration of self too easily spreads to seeing others as equally worthless. True humility sees both self and other as worthful; it exalts neither, devalues none. The character of humility is a compound of tentativeness replacing dogmatism, openness instead of closedness, flexibility rather than certainty, negotiability not obstinacy. It embraces imperfection as an acceptable self-image, not striving for perfection.

In perfectionism one pride is substituted for another. Subtle pride in the absence of pride both conceals and justifies the comparative process of believing I am "holier and humbler than thou." Pride is essentially comparative, C. S. Lewis argued. When the element of competition is removed, what remains is a humble self-assessment of great or small abilities. Pride is claiming to have greater or lesser abilities than the chosen competitor.

Humility is the refusal to compare oneself with others. One is not proud simply of being brilliant, handsome, beautiful, or successful; one becomes proud by evaluating the self as more brilliant, handsome, beautiful, or successful than another.

Humility is an unselfconsciousness that becomes wholly aware of the other by escaping, for the moment, the habitually self-conscious self.

> When we are *self*-conscious, we cannot be wholly aware; we must throw ourselves out, first. This throwing ourselves away is the act of creativity. So when we wholly concentrate, like a child in play, or an artist at work, then we share in the act of creating. We not only escape time, we also escape our self-conscious selves. The Greeks had a word for ultimate self-consciousness which I find illuminating: *hubris*: pride: pride in the sense of putting oneself in the center of the universe. (L' Engle 1972, 11)

Humility is often equated, mistakenly, with self-abasement, and pride with self-exaltation. Madeleine L'Engle argues that the moment humility becomes self-conscious, insofar as it is being aware of itself it is not being truly humble. "Humility is the act of throwing oneself away in complete concentration on something or someone else." Whether this happens in the creative moment, in love for the neighbor, in an act of compassion for another's pain, in the practice of service to others, in the performance of any skill, art, or profession, such concentration on the welfare of the other is both the deepest forgetfulness of the self and the fullest realization of the self. Like self-exaltation and self-abasement, self-realization and self-forgetfulness can be essential parts of true humility, but they can also be constituent elements in pride and arrogance. Perhaps they are better visualized as separate variables, each with two faces, as in figure 1.

Pride as self-abasement can be largely self-absorbed in its centered focus on the worth and welfare of its own being, or it may be obsessive in its narcissistic goals, ignoring and blind to the other. In extreme form, self-flagellation has an arrogant, although masochistic, trust in the atoning power of self-inflicted pain and suffering. Pride as self-exaltation needs little explanation. Egotism grows into egomania and self-idolatry.

Humility is more complex. In self-abasement it can be gently self-effacing, genuinely self-forgetful and unselfconscious. In its deeper levels it moves toward a no-self spirituality in which the person becomes virtually selfless, beginning all conversation and action from the middle ground, the point of meeting with the other, not from a self-center. Humble self-exaltation, although it sounds like a contradiction, claims its full equal position and role with the other, acts out of full mutuality and balanced dignity. It may fulfill the self by voluntarily sacrificing the self for principled vision and commitment.

Figure 1 depicts types of self-appraisal in spirituality. In quadrant 1 is the present and equal "I-thou" spirituality that delights in no more and no less than full equality, mutuality, and equal regard. In quadrant 2, the "holier than thou" spirituality of perfectionism, pursuit, and quest. In quadrant 3, the "humbler than thou" spirituality of pseudosainthood, which pretends nothingness, humbling the self in order to be exalted. In quadrant 4, the "humor in humanity, joy in service" spirituality that is self-forgetful and self-surrendering, achieving realization through renunciation.

Obviously, the argument of this chapter supports quadrant four as the pathway of humility that leads to a spirituality of recognized imperfection expressed in nondefensive renunciation and surrender, classically known as *Gelassenheit*—that is, an active practice of habitual humility. It sees the quadrants on the right as the darker side of authentic spirituality that is alloyed with pride, and the quadrants on the left as the lighter side that takes one's

Figure 1

SELF-EXALTATION

"I-Thou" spirituality	**"Holier than thou" spirituality**
• self and other equally prized in principled vision	• spirituality tempted by superiority and disdain
• self-other equality lived out in mutual dialogue	• self-confident domination and use of others
• candid self-assessment and respect for others	• egotism in being right and disregard of others

HUMILITY   1 | 2   PRIDE

    4 | 3

"Humor in humanity, joy in service" spirituality	**"Humbler than thou" spirituality**
• humorous self-effacing and other-respecting	• self-absorption/ignoring of others
• self-forgetful consciousness of other	• self-obsession/blindness to others
• self-surrender in service; relinquishment in concern for other	• self-flagellation/comparison with others

SELF-ABASEMENT

achievement of any special status in the world of spirituality as highly suspect, realizing that pride casts a long and sometimes almost invisible shadow.

The self-abasement affirmed here is a kind of self-emptying (kenosis) that welcomes the other into conversation and communion without imposing its own agenda, definitions of the world, or formulations of how relating and collaborating should happen. Pastoral care, for example, requires humble openness. We enter any pastoral conversation with open humility. This is self-emptying but it is not emptiness, since the one extending the care is enriched and equipped with all past learning, experiences, and encounters. It is an absence of agenda either for the self or for the other.

Pastoral care is similar to the work of the chef on a popular television show who enters a home and prepares a gourmet meal using only the ingredients and the equipment found in the resident's kitchen and pantry. The chef, with a rich knowledge of techniques and recipes, enters with empty hands and explores with the hosts what they will prepare together from what is available. Humility welcomes the other without any need to control, cares without any need to be thanked, serves without thought of being humbled by service.

The practices of self-abasement create a kind of humility that is invisible to the self, but easily identified by the onlooker. Humility, the tangible evidence that one loves God with heart, soul, strength and mind is visible to others, but not so visible to the self. This is the nature of humility. Humility claimed is pride reframed, or with surprising self-aggrandizement, pride renamed. Although humility is the concrete embodiment of faith, to claim it is presumptuous. It can be noted in others, but not in the self.

Humility is a way of being in the world that permeates an entire worldview with its willingness to live out self-renunciation in noncoercive mutuality that refuses domination. "Christian humility is a voluntary letting go of coercive power in a way that reflects the very character of God. Its best exemplar can be found in the pattern of Jesus Christ" (Roth 2002, 104). Christ emptied himself, taking the form of a servant. He humbled himself and became obedient to the point of death (Phil. 2:7–8). A humility of self-renunciation is rooted in a spirituality of imitation of Christ in which a self that seeks security and safety through domination is renounced and a new self is found in the love of God and neighbor.

"If we get much praise," Dom Helder Camara used to say, "It is a sign that we are opaque, visible instead of transparent."

> God wants our works to be visible,
> Wants the good that we try to do to be known,
> But those good works are to be done with humility,
> An inner humility that is absolutely genuine.
> The ideal is that the person who sees us
> Shouldn't even notice how wonderful and great we are.
> They should find us so transparent
> That instead of noticing us
> They should discover
> The living presence of Jesus Christ.

>   (in Schipani 2002, 1)

On the Other Hand

When it comes to our need for humility, perhaps there is no other hand?

For Peditation

The following is for a meditative walk called a peditation, in which you meditate while walking. One's walk is a biblical metaphor for spiritual and moral life encompassing the whole of daily experience. Peditation on a parable allows you to review a narrative that is foundational to a disciple's life. The story can be reexperienced as you walk to these couplets, matching the "feet of the line" to your feet. Copy the following on a bit of paper and walk to the parable in peditation, asking "When, where, how do I do the same?" *(Rhythm for walking to the text—recite a line of three syllables, rest, then recite the next line of three syllables: 1,2,3, rest, 1,2,3, rest, etc.)*

The Proud and the Humble

Pharisee
in front pew,
billing God
credit due.

"I'm unlike
common men,
note how I
disdain sin."

"Never stole
cent or pound,
never once
fooled around."

"See how I
tithe and fast?
I'm not like
that outcast!"

Taxman kneels,
humbly pleads,
"Mercy please,
for my deeds."

Jesus asks,
"Can you guess
which of these
God will bless?"

(see Luke 18:10–13)

For everyone who exalts self will be humbled; And whoever hum-
bles the self will be exalted. (Luke 18:14, NEB)

5

The Practice of— Resolute Nonviolence

"Because my life is in God's hands, I will never take my enemy's life into my hands."

John Howard Yoder

Resolute nonviolence is the true evidence of love for neighbor, enemy, or persecutor. To believe what Jesus believed is to practice active, nonviolent concern for the welfare of the other in all circumstances.

The Way of the Cross

In the early 1990s, gang violence erupted in Boyle Heights, a section of East Los Angeles. Eight gangs were in conflict in the parish around the Dolores Mission Catholic Church. Killings and injuries happened daily. A group of women who met for prayer read together the story of Jesus walking on the water (Matt. 14:22–33).

125

Then one of the mothers, electrified by the text, began to identify the parallels between the Jesus story and her own.

The gang warfare in Boyle Heights was the storm on the Sea of Galilee; the people hiding behind locked doors were the disciples huddled in the storm; the crackle of gunfire was the lightning; in both cases death was imminent. Then Jesus appeared and they hoped for a magical rescue. Instead, he said, "Get out of the boat." "Walk on the water." "Enter the violence." "We will calm the storm together."

That night, seventy women began a *peregrinación*, a procession from one barrio to another. They brought food, guitars, and love. As they ate chips and salsa and drank Cokes with gang members, they began to sing the old songs of Jalisco, Chiapas, and Michoacán. The gang members were disoriented, baffled; the war zones were silent.

Each night the mothers walked. By nonviolently intruding and intervening they "broke the rules of war." The old script of retaliation and escalating violence was challenged and changed. It is no accident that the women christened their nighttime journeys "love walks."

As the relationships between the women and the gang members grew, the kids told their stories. Anguish over the lack of jobs; anger at police brutality; rage over the hopelessness of poverty. Together they developed a tortilla factory, a bakery, a child-care center, a job-training program, a class on conflict-resolution techniques, a school for further learning, a neighborhood group to monitor and report police misbehavior, and more.

And it began with the challenges "Get out of the boat" and "Walk on the water" (Butigan 2002, 39–90).

Love Walks

This is a spirituality of active nonviolence. It is not rational behavior, according to common wisdom. The streets are a war zone. Mothers should be protected and they should be protectors—or protestors. But a higher rationality took hold of these mothers' souls—a rationality with a long view, a deeper understanding, a radical wisdom that violence begets violence, which begets violence again.

The common wisdom on the streets of L.A., like the wisdom on the streets of most cities, holds that violence is the ultimate reality. This is the conviction of people in democracies and dictatorships, in "developed" as well as "undeveloped" countries. Here are its basic assumptions:

- The world is a dangerous place.
- Human beings are innately, intrinsically violent.
- The enemy is evil, more violent than we are, and beyond change.
- We have only three alternatives: accommodate violence, avoid violence, or use violence ourselves—go along with it, run from it, or do it before or when they do it.
- The answer to violence is more violence. Evil is the bottom line, and violence its language, logic, and ultimate reality.
- Violence can solve our problems decisively. Power, domination, and extermination of evildoers will stop the spiral, prevent the violence from feeding on itself, extinguish resentment, intimidate those who would seek revenge, render retaliation against us impossible, allow us to dominate benevolently.

These are the storm-waves of violence, beating on countercurrents of equal violence. Each side justifies its actions as self-defense, each is willing for the other to die to insure its own safety.

Active nonviolence steps out of the pitching boat and onto the pounding waves and does the suprarational. It walks on the water and finds it firm. It summons its courage and reaches out to the enemy as a person. It thinks of the enemy's needs and fears; it acts in commitment alloyed with compassion. It chooses the surprising.

—ɯ—

One evening when he was in Hamburg, Germany attending a conference, Jonathan Roth boarded a commuter train and dozed as it crossed town. He was awakened by the sounds of four teenagers jeering an old man in rags. They sprayed the man with beer and soon began to attack him, kicking him with heavy boots and punching him in the face. Jonathan, a foreigner, a Christian, and a pacifist with no training in martial arts, looked on powerlessly as the violence became a merciless beating.

Then, whispering a prayer for help, he sprang to his feet and ran to the fallen man. Pushing between the teenagers, he said in his best German, "Hans! How are you? It's been a long time since we've seen each other. Come, sit with me, Hans. We have so much to catch up on." In the sudden silence, the old man rose and followed him to the other end of the car, and slowly began to answer Roth's questions. The teens looked on, talked among themselves, and at the next stop, got off the train. "Hans," murmuring thanks, left soon after (Roth 2002, 3, 4, 9).

—⚏—

"I have a special assignment for you," the president of the steel company said to his chief of sales.

"Tomorrow morning you are booked as the first appointment at Lima Tank Depot. I want you to land the contract for all the hardened steel required in their new military contract." It was in the 1970s, in the Cold War period of stockpiling weapons and arming the world.

The sales director, my older brother Dan, listened without comment as the president described the multimillion-dollar Pentagon contract, emphasized the importance of this sale to the company's future, and laid out the details of the already scheduled appointment. When the president, a veteran Vietnam helicopter pilot, paused to take a call, Dan excused himself.

In the executive washroom Dan faced himself in the mirror. His Anabaptist convictions about opposing war and refusing participation in or profit from the military industrial programs that arm the world confronted him from the face in the glass, as did the memory of his dad resigning from a high-paying job in the 1940s over the same issue at the Lima Locomotive Works, next door to the tank depot, where today the Abrams tank is produced.

"I'm going to say no to the boss for the first time," he confided to one of his salesmen.

"Then you can pack your bags," the man answered.

When back in the president's office Dan said to him, "I cannot make this sale for you tomorrow. I have two sons who will soon be making decisions about military service. I want to be able to talk with them about war, about how wrong it is to base our whole economy on death and destruction. If I do this, I cannot do that."

"I suspected you might say that, but I had to ask. Keep your sons' respect. Stick to your guns—whoops, wrong words," the president said.

—⁂—

After my colleague Nancey Murphy delivered an address in London, two Muslim men sought her out to ask, "Did we hear correctly? You are a Christian and you believe in nonviolence?"

"Yes, I come from a long tradition, Anabaptism, which, like Jesus did, refuses violence."

"And you would not kill, even to protect your family?"

"I've told both my husband and my son that I would gladly die for them, but I will not kill for them."

"This is part of the Christian tradition?" they asked, surprised. "This is not the Christianity we know about."

—⁂—

In a war-torn country an acquaintance of mine looked up to see five resistance leaders walk into his office. A teacher and practitioner of nonviolence, he knew his guests as underground saboteurs and assassins.

"We have come to learn your techniques of nonviolence," they said. "We have seen changes brought about by your way. Our way leads only to retaliation, revenge, and further violence. Will you teach us?"

"No," my friend said, "I cannot teach you. You are too weak to learn nonviolence. When threatened you have always struck back. You are not strong enough to learn the nonviolent way. Perhaps I can teach your sons and daughters, but not you. Send me your children, there is hope for them." They left, puzzling over this strange strength they did not understand.

A Spirituality of Cross and Sword

Theologian Harvey Cox once put forward an intriguing proposition.

> We should read history more as a cautionary tale than as a treasure house of available inspiration. We Christians today need to understand our history as a compulsive neurotic needs to understand his—in order to see where we veered off, lost genuine options, glimpsed something we were afraid to pursue, or denied who we really are. (Cox 1978, 159)

Let's begin with the great moment when oppressed and persecuted Christianity became—through the conversion of the emperor—itself the oppressor and persecutor. Perhaps we can understand something of what went wrong.

In 313, Constantine, the emperor of Rome, published the Edict of Milan. This event signifies the union of church and state in the Roman Empire, a day to be celebrated by the Catholic Church and the Church of England, which consider Constantine a saint; a day mourned by those in the free church tradition, who think of it as the co-option of the church to become servant of the state. Constantine understood that his people were leaving classic paganism for Christianity. If they could not be loyal worshipers of the state in pagan belief that the emperor is God, then they could be imperially Christian.

Russian novelist and Christian activist Leo Tolstoy retold the story of this supposed triumph of Christianity, when the church welcomed, blessed, and sanctioned Constantine, whom he calls the "robber-chief." In Tolstoy's version, it is Constantine who triumphs over Christianity:

No one said to him: "The kings exercise authority among the nations, but among you it shall not be so. Do not murder, do not commit adultery, do not lay up riches, judge not, condemn not, resist not him that is evil."

But they said to him: "You wish to be called a Christian and to continue to be the chieftain of the robbers—to kill, burn, fight, lust, execute, and live in luxury? That can all be arranged."

And they arranged a Christianity for him, and arranged it very smoothly, better even than could have been expected. They foresaw that, reading the Gospels, it might occur to him that all this [true discipleship] is demanded. . . . This they foresaw, and they carefully devised such a Christianity for him as would let him continue to live his old heathen life unembarrassed. On the one hand Christ, God's Son, only came to bring salvation to him and to everybody. Christ having died, Constantine can live as he likes. More even than that—one may repent and swallow a little bit of bread and some wine, and that will bring salvation, and all will be forgiven.

But more even than that: they sanctify his robber-chieftainship, and say that it proceeds from God, and they anoint him with holy oil. And he, on his side, arranges for them the congress of priests that they wish for, and order them to say what each man's relation to God should be, and orders everyone to repeat what they say. . . .

And as soon as one of the anointed robber-chiefs wishes his own and another folk to begin slaying each other, the priest[s] immediately prepare some holy water, sprinkle a cross (which Christ bore and on which he died because he repudiated such robbers), take the cross and bless the robber-chief in his work of slaughtering, hanging, and destroying. (Tolstoy 1967, 278)

So Christianity became the religious worldview of the state. The gospel was defined, trimmed, smoothed to fit imperial policy. From this Constantinian project comes the long stream of efforts to make the faith credible to the world, to bridge the contradictions between the state's needs and the gospel's central truths. The translation of the message into socially, politically, economically viable, acceptable, assimilable beliefs took on fresh forms with Augustine, Anselm, and Aquinas, and was updated by modern thinkers who sought "to relate the ancient world of faith to a modern world of disbelief" (Hauerwas and Willimon 1989, 20).

Co-opted by the emperor, allied with the state, merged with the political powers, Christ's followers became Christianity, then Christendom. The gods are on the side of the stronger, said the great Roman historian Tacitus. Christians after Constantine came to agree with Tacitus, even though the Hebrew scriptures portray a God who went to prison with Joseph, into captivity with the Jews. And the Gospels tell of a God who can, in his strange way of standing with the powerless, wind up on a cross. After the Reformation, Lutheran and Reformed churches struck a new deal with the state. As national governments chose a secular path to separate from the church, the Christian church in a secular society continued the Constantinian contract by finding new ways of joining with the domination systems of this world.

The Constantinian question is how to attain and exercise power in a morally responsible way. This is not a Christian question. Followers of Jesus do not ask under what circumstances Christians should kill to serve the political good, and how to do it in a morally permissible fashion. Instead, they ask how to bear a faithful witness to the Jesus way of creating and sustaining peace.

I have seen political cartoons that concentrate this truth into laser sharpness. In one, Jesus is standing at a Northern Ireland airline counter in the midst of the Protestant-Catholic wars. He pleads with the attendant: "Please, fly me anywhere where there are no Christians." In another, a Crusader sits astride a white horse, his shield emblazoned with the classic Crusader's cross. The Arab man on the ground beneath his spear says, "Tell me more about this Christianity of yours, I'm terribly interested."

What Kind of Spirituality?

Those who read the Bible from a spiritualizing, other-worldly perspective will have a spiritualizing, other-worldly faith and go to spiritualizing, other-worldly churches.

Those who read the Bible from a prosperity-promising, greed-promoting, materialistic perspective will have a prosperity-seeking, greed-satisfying faith and go to prosperity-baiting, greed-manipulating churches.

Those who read the Bible from an individualistic, self-actualizing, autonomous-spirituality perspective will have a privatistic, personally tailored, egocentric faith and go—if they should choose to go—to ego-oriented, individualistic, self-fulfilling churches.

Those who read the Bible from a patriotic, nationalistic, "God Bless My Country" perspective will have a security-based, trust in armaments and military as God's way of making us "the possessors of *might* and the heirs of what is *right*" and will go to a church where they and the Christ they follow recognize Caesar's prior claims to our sons and daughters when we are threatened.

Those who read the Bible from an Old Testament prophets perspective, like Micah, Joel, Amos, and Isaiah and from the perspective of the Jesus of the Gospels will have great difficulty reconciling their faith with other-worldly spirituality, materialistic, individual fulfillment, nationalistic, rationalized perspectives and find themselves outside the mainstream of Christianity as dissident disciples and go to a church where discipleship to Christ is valued above spirituality, prosperity, security, or success—or will try fruitlessly to find such a church.

August 9, 1945, Catholic chaplain George Zabelka, stationed on Tinian Island with the U.S. Army Air Force, blessed and prayed for the safety and success of the pilots and the planes about to deliver the bomb they called the "gimmick" and drop it on Nagasaki. A half century later he wrote:

> It seems a "sign" to me that seventeen hundred years of Christian terror and slaughter should arrive at August 9, 1945, when Catholics dropped the A-bomb on top of the largest and first Catholic city in Japan. One would have thought that I, as a Catholic priest, would have spoken out against the atomic bombing of nuns. (Three orders of Catholic sisters were destroyed in Nagasaki that day.) One would have thought that I would have suggested that as a minimal standard of Catholic morality, Catholics shouldn't bomb Catholic children. I didn't.
>
> I, like the Catholic pilot of the Nagasaki plane, "the Great Artiste," was heir to a Christianity that had for seventeen hundred years engaged in revenge, murder, torture, the pursuit of power, the

prerogative of violence, all in the name of our Lord. (Wallis 1994, 230)

Forty-five thousand human beings were killed by the single bomb dropped by "the Great Artiste." Father Zabelka concludes,

> Well, I was there, and I'll tell you that the operational moral atmosphere in the church in relation to mass bombing of enemy civilians was totally indifferent, silent, and corrupt at best—at worst it was religiously supportive of these activities by blessing those who did them.
>
> I say all this not to pass judgment on others, for I do not know their souls then or now. I say this as one who was part of the so-called Christian leadership of the time. So you see, that is why I am not going to the Day of Judgment looking for justice in this matter. Mercy is my salvation. (Wallis 1994, 231)

Leo Tolstoy, in sharp critique that is serious judgment not satirical comment, confronted the contradictions between the way of the cross and the way Christendom has chosen to go:

> A Christian nation which engages in war ought, in order to be logical, not only take down the cross from its church steeples, turn the churches to some other use, give the clergy other duties, having first prohibited the preaching of the gospel, but also ought to abandon all the requirements of morality which flow from Christian law. (Tolstoy 1967, 82)

Habitual Nonviolence

Habitual nonviolence is a way of living with as little coercion as possible. Coercion is the opposite of genuine human relations, and any increase in coercion causes a corresponding decrease in humanity. The opposite—any increase in noncoercive yet truly collaborative relationships—increases humanity.

A discipline of habitual nonviolence takes the way of Jesus as the prototype for one's own way and refuses—in threat or stress—to resort to violence.

In figure 1, the horizontal continuum indicates degree of stress or threat necessary for the person to turn from nonviolence and act coercively. How soon, and under what circumstances is the person willing to give up civility, lay aside nonviolent responses, and become coercive?

As a case example, the use of or the willingness to support the use of military force in warfare can be visualized on this continuum with the following positions.

Figure 1

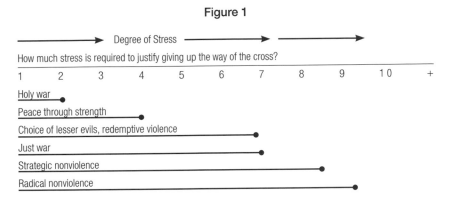

How much stress, threat, endangerment is required for us to have moral permission to react with violence? Some of the positions charted above, like the holy war perspective, require little threat; others demand evidence of impending attack; still others insist upon actual injury or violation. For the classic just war position, there must be moral evaluation of the feasibility, proportionality, moral necessity, and so on. According to the nonviolent positions, stress does not justify resorting to violence of either retaliation or prevention.

For many religious persons, this determination is completely divorced from spirituality. The decision to use violence is made "in the world of reality," whereas the commitment to compassion and care for the neighbor lies in "the world of faith." The two need not meet. Among Christians, the situation is more complex, since the use of violence stands in direct opposition to the teachings of Jesus.

In dialogue with fellow disciples of Jesus who take sharply contrasting positions along the continuum of figure 1, I often offer the following propositions as interpretations of the diagram.

1. *All followers of Jesus are pacifists.* There are no other kinds. Essential to my belief in the uniqueness of Jesus is the conviction that love, not hate is the way; compassion, not coercion is the means; redemption, not retaliation is the end. The cross is God's intention for our response to evil. "I will seek to live habitually, completely in the way of Jesus."

2. *All followers of Jesus are fallible.* Each has a breaking point where he or she may fail the spirit of Jesus; falter in following his way; fall short of his model, teaching, and call to refuse violence; and respond with evil for evil. "I want to live in imitation of his way, but I am broken, vulnerable."

3. *All choices are flawed, finite, and imperfect.* When one sees no alternative, finds no better way, and chooses to react defensively, coercively, or violently, one cannot say that it was the right way or the only way, but simply that it was the best way one could see in that desperate or troubled moment. "If I react in coercion or violence, it will be a last resort, and never in taking another's life into my hands."

4. *Any choice to take part in coercion must be open to correction.* If one resorts to coercion, one pledges to be consistently open to correction and confrontation by sisters and brothers, to be repentant and willing to learn. "My choices are not 'right.' They are the best I can see and do in my circumstances. I will not defend them; I am willing to be corrected."

A spirituality of resolute attachment to Jesus calls us to steadfastly, stubbornly, courageously remain true to the cross, even at great cost. These are painful, not easy words; costly, not superficial commitments. Nonviolence is a demanding path of discipleship, not a way lightly taken.

Habitual Nonviolence as Attachment

The habitual nonviolence of Anabaptist spirituality has a particular and unique focus and locus. It is attached to the way of Jesus (the focus) and grounded in the cross (the locus).

This differs sharply from:

- biblical fundamentalist pacifism with a nonviolence of absolute principle,
- conscientious objection with a refusal to violate one's own conscience by participating in violence,
- pacifism of a moral ideal such as Quakerism or liberal Protestantism,
- strategic pacifism that claims political and social effectiveness as its warrant and validation, and
- many other types of abstention from violence and from participation in its use (Yoder lists twenty-five varieties of pacifism, all intriguing commitments to reverence for human life and dignity [Yoder 1971a, 11–14]).

In contrast, Anabaptist pacifism is grounded in resolute Jesus-attachment. *"The person of Jesus* is indispensable," Yoder argues, as is the community of disciples who gather to follow Jesus in daily life. Anabaptist pacifism does not claim to be politically effective, nor does it trust in the good will of people who naively insist that nonviolence is a pragmatic option. It does not justify itself by the hundreds of instances of its effectiveness in ending oppression or halting violence.

Christians can no more base their nonviolence on success or on evidence of effectiveness than Jesus did. He chose the way of the cross as the clearest expression of how God confronts and deals with human evil, not by responding in kind, giving evil for evil, but by extending self-giving, nonresistant love. Christians refuse to use violence not because of an absolute commitment to the sanctity of life in and of itself, nor because it is totally abhorrent to use coercive resistance, but because of the One they seek to mirror and reflect, the Lord, who took the way of the cross.

Nonviolence is right not because of what Jesus taught, although that guides our thinking on the nature of love for God and neighbor; nor because of the individual acts of compassion that Jesus performed, although they model the selfless life of concern for the other. It is the cross, the radical confrontation with evil, that refuses to return evil for evil.

Nonviolence is right not because it works but because it is the way of Jesus. It anticipates the triumph of the Lamb that was slain; it reveals the heart of God.

The way of the cross is not an inner spiritual surrender as Luther taught, or a profound sentiment of spirituality as pretension holds, or any of the many other inner conceptual, emotional, volitional, spiritual definitions of experience that identify the cross with physical, familial, or vocational hardships. *The way of the cross is the willingness to die.*

Love Not the Domination System

The *world*, in the way Jesus used the word, refers not to geography or place, but to "the domination system" by which human societies control, compute, and conflict. This is biblical scholar Walter Wink's best translation of *cosmos*. The domination system is a set of cultural values, basic survival assumptions, and political structures that actively control, impose upon, and exploit humankind through violence and domination (Wink 1992, 139–55).

Of his disciples Jesus said, "They are strangers in the world, as I am"; in other words, "they are strangers to the domination system as I am a stranger to the domination system" (John 17:14, 16 NEB). We too live within a domination system of organized fear, institutionalized greed, rationalized violence, and socially accepted hatred, but we are strangers to its creed of greed, fear, coercion, and we-they thinking. There is no true spirituality at the end of the pursuit of greed, none that is motivated by fear, none that is nourished by violence, none that carries out the practices of hate. These are acts of obedience to the domination system and not to the reign of God.

Every violent action is an act of faith in the domination system.

Every commitment that answers violence with violence is an act of obedience to the domination system.

Every allegiance to the values embodied in the domination system is an affirmation that men are superior to women, whites to people of color, and the wealthy to the poor; that the northern hemisphere is better than the southern hemisphere, the West than the Third World, and human beings than nature.

Every surrender to the domination system legitimates the unquestioning validation and justification of the use of force and violence. Then even when violence fails to resolve conflicts, it is merely discredited.

Clarence Jordan, farmer, Bible scholar and translator, and founder of Koinonia Farm in Georgia, where people lived in interracial harmony during the height of the civil rights struggle of the 1960s and 1970s, thought deeply about the kinds of retaliation he observed in the tit for tat interactions in Southern society.

> Jesus pointed out the stages through which the law of retaliation had passed, and how it finally came to rest in the universal love of the father's own heart. There were four of these steps, each clearly defined and each progressing towards God's final purpose. First, there was the way of unlimited retaliation; second, that of limited retaliation; third, that of limited love; and fourth, that of unlimited love. (Jordan 1952)

Obviously, the first is both eyes for an eye, all teeth for a tooth. The second is an eye for an eye, a penny for a penny and no more. The third is "love your neighbor and hate your enemy" (Matt. 5:43 NJKV; see also Lev. 19:18). The fourth is to love as God loves, drawing no lines between friend and enemy, between those who reciprocate and those who do not. One loves in this fourth way not because it works or is guaranteed to change enemies, but so that they will be "children of [their] heavenly father" (Matt. 5:45 NEB).

A Spirituality of Enemy Love

Love for the enemy, Martin Luther King Jr. argued, is not to be confused with some sentimental outpouring. It is a struggle in which the enemy is conquered without the use of military weapons, and it enables the enemy to share in the benefits of the freedom that is won (King 1963, 39–41). Love of the enemy means maintaining a posture of nonviolent resistance, enacting a "bloodless coup" through a direct appeal to the foe, no matter how relentless the foe is. "We shall match your ability to inflict suffering by our capacity to endure suffering. We cannot in all good conscience obey your unjust laws, because noncooperation with evil is as much a moral obligation as is cooperation with good. Throw us in jail and we shall still love you" (40).

Enemy love is fundamental to all Christian concerns, but an observation of Christian behavior reveals a wide range of interpretations of this concern for the adversary. In this argument I shall follow and adapt a set of types by David N. Duke (Duke 1983, 986–89).

1. *Reciprocal enemy love*: Respectful, evenhanded, reciprocal fair treatment, fair representation, and fair exchange with the enemy wherever possible. This is the conventional moral standard of most cultures and of international law. We both offer and expect fairness in our relationships; we seek to act with generosity to show good faith although we recognize that full reciprocity may be unlikely. We expect, at a minimum, that proportional decency will be shown in response to our civility. The commitment to reciprocity usually means that a nation will practice policies of deterrence but repudiate preemptive action even when threatened. Fair-treatment reciprocity seeks to work constructively until survival is actually endangered, or until the proponents of preemptive action can create the illusion of actual endangerment!

2. *Pragmatic enemy love*: Practical, pragmatic, tolerant, sometimes tough love of the enemy. This is a commitment to act positively toward the other even when positive action is not returned, to love the enemy who does not love us, but only as long as it is practical. There are limits to altruism, lines that must be drawn in generosity. There must be some promise of growth toward reciprocity. The goal of this tolerant, practical love of enemy is to invite change, to evoke shame, and elicit a quid pro quo. Such a pragmatic strategy insists on commonsense limits, on practical terms that realize the inadequacy of good will to change some enemies, on the need in extremity to deal with enemies on their own terms, in which case violence is justified.

3. *Righteous enemy love*: Morally responsible, loyally obligated, socially committed enemy love. Those who adhere to this perspective are committed to love of enemy but balance this concern with responsibility for the family, for fellow community members, for those who own their loyalty, and for the nation that claims them. Loyalty and obligation require that we render faithful support to those to whom it is due. Thus when the enemy's cause is unjust, we, for just cause, must resort to returning the same tragic violence the enemy initiates. The cause is righteous, in rational terms of responsibility and solidarity, and the survival of loved ones is morally mandated if we have any possibility of ensuring it. Love for the enemy is constant while love for a greater justice for all may require us to destroy the enemy even while loving the enemy. Defending the innocent, freeing the oppressed, and stopping unjustified aggression takes precedence over concern for the welfare of the enemy as a person.

4. *Critical enemy love*: Morally responsible, critically thoughtful, attributively just, tragically committed enemy love. This critical love is radically committed to the survival of those who are our personal responsibility—family, friends, neighbors, community, nation—yet recognizes that there is no truly righteous national defense. It recognizes that destroying the enemy is ultimately self-destructive, that violence begets violence, that even at its best violence is only a temporary and morally questionable measure that seeks to minimize innocent suffering. Nevertheless, critical love of enemy may in the final analysis be no less violent than the enemy, or than any of the preceding forms of enemy love. Its distinctive character lies in the critical thought given to attributive justice—give to each his or her due—and in the tragic honesty and humility in its refusal to claim righteous superiority and absolute moral justification for its actions.

5. *Uncalculating enemy love*: Persistent, unrelenting, unqualified love of enemy. This love recognizes consequences but refuses to use them to justify absolute actions of violence. The end cannot justify the means when the means contradict the end desired. In seeking the ultimate good for all humankind, uncalculating enemy love is unwilling to seize responsibility for determining who shall live and who shall die. In recognizing the sovereignty of God, it refuses to

take God's place in absolute decisions or ultimate actions. It gives up the need to dominate. Taking the meaning of Christ's death on behalf of his enemies with final seriousness, it recognizes that "no one for whom Christ died can be to me an enemy." "Christ died for his enemies, and therefore Christians have the responsibility of preserving all life, especially the enemy's" (Duke 1983, 988).

The great call of both the Law and the prophets, to take up the cause of the innocent and oppressed, which Jesus declared as his mission, was more faithfully fulfilled by Jesus's nonresistant and nonviolent love than by any righteous, calculated, benevolent, or any other form of concern for those in need.

A Spirituality of Nonviolence

There have always been Christians who, like the followers of Jesus in the first two hundred years after his life, death, and resurrection took the path of nonviolence as the practice of spirituality in life.

A spirituality of active nonviolence chooses faithfulness to the way of Jesus, the way of the cross, over personal security; chooses the practice of nonviolent love over defensive, reactive rage; rejects even regretfully or remorsefully resorting to violent self-defense as less than the spirituality of the cross.

A spirituality of active nonviolence refuses to join the spiral of violence–retaliation–violence–revenge–violence–recrimination–violence–retribution.

A spirituality of active nonviolence seeks a constructive process for addressing, resolving, and reconciling conflicts, and it seeks to transform the system that engendered the conflict in the first place.

A spirituality of active nonviolence is an act of faith in the nonviolent God revealed to us in the nonresistant Jesus, who confronted evil with all his power but without abuse of power.

A spirituality of active nonviolence seeks the truth, the opponent's truth as well as its own; seeks genuine human social concern, believing that humans are meant to love and to be loved.

A spirituality of active nonviolence is a politics of repentance and reconciliation that works for transformation of broken systems, for healing of wounded persons, for change in the human order.

A spirituality of active nonviolence is not optimism about human conflict—it takes evil very seriously—but it believes in the reality of good even more than in the reality of evil.

Living nonviolently is a deeply spiritual thing, a profoundly religious commitment. For Anabaptist spirituality, nonviolence is not a technique; it is a habitual expression of the imitation of Christ. It is not a tactic or tool; it is the primary evidence of attachment to Jesus.

When early Christians dared to call Jesus Lord, saying *Kyrios Christos*, Lord Jesus instead of Lord Caesar, it was a political statement first and a religious confession second. In a world where only Caesar could be called Lord—the official words were *Kyrios Kaesar*—Christians pledged allegiance to the nonviolent, suffering prophet Jesus as their exclusive master, final authority, and political head of the state beyond and above all earthly states. No wonder they were seen as subverting the established political order.

A spirituality of nonviolence makes these affirmations:

- Love for God and love of neighbor are two aspects of the same love. Jesus was wholly faithful to God and truly faithful to fellow humanity. We live out his love.
- No one for whom Christ died can be to us an enemy. If Christ already suffered the death penalty for a person who has committed a capital offense, how can I reenact it without invalidating all Christ offered and suffered? We carry out his mission.
- No one is expendable or disposable. No one is absolutely or irrevocably incapable of loving; no one is absolutely or unapproachably incapable of being loved. All persons are within the love of Christ. We join him in this work of love.

- We do not fear or avoid conflict. We refuse to believe the lie that violence is the answer to conflict. We believe in peacemaking.
- To love God, our neighbor, our enemy, and ourselves requires persistent, relentless commitment to the way of Jesus.

On the Other Hand

Seventeen hundred years of Christian cooperation with those who rule, collaboration with Caesar, and attempts to Christianize the state cannot be lightly ignored or written off. The history of great thinkers, sincere believers, and earnest followers who, often with great struggle of conscience and elaborate theological construction, have found ways to bring church and state into mutually supportive contracts has much to teach us.

Those who teach just war ethics are not on the opposing side from those who teach nonviolence because both seek to limit the use of violence—the just war believers through a limited participation in war, the nonviolent disciples through constructive practices of peacemaking that, if followed, point toward the elimination of war. As friends we press one another to be more faithful to our goals, more consistent in our practices. There are many forms of spirituality that, in the Constantinian tradition, see the goals of seeking shalom as primarily internal to the believer and only secondarily actual and visible in times of war. They find ways of affirming love of the enemy even as they are forced by their allegiances and loyalties to take that enemy's life. In Anabaptist spirituality this is unthinkable, and reconciling it with the teachings of Jesus, appears impossible. This is not to deny that spiritualities of accommodation to political strategies can be spiritual; but the question of what sort of spirituality remains. And the questions raised by Jesus, Paul, John, Peter, Origen, Clement, Tertullian, Peter Waldo, Francis of Assisi, Menno, Hans Denck, George Fox, Leo Tolstoy, Mahatma Gandhi, Dorothy Day, John Stott, Martin Luther King Jr., Clarence Jordan, Will Campbell, John Howard Yoder, Ron Sider, Jim Wallis, John Stoner, and many others in the Jesus stream of followers, remain to stir up a counterspirituality of shalom. Such peacemakers—we have it straight from the top—are children of God.

On the Shadow Side

What if everyone believed in nonviolence? What then? What if all believers in Jesus covenanted that they would not kill each other? If that had happened from the start of the Jesus movement, there would have been no Holy Roman Empire, no Crusades, no Thirty Years War, no Hundred Years War, few revolutionary wars in the West, and no world wars in the last century.

But what kind of a world would it be? Does creative change happen only through violent conflict, as has often been argued? How then would we explain the end of the last century, when over half of the world was affected by nonviolent revolutionary changes? Would the shadow side of nonviolence be a world in passive coexistence? Or might we find other motivations for growth, for breakthrough, for discovery? Does not a balanced view of history indicate that creative breakthroughs are not correlated with war except in the rationalizations of those who seek to justify war?

The shadow side of nonviolence has not been demonstrated to be passivity; it is not shown to be buried, potentially explosive, over-controlled hostility; it is not proven to be accumulated anger and rage. And the nonviolent followers, do they use passive aggression? Some do. Are they useless in a military-defense-based economy or a patriotism-equals-militarism society? No, they contribute to the wider world in service and development in ways that are out of proportion to their numbers. So what keeps us from clearly and forthrightly exploring the spirituality taught by the Jesus we claim to follow? What if we took seriously the modest proposal that the children of Abraham refrain from killing each other?

For Meditation

From Hymn 11 in the *Ausbund*, the 1564 hymnal of Anabaptist martyrs:

Who now would follow Christ in life
Must scorn the world's insult and strife
And bear the cross each day;
For this alone leads to the throne,
Christ is the only way.

Christ's servants follow him to death
And give their body, life and breath
On cross and rack and pyre;
As gold is tried and purified
They stand the test of fire.

Renouncing all they choose the cross
And claiming it count all as loss
E'en husband, child and wife;
Forsaking gain, forgetting pain
They enter into life.

6

The Practice of–Concrete Service

Those who are happy
are those who have learned to serve.

Concrete service is the practice of serving Christ by serving
the neighbor. Service is not about me, but about the one being
served. Serving others is voluntary, inner-directed, sometimes
naive, and truly collaborative.

Concern for Others

"I listen to people complain about having to do little things for
others, and I wonder how they would feel about being available
to help someone around the clock?" The doctor's wife is talking
not about his being on call for thirty years, but about her own
present situation.

"All our lives we've done things for each other, back and forth,
the give and take of love," she says. "A stroke changes the balance
of all that."

I look across at her husband, a tall, gentle physician whose life has been given in serving others in a small-town medical practice. Now a postsurgery stroke has taken away his freedom to rush to the aid of others, and requires him to often wait for another to reach out to him.

"It's ironic," he says. "All my life I give, and now I have to receive; all her life she gives, and now she has to give." He smiles a slanted smile, "I liked it better on the giving end. Didn't St. Paul say, 'It's more blessed to give than to receive'?"

"Both of our lives are lived on a different basis. He offers me constant affectionate attention; I offer him loving care around the clock. And each step of new mastery in standing, walking, and self-care is a victory for both of us. And what I've learned is, when we do things for another gladly, it's not about me, not about the one doing the service, it's about the other."

She's understood what so few understand. Real service is not about me. Do you get it?

—⁊⁊—

The speech therapist preens herself in front of the gathered audience. "I take the limited child and give them the gift of communication," she says. "When I can elicit the first word, and the child begins to name its world, well, it's a service only a privileged few get to offer." As we listen, we discover how highly selective she is in picking her subjects: only those with real promise, only those whose influential parents can contribute to her research, only those who will shine as brilliant case studies. The service is not about the child, it's really about her.

A CEO is defining the art of servant leadership. "First, you've got to know where you will hide the body before you pull the trigger," he says in an oft-quoted aphorism. Consequences. Every decision has consequences, and if it happens on his watch, if it looks bad to the board or to the public. . . . His "servant leadership," it seems, is really about him.

A politician is extolling the honor of public service. "If you want to earn the respect of your public, you must listen to the polls, you must have an ear for the vox populi, you must know which way the wind is blowing even when there is only the promise of a breeze, and it pays off." His public service, it is not hard to hear, is really about him.

"It's Really about Me"

Much service begins and ends with the servant. The one being served, no matter how much the service is needed, is only an auxiliary to the real drama. But service whose goal is to elevate the servant is no service at all. It is egocentric at best, exploitive at worst. It seizes the opportunity to seem compassionate, appear benevolent, while in reality it uses another gratuitously.

Many lives lived in pursuit of self-aggrandizement may reach a triumphant conclusion in long and highly acclaimed service that, in retrospect, served primarily the self. Egocentricity, held up before one's face in a review of life, sometimes collapses inward: the memories of a meaningless Christmas past and the certainty of an empty Christmas future can shake a Scrooge awake and make the invisible neighbor visible. Then the Cratchets of the world exist for their own sakes, not just to serve the Ebenezer Scrooges of management. Only when employees become persons, not producing units, ends in themselves rather than means toward greater profits, does servant leadership become more than a cloying cliché.

When the egocentric leader looks back over a lifetime in the inevitable process called life review, the experience may remain superficial, a sort of basking in the light of recalled brilliance while rationalizing and excusing the misuse or exploitation of others' services as something that was necessary. An autobiography written to justify the author's expenditures of persons, time, and resources can celebrate the great man or woman in fantasy, and those whose labor, health, and basic needs were overlooked are footnotes invisible to us, but visible to God.

"I myself am proud of what I spent my life doing," I hear a voice on the morning news as I write. I look up and recognize the candidate for public office. He has made his reputation as an attorney often cited as exploiting the systems of health care, insurance, and retirement benefits. How will that look in life review?

Seen in the dim light of the private conscience, the murky actual past disappears and the fantasy past explains the millions accumulated at the expense of others. A life of service is proclaimed, the dignity of service is extolled, but in the end it is all about the hero of the autobiography. The person who has truly served thinks less about the self and more about others, recalling the persons served, the relationships created, the good accomplished for those in need.

When service is primarily about me, it tends to seek the large need or opportunity, not the small one. It looks for publicity rather than preferring to stay hidden or anonymous. It becomes selective, serving those who will offer advance or advantage rather than those who offer nothing but their human need. It is concerned with results and reduces the care given when those results fall below expectations. It tends to be immediate and temporary rather than consistent in enduring the long haul.

When service is primarily about the other, it does not need triage to sort out the small or insignificant. Public approval is optional, not essential. Personal or institutional profit is not the sole deciding factor; good results are desirable but not crucial; the care continues when others drop away. The service can be given when it is clearly constructive or withheld when aid would be destructive. Since this service is not about the giver's own success or image, the effect for the recipient is what matters.

Service comes in widely contrasting types. We can identify six different types of service by examining their essential, not their publicly stated, goals. Is the service done for the benefit primarily of the server or of the one served? Is the motive self-advancement or ego enhancement, or is it genuine concern for the other? These are not pejorative questions; nor do they have elusive answers. Service and its benefits to the giver and the receiver are open, visible, and self-evident to the recipient, the observer, and, if the actors are at all self-reflective, to the "servant" as well. Let us visualize a range of motivations for service, as portrayed in figure 1.

All six types of service are commonly seen in a day's work. A person may do one act that is egocentric followed by another that is benevolent. Some persons consistently choose a single style of service; others are highly situational and utilitarian.

Figure 1

Motivations for Service

"It's really about me."   **"It's truly about you."**

	Self-serving other-using			Other-serving self-forgetting	

$\longleftarrow$ ———————————————————————————————— $\longrightarrow$

1	2	3	4	5	6
Exploitive Service	**Egocentric Service**	**Egalitarian Service**	**Obedient Service**	**Benevolent Service**	**Sacrificial Service**
Service done solely for self-advancement achieved, profit gained, righteousness demonstrated, moral superiority proved, power seized, political clout claimed.	Service that fulfills ego needs, inflates self-esteem, justifies the giver's pride, raises the giver above others, or claims virtue.	Service that is of equal benefit to both parties, a quid-pro-quo exchange of help and of the benefits of reward or repayment.	Service that fulfills a moral imperative to care for the neighbor, help the needy, even aid the enemy out of a committed, willing obedience to a core of internalized values.	Service that is freely given, offered as a gift, that goes beyond mere payment. It is primarily offered out of caring, mercy, or compassion.	Service that is self-forgetting concern for the other's needs, that helps even though the cost is real sacrifice and voluntary self-investment.

Eros	**Philea**	**Agape**
(self-satisfaction, self-pleasing)	(fellow-feeling friendship)	(care and concern for the other as other)

Public service may vary from exploitive machination with a public-relations spin to action motivated by actual social concern for the good of fellow citizens. Egregiously egocentric service is unmistakable in those who are eager for recognition, quick to do the visible tasks but unavailable for the invisible. Routine service, the give-and-take exchange of daily life, when accomplished with civility and social responsibility, is the stuff of good business, good citizenship, good social judgment and behavior, and much of normal church life. Obedient service suggests that the person is responding to a higher standard than the quid pro quo of routine transactions. This higher standard may be a principle of internalized values or simply the expectation of inner parents. It may be the requirements of a moral conscience or a sense of divine command to serve the neighbor.

Benevolent service and sacrificial service answer to yet a higher call. Both arise from a deep commitment to act in love toward the neighbor, to serve out of concern or compassion for the other's needs, to offer help even at one's own expense because it believes that love is something one does. Participation in community requires doing more for others than expected, offering more than one must and more than is asked for. *A spirituality of service calls one toward benevolent and sacrificial service.*

"It's Truly about You"

There are those extraordinary people who serve others for the others' sake, not for their own. We expect such service from people in the professions—for example, that my physician will not decide which medications to provide on the basis of fringe benefits given by the drug companies; will provide care for reasons other than just the fees received, and will not allow medical decisions to be dictated by the policies or profits of the HMO. The ethics of the practice of medicine define a service that is centered in the welfare of the patient. However, self-giving service is more often the product of personal character, not a professional code of ethics.

We expect that the help we receive from an attorney, an investment counselor, a police officer, and so on will be unbiased, disinterested, eminently fair, genuinely altruistic service. We know that this is not always the case, so we look for a certification that vouches for the quality of service given. Our expectation is that it will be at least egalitarian service, level 3 in figure 1, above.

Each of us seeks service that is not primarily to the advantage of the one serving; we want service that is truly about us. But we feel the warmth of surprise when another goes beyond the socially expected minimum or the professional norm to offer benevolent care or even sacrificial service that is not convenient, not routine, better than the standard.

Ancient proverbs record the breakthrough to reciprocity common to many cultures that taught the possibility of the mutual, reciprocal exchange of aid that is central to civility, social cooperation, and the basic ethics of relationship. "The sort of thing you say is the thing that will be said to you," Homer wrote. "What you do not want done to yourself, do not do to others," Confucius advised.

"He who loves others is constantly loved by them; he who respects others is constantly respected by them," Mencius taught. "What is distasteful to you do not do to another," Rabbi Hillel wrote. And in Jesus's eloquent and proactive words, "Always treat others as you would like them to treat you" (Matt. 7:12 NEB).

The step from self-service to mutuality, from self-advancement to equality, from self-profit to reciprocity is a great step upward in human relationships. It is not only the basis for fairness in the practice of service and justice in the business of service, it is the foundation of fair and equal economic community, something seen all too rarely in either democracy or autocracy.

Outer- or Inner-Directed Service

The higher forms of service rise from internalized motivations that are not dependent on context or external approval.

Service that arises from deeply held values that form the solid core of person and personality is principled service. The care that such service gives to the task, to the recipients, to the larger meaning of the service being rendered extends from the deeply held values that motivate action and attitude.

When outer-directed, a person gathers values and constructs the self from secondhand commitments and concerns. Approval by others, affirmation by those who matter most, applause from the real or imagined audience direct the construction of a pseudoself, a putative model of what is significant in one's society and personal circle.

There are many values that can guide a life as central, indeed sacred passions that organize and direct the self in its primary choices. These ultimate concerns are *god* for the individual, and any failure is *sin*. It is useful to reduce such views to terse paragraphs to feel their power and see their patterns of influence and life formation.

If ambition becomes your driving passion, you are swept into worship of the god of success. Sin is failure. Triumph presupposes virtue. Success is the meaning of life. The winner takes all. Service is the path to success.

If wealth is your consuming passion, you are drawn into worship of the god of prosperity. Sin is insufficient resources. Greed is longing for the good. Possessions self-evidently justify the life and work of the possessor. Riches are the undeniable evidence of God's blessing and favor. Service is a means to prosperity.

If control is your overriding passion, you serve the god of dominance. Sin is submitting to domination by others. Power and control are their own justification. Might makes right. Service obligates others to you.

If fame becomes your ultimate goal, you pursue the god of historical records. Sin is being forgotten, ignored by the guardians of fame. The dream "I shall live forever; they will remember my name" offers the eternal reward. Service is a way to be remembered.

If social superiority is the last word, you prize the privilege of looking down in disdain from the high ground of status and worship the god of social class. Sin is being seen as inferior, coarse, or common. Service is given to those above, expected from those beneath.

If style becomes your reason for being, you set the benchmarks of haute couture and worship the god of elitism. Sin is being outmoded, dated, lacking in panache. Service is done with a flair if it is done at all.

If eternal youth, beauty, and the power to evoke admiration, awe, or envy are supreme, you pursue anything that will stop the ravages of time. You worship the god of divas, stars, models, and pop-culture idols. Sin is aging, sagging, wrinkling, or liver spotting. Service is what you get from your hairdresser, masseuse, and manicurist.

If excellence is your primary, secondary, and penultimate goal, your god is perfection. Sin is mediocrity, the discovery of the fatal flaw. Service, when purchased, should be perfect; when given it is a point of pride.

If righteousness becomes the surpassing goal, your god is the image of goodness, holiness, and immaculate public virtue. Sin is the shame of exposure, discovery, rumor, or the appearance of reality that may gainsay all your pretensions. Service is done when it displays your benevolence or perfection.

If public approval becomes the overwhelming goal, your god is affability, people pleasing, niceness, and the delight of agreeable company. Sin is offending anybody, sticking out as disruptive, failing to fit in and be liked. Service is the art of winning admiration and the gratitude of others.

If sheer pleasure and enjoyment of ease, sensory excitement, comfort, sensuality, and other delights become your reason for being, then your god is hedonism and perhaps even excess. Sin is missing out on the thrill, failing to seize the moment of delight. Because service is not a pleasure, it is chosen only for ego-fulfillment or self-advancement.

If order and decorum is your highest value, your god is what is proper and perfectly correct. Sin is being inappropriate or out of place. Service is done according to the rules of propriety.

But if benevolent or sacrificial service is the goal of your life, your ultimate good is found in contributing meaningfully, your God is the One who loves, gives graciously, shares in mutuality, cares sacrificially, is ultimately a suffering servant. Sin is self-seeking, self-serving, self-aggrandizing refusal to serve. Service is the work of mutual regard.

Naive or Strategic Service

Naive service does not consider all the options, weigh all the consequences, explore all the complexities of a situation before acting. Naive service sees the human need, recognizes that there are many levels of responsibility, refuses to get caught up in the ambiguities, and simply goes ahead and does the right thing.

Calculated, strategic service is more astute. It examines all the factors contributing to the dilemmas of human pain, projects the statistical likelihood that the assistance being contemplated will have long-term effect, and proceeds with strategic selectivity.

Naive service sees the human need, feels the pain of the suffering, and reaches out in compassion; calculated service assesses the viability of the project, recognizes the futility of giving aid where the end is already in sight, and moves on.

Naive service sees the abandoned dying of Calcutta and offers care by creating a house for the destitute and dying; strategic service sees the hunger and plans research into agricultural changes and the development of higher-yield rice varieties to promote a green revolution. Naive service motivated Mother Teresa; strategic service motivated an agronomist who pioneered the development of high-yield rice. Each possesses a unique genius for caring, each has a spirituality of concern for the other. There is a profound spirituality of naive service grounded in the call to care for the orphan and widow (James 1:27), to clothe the naked, feed the hungry, and care for the suffering (Matt. 25:31–46). There is a wise spirituality of strategic service that envisions, explores, experiments, extrapolates, and acts in constructive change. The call to dream dreams of transformation, to see visions of what might, should, and then can be empowers individuals to challenge the way things have always been done and to create something new.

Necessary or Voluntary

Service that is necessary—required, owed, obligated, contracted—may be offered with genuineness, concern, compassion, and thoroughness. Or it can be done grudgingly, of necessity, under duress. One does what has to be done.

Service that is voluntary falls into a completely different category. It arises out of unbidden concern, undemanded interest, unowed compassion. This is the service that comes close to being the actions of love. It is offered by free choice because of the nature of the servant. One does what one sees as needed.

Most service is mixed, with necessary and voluntary aspects occurring together. Perhaps one serves because it is a career—a chosen course—and for a salary does what is necessary, fulfilling all requirements. But when one goes beyond the expected, the service becomes voluntary; when one gives without self-centered motivation, the caregiving becomes an act of freedom; when one transcends what is expected or required, one serves joyfully, freely, out of the exuberant excess called love. Service moves from the quid pro quo of "you scratch my back and I scratch yours" to the practice of benevolence and sacrifice in meeting others' needs.

Spirituality meets service as it calls one to go the second mile, to offer the second act of caring, to reach out without first asking "But what's in it for me?" Spirituality is the voluntary element in serving another that links persons with loving concern; spirituality is the voluntary connection of social interest, fellow-feeling, and mutual aid.

Spirituality and service are sometimes viewed as direct opposites. Spirituality is believed to be detached from the tasks of life, the concrete acts of caregiving, the mundane, the routine, the earthly, the material; the spiritual reaches toward the transcendent, the ineffable, the heavenly. Some can be so heavenly minded that they are of no earthly good. Anabaptist theologian and martyr Hans Denck wrote, "He whose heart is directed towards heaven would do better to align himself with the despised and humble people of this earth" (in Bauman 1991, 50).

Spirituality in a tripolar key does not divide the heavenly from the earthly, the sacred from the mundane or even the profane. All of life can be viewed as service when service is defined as work done in voluntary, caring relationship. Work may be obligatory, compulsory, and coerced, but spiritual service is labor done out of concern, conviction, and commitment to a person or goal. Work is about the task and the toil required to complete it; spiritual service is about the higher goal, the welfare of persons and community. In tripolar spirituality, service to neighbor and service to God cannot be divided; like two sides of the same coin, they are the same reality. As I serve the needs of others, the spirituality of service elevates work to something more than mere employment.

Service as Work; Work as Service

The paradigm for work that one carries in the unconscious is the inner muscle that carries one through the long day from nine to five. In fact, the paradigm shapes the whole of one's life, for working and loving and sometimes playing are the stuff of life, and mature individuals work when they work, love when they love, and play when they play, without loving only their work, playing at love, and competitively working at play. The two central paradigms for work are "working to live" and "living to work." Those who operate according to the first see work as a hated necessity. They work only to make money, and they live to escape from work to do something else. Those who adhere to the second tend to look at work as a means of self-fulfillment. They see the money earned as making it possible to devote themselves more freely to what they want to pursue with a passion. Those who love work are not just artists, scholars, and scientists but all who find expression of their love of life in the privilege of creation and service. Those who hate work are not only those who do the hard, repulsive, and uninteresting or ill-paid jobs; they also include the idle rich (Sayers 1946, 122–23).

Since work consumes a major part of each person's time and energy, it has a close relationship to spirituality. The two intertwine as interdependent parts of vocation, calling, and a personal sense of life project. Among the many metaphors possible, six predominate.

Metaphor 1: Work is *achievement* (success is evidence of likely election, a sign of probable salvation). This is the Puritan articulation of the Protestant work ethic. One cannot earn salvation—that is unilaterally up to divine discretion—but industrious labor and material wealth are signs of one's election. So the harder one works and the more prosperous one becomes, the more certain one is of personal salvation. According to this managerial theology, motivation, moral intolerance for laziness, and workaholism are synonymous with virtue. "Give diligence to make your calling and election sure" (2 Peter 1:10 KJV).

Metaphor 2: Work is *identity* (what one does and who one is are one and the same). When one chooses a career or profession as the primary way of identifying who one is, work can become the master identity. "I am what I do" has been true to some extent at some times in my life, but I am more than my set of skills, the shape of my role, the place of my appointment, and so on. Reducing the person to a set of functions is a violence to human nature and destiny, and it leads to a functional theology: I am my performance, profession, product, social standing. When professional identity usurps personal identity, the soul is being absorbed by external forces. Having described all the role relationships of his professional life that had usurped his identity, Paul dismissed them as useful nutrients now digested and discarded. Then he identified the central pursuit of his identity, life project, and vocation. His work was not his person (Phil. 3:3–16).

Metaphor 3: Work is *a commodity* (a unit of value that can be exchanged for or cashed in as money). The industrial revolution was built on this understanding. The worth of a person was now shown by the price his or her time commanded: I am worth less than those above me; the CEO is worth millions. This leads to a mercantile theology: monetary value is the measure of all things. James personified wages when he wrote that "the wages you never paid to the men who mowed your fields are loud against you" (James 5:4 NEB). Money talks. It cries out against those who have held it back from those to whom it was owed. The outcry of the millions of dollars CEOs have skimmed from the pay and pension funds of their employees is audible to God.

Metaphor 4: Work is *a basic human right* (every person deserves the privilege of meaningful work). Unionists, humanists, philosophers, and theologians have maintained that everyone seeking a job must have the opportunity to find employment that befits human dignity. By working we reflect our Creator, whose work we are. The Reformation concept of vocation includes the propositions that each one's work contributes to the greater good; that work is an end in itself, not just a means, so that its every activity has meaning; that vocation is universal, specieswide, for all persons; and that vocation is particular, each person having a gift, a capacity, a place in community to fulfill, a way to serve and contribute. This is a vocational theology that regards a calling as a gift. "As God has called you, live up to your calling," Paul says tersely (Eph. 4:1 NEB).

Metaphor 5: Work is *a curse* (work involves sweat, toil, weeds, and suffering). Work is the enemy. Work is worthy of our hate, but because it is our natural state, it must be endured. An African-American tradition arising out of the bondage labor of slavery is notable here—labor was a vehicle of the curse, an oppressive task that imposed sweat and suffering, not a symbol of blessedness or opportunity for service. A slave theology demands of workers: "accept your station and situation; work in the state where you were called." It all began with the curse spoken to Adam: "Gain your bread by the sweat of your brow" (see Gen. 3:17–19 NEB).

Metaphor 6: Work is *service* (it is an act of human compassion, communal participation). The Pietists believed that experience is more important than doctrine, and they taught that the activity of work is in and of itself meaningful, as an expression of one's faith and as an act of loving service to the neighbor and the community. Calvinists believe that doctrine is essential and that it is gratitude that motivates us to do our tasks obediently. And Anabaptists believe that work is service in following the way of Jesus. They all see work as virtue and vocation. We are blessed in joyful labor. This is labor theology, which asserts that loyal service is a virtue. Paul advised that we work "with good will, doing service, as to the Lord and not to be approved by others" (Eph. 6:7, author's paraphrase).

The metaphors of work—as achievement, identity, a commodity, a basic human right, a curse, or an act of service—are not mutually exclusive. One may recognize them all at different times or in differing jobs, but usually one metaphor predominates. Spirituality from the first becomes material; from the second, depressive; from the third, political; from the fourth, endurable; from the fifth, despicable; and from the sixth, meaningful and fulfilling and, at best, even redemptive. Work can be seen as a creative activity that can be done with a vision and in a vocation of service.

Service as Competition; Service as Collaboration

Competition and service are not antonyms. Service can be competitive in its striving for excellence, but the crucial thing is the nature of the competitive spirit—is it malevolent and destructive or benign and constructive?

Malignant competition competes for its own sake, for the gratification of winning and seeing the other lose, not for the reward that comes from excellence in performance or service. It may become more invested in the others' losing than in its own winning.

Benign competition competes with itself, attempting to go beyond its own level of performance, seeking to better its service, and working for the betterment of the welfare of the larger group or community.

Malignant competition becomes obsessive since one must win or the comfort zone is destroyed, the internal balance is damaged, and one is nothing. It is often narcissistic, as the ideal image of the winner is attached to the outcome, and losing causes a deep wound to core self-esteem.

Benign competition is collaborative; each party strives to achieve a personal goal and to facilitate others in reaching their highest aspirations. It is dialogical because in debate one side presents the best arguments for its position yet also contributes to strengthening the other side, when appropriate, to bring out the best in both positions. It sees the dignity and beauty in a performance, the art in a project, the integrity in a piece, and cares for the highest expression of the work, seeking to express all that is possible in excellence. The spectrum between these two types of competition is illustrated in figure 2.

Mature service leans toward the collaborative; it questions competitive striving that elevates ego, requires the other's defeat, and accelerates self-inflation. Competitive striving is better associated with pride than humility, with monopolar spirituality than tripolar integration of one's working relationships with one's deepest commitments of character.

Service that cares about the work being done and the workers participating in that service leans strongly toward the collaborative, the constructive, the benign forms of goal setting and outcome seeking. The more the goal of service becomes competitive, the less it truly involves the welfare of the recipient and of the persons providing the assistance. For the healthy person ego is not everything; nor is it the only thing. One exists for the sake of others, as well as for oneself. It is the nature of true maturity to learn to love the work one does for the work's sake, to value the service one can provide for the worth of the service itself, not for the acclaim or esteem it may earn. Competition is a useful motivation, but not our highest calling. Worthwhile work, self-rewarding service, the daily practice of care and compassion rise from a deeper place in

Figure 2

The Competition Spectrum

Malignant				Benign
1.	2.	3.	4.	5.
Chronic destructive competition; the ends justify the means; used in intractable feuding with the goal of eliminating the other.	Competitive conquest that is obsessive; winning is everything and the only thing.	Competitive contest that is sharply win/lose; "My way is Yahweh" — that is, it's the only way.	Collaborative competition; joint and mutual problem solving.	Celebrative competition that achieves everyone's best.
The goal is to see the other lose even if I must lose as well.	The goal is to win and to see the other lose. My triumph must be visible, and the other's defeat public.	The goal is to win and to let others take care of themselves. I regard my opponents with disinterested respect.	The goal is for both to win, where possible, and to achieve mutual satisfaction of both parties.	The goal is to win by excelling, to achieve one's best and to bring out the best in others.
Actions that expose the evil in the opponent or weakness in the other side.	Service that wins first place, rising above others in victory and superiority.	Service that exhibits my ability and my care for true excellence.	Service that brings out our mutual best in joint success.	Service that is my best and invites your best performance.

the soul than conquest, competition, conflict, and the need to be seen as first and best or to be on top.

Service as Worship; Worship as Service

Worship falls under the theological category of service, and vice versa. When we speak of a service of worship, or of a worship service, we repeat ourselves. The two words mean the same thing. As Frederick Buechner writes:

> To worship God *means* to serve him. Basically there are two ways to do it. One way is to do things for him that he needs to have done—run errands for him, carry messages for him, fight on his

side, feed his lambs, and so on. The other way is to do things for him that you need to do—sing songs for him, create beautiful things for him, give things up for him, tell him what's on your mind and in your heart, in general rejoice in him and make a fool of yourself for him the way lovers have always made fools of themselves for the one they love.

A Quaker meeting, a Pontifical High Mass, the Family Service at First Presbyterian, a Holy roller Happening—unless there is an element of Joy and foolishness in the proceedings, the time would be better spent doing something useful. (Buechner 1973, 97–98)

"You shall worship the Lord your God, Him only you shall serve," Jesus replied to the tempting offer of power and glory (Luke 4:8 NKJV). To worship God is to serve him exclusively; every act of service given to the neighbor is, on a deeper level, service given to God—it is to "run errands for him, carry messages for him." In serving others, we are living out the daily, concrete practice of worship.

"For me, counseling is not just akin to worship, it is the experience of worship," Frank Kimper, my professor and clinical supervisor would say thoughtfully. "Not just when I see persons celebrating breakthrough and reconciliation—it's easy to worship then—but when they are locked in the struggle with depression or despair, I worship because I know God is there."

Every act of caring, support, confrontation, and healing truth-telling is a form of service and therefore an act of worship. It is done to and for the neighbor as a recognition that we stand before and in the presence of God. This is the core of tripolar spirituality—knowing that in the moment we receive aid from or give aid to another, God is there.

Service as the Way of Jesus

Service is a recurring theme in the teachings of Jesus. It was a virtue he prized and practiced. If Jesus was a man who lived to serve others, Dietrich Bonhoeffer argued, then it follows that the church is only the church when it exists for others in the practice of agape. This agapaic love, he noted, results in three kinds of service: the service of listening to others that is an extension of the work of God, the great Listener; the service of active helpfulness with the bothersome things of life, the little irritations that offer us an opportunity to respond to none other than God—because we must be ready to be interrupted by God; and the service of forbearance, in which the strong help the weak, the healthy help the ill, and the righteous help the fallen. In Christian forbearance we are drawn together toward God. "Nobody is too good for the meanest service. One who worries about the loss of time that such petty, outward acts of helpfulness entail is usually taking the importance of his own career too solemnly" (Bonhoeffer 1952, 96–99).

It was Palm Sunday, a traditional time for self-examination one week before Easter communion according to the practice of the Virginia Mennonite community where I was a young pastor. After a sermon on self-reflection—"Are you at peace with God and all others as far as you know?"—tubs and towels were brought in as the women retired to the adjoining room for their own foot-washing service. The men, now barefoot, began gathering in groups by the tubs in the aisles. They paired up randomly to kneel, wash, and dry each other's feet, then rise for a brotherly embrace.

Then a movement caught my—and everyone's eye. One man was making his way across the room, shaking his head no to those who reached out, offering to share foot washing with him. He approached another man, whose back was turned. All eyes followed and silence fell. The two had been business partners, but the enterprise had faltered and had sunk into the red. It was the man crossing the room who had put up the capital and sustained the most visible loss. Reconciliation attempts had been unsuccessful; they had not spoken for months.

The other, puzzled by the silence, turned to look and saw the big man bearing down on him. He froze for an instant, then turned and walked to meet him. The men in line by the front tub stepped back, and the former business partners took their places. As one knelt and took the other's foot, and the sound of poured water softly rippled through the church, all looked away in respect for a holy moment or to hide the moisture in their own eyes.

Following Jesus is joining in the service of humanity. All through-out his teaching one finds the recurrent themes of the necessity and the dignity of service.

- He defined greatness as serving, not dominating (Mark 10:44; Luke 22:25–26). *The truly great are great servants.*
- He defined leadership as serving, not commanding (Mark 10:44; Matt. 20:25). *To lead is to serve.*
- He defined vocation as serving, not being served (Mark 10:45; Luke 22:27). *It is in caring for the other that we find our true calling.*
- He described motivation as serving God, not serving greed or gold (Luke 16:13; Matt. 6:24). *It is in serving that we become rich.*
- He described self-forgetful service as sacrificial discipleship (John 12:24–26). *It is in giving that we receive, in losing life that we find it.*
- He declared that serving the innocent is serving God (Mark 9:36–37). *To serve a child is to serve God.*
- He described service as authentic humility, a new authority of actual involvement, not rank (Matt. 23:11; Luke 22:24–27; Matt. 20:25–28). *Service nourishes humility; dominance feeds arrogance.*
- He equated service and friendship with mutual loyalty and reciprocal care or collaboration (John 15:13–17). *Friendship is availability and openness to mutual service.*

The ancient hymn that tells the Jesus story reaches its focal point in the words, "he humbled himself" and "he took the form of a servant" (Phil. 2:7 NKJV). To follow him in life is to "be servants to one another in love" (Gal. 5:13 NEB). A spirituality of discipleship is a spirituality of service that truly appraises and responds to the needs of others as an expression of agape. True spirituality is seen in the love that expresses self-giving on behalf of another. The first requisite for Christian service is not love but solidarity with the world. Love without solidarity is nothing but spiritual pride. I am, first of all, a person like other persons—Catholics, Muslims, communists, and those of all other backgrounds. Where this solidarity is denied or played down, there is also good reason to question the quality of the love (Dyck 1968, 7).

In the dominance system of the world, the way to power, authority, public esteem, greatness, and self-confident assertiveness is in serving the system, serving those who can profit one, and ultimately, serving oneself. In the way of Jesus, serving others is the way to a loving spirit, concern for the neighbor, and the authentic authority of compassionate service. Then the service is really about others and is done out of love for the Other. The service is faithful even when the times get hard. As Terry Barringer paraphrases the magnificent closing words of the Hebrew prophet Habakkuk (3:17–19):

> Though the contract finishes, and there is no work to be had;
> Though there is no demand for my skills, and no one publishes
>   my work.
> Though the savings run out, and the pension is not enough to
>   live on;
> Yet will I rejoice in the Lord. I will rejoice in God my savior.
>
> (Barringer 2004, 215)

On the Other Hand

Some see spirituality as a quality that lifts one out of the routines of service to others and allows a time of quiet and withdrawal from task and deed. Yes, such quiet may suffuse service with a gentle spirit, but tripolar spirituality, with its emphasis on praying as you act, loving as you serve, meeting God in those you serve, and following Christ in taking the form of a servant stresses action as the place where true reflection takes place. Other traditions see withdrawal as the proper setting for meditation and reflection that then results in action. Is it possible to get caught up in action and fail to take time for contemplation of its meaning? Is so much outward focus inevitably achieved at the expense of inwardness? Perhaps the call to the desert for meditation should always precede the command to the world for mediation and service.

All action and no reflection makes the disciple an empty vessel. All work and no withdrawal exhausts resources and depletes the soul. All effort and no comfort drains away the energies of the spirit. So the activist may stand tall, but she may also cast a long shadow of self-righteousness because of her own sacrificial achievements. The servant may be selfless and other-centered while gaining his own rewards from his virtuousness. Self-discipline, self-investment, and self-effort may result in self-worship. Such shadow-side risks deserve second thoughts.

This focus on concrete service prizes work done with a gentle and humble spirit in mutual and reciprocal ways that may be benevolent and sacrificial when necessary, and sees it all as participating in the way of Jesus. It assumes that the servant can truly walk in the steps of the greatest servant, that service and worship can be one, and that service should rise out of the gratitude of spirituality and that the two can meld.

Are a spirituality of the feet and a spirituality of the knees inseparably welded into one? The tripolar spirituality espoused by such groups as the Anabaptists believes that we follow the path of service simply because it is the way of Jesus, and we go into service because that is where we truly meet Jesus. We know the three places where Jesus can be found—where two or three gather in his name (Matt. 18:20), where walls come down in reconciliation (Eph. 2:11–22), and when we serve another in need (Matt. 25:40). Because all three of these are concrete forms of service, we can say with certainty that authentic Christ-encounters happen not only in the desert or the closet or the place of retreat, but also as we serve.

For Meditation

The following hymn text addresses the call to serve. It is from Hymn 56 in the *Ausbund*, the 1564 hymnal of Anabaptist martyrs.

What about the neighbor?
When God's will is done,
Love of God and other,
Two loves become one.
Jesus asks the question,
We dare not ignore,
"Will you *be* a neighbor?"
"Do you love self more?"

What about the neighbor?
Do we know their needs?
Do we seek to meet them,
with both words and deeds?
Christ is our example.
He did not divide
love for God and others.
Both stand side by side.

What about the neighbor?
God requests reply.
Though we claim to love them,
do our acts belie?
No matter what others
may do in return,
they're our sisters, brothers,
our equal concern.

Parable for Peditation

Copy the following on a bit of paper and walk to the parable
in peditation.

(Rhythm—three syllables, rest, then next three syllables.)

Good Samaritan

Lone man mugged,
beat and fleeced,
scorned by saint,
passed by priest.

Good men look
other way,
Much to do!
Seize the day!

Alien stops,
sees his hurt,
gives first aid
in the dirt.

Cares, although
not his class,
lifts him on
his own ass.

Picks up check
at the inn,
on return,
checks again.

Jesus asks
critics dim,
"Which of these
neighbored him?"

(see Luke 10:30–37)

7

The Practice of—
Authentic Witness

Preach the gospel at all times;
If necessary, use words.

> St. Francis of Assisi

Live the answers faithfully;
Listen, be patient for the questions.

Authentic witness is the practice of genuine presence with, sensitivity to, modeling for, and then sharing with others about one's deepest beliefs, values, and hopes.

Faithful Presence

David Shank, a pastor in Belgium, followed a translator into a room filled with Greek, Spanish, and Serbian miners. At a minute's notice, he was to tell the Christian story.

"Fellows, would you agree to play a game with me?" he asked. "Let me try to tell you about yourselves. If I am wrong, you stop me. But as long as I tell the truth, you let me go on. Agreed?" They nodded in skeptical consent.

"You've never had a real chance to get ahead in life until now, so every day you risk your lives to go down into these dirty Belgian mines to give your children a better chance, right?"

"Yes, that's right, go on."

"So you work like a slave, day after day, so your kids won't have to do the same. That's your ideal. You get paid on Saturday. You stop at the café for a drink or two, a few hands of cards and a couple bets, and when you get home your wife looks at what's left of your pay and says 'Not enough for the week.'"

"Yeah, go on."

"When she criticizes you, and what's even worse, you know she's right, you get mad at her, and you lose you head and hit her?"

"Right, but how did you know?"

"Then you feel ashamed, and you ask yourself, 'Why did I do that?'"

"True."

"Then you can't sleep and you lie there thinking 'My kids are no better off than before, I've failed them,' And you get mad at yourself, at the filthy job, then at your wife, your kids, the whole world. After you fume awhile you say, 'Next week will be different.' So you go back to the dirty mine."

"Yes, that's about right."

"And when you're a mile or two down under the earth, you start to wonder, 'What about all the gases down here? What if there's an explosion? What about a cave-in? What then? What about the wife and kids? What about me?' But there's no one to talk to about this. You're alone, and you feel rotten."

"Yes, that's true."

"Do you know how I know all this?"

"No, that's what we want to know. You're no miner. How did you get to know about us?"

"I got it out of this book."

"What book?"

"It's called the New Testament. It tells about our hopes and God's hopes for us. Do you want to hear the rest of the story?"

"Yes, tell us the rest."

"It says that at the very point where we fail, where we betray our ideals and we are guilty and afraid, God wants to help. And if we accept that help, there's hope for our children." (Shank 1969, 32)

—∞—

Charles Cristano, an Indonesian pastor and the former president of the Mennonite World Conference, tells of the man who influenced him most.

He was Christian, as was his family of seven children. He was generous, hospitable. He welcomed strangers.

During the war against the Dutch colonialists, in the early twentieth century, since the family was Christian, it was assumed they were collaborators with the Dutch, so they suffered abuse, assault, and beatings. During the most intense attacks, they sought sanctuary as refugees in a large city.

Then the father was abducted, the family thought him dead. When he returned, he bore the scars and burns of torture, and reported that the leader of the torture squad was a close family friend, a man who had been a frequent guest in their home.

Several years later, the family, having reclaimed their home, rebuilt their business, reclaimed their place in the community, were paid a visit by this same man. The father received him kindly, insisting that he join the family for lunch. As they ate and talked, the man grew angry and the old malice poured out. "How did you survive the war? Who protected you? How did you start your business again? Did you get money from your Dutch masters?"

"No, we survived the great hardships because our God cares for us," the father said calmly, and the lunch went on with a return to friendly talk.

"How could you forgive and tolerate such a man?" the children asked later. "You were nearly killed because of him."

"To be honest, I cannot forget what he did to me, indeed, what he did to us, but we are to love, even our enemies. I shall find a way to make him my friend."

"He was an amazing man," Charles Cristano concludes, "I shall always remember him. He was my father" (Peachey and Peachey 1984).

—∽—

Nobel Peace Prize–winning author Rigoberta Menchú Tum
was being hosted by various universities in greater Los Angeles,
and a *Los Angeles Times* writer was seeking a local connection:
"Your appearances in Los Angeles were arranged by Phil Hofer
of University of LaVerne, who said he was acquainted with you.
Do you know Phil Hofer?"

"Do I know him?" she replied. "He saved my life. He and his
community hid me, cared for me when the government sought
my life, helped me escape certain death, at the risk of having all
Mennonite development workers expelled from Guatemala—or
worse—if they were found out."

"Mr. Hofer," the reporter asked, "how did you decide to give aid
to this woman speaking out about alleged massacres of indigenous
peoples?"

"Why do you ask?" Phil replied. "We did it because it was the
right thing to do" (*Los Angeles Times*, April 2000).

—∽—

The mood in Sevastopol, Russia, was nasty in 1905. The Russian
war with the Japanese (1904–1905) had been a disaster, and those
unsatisfied with any reasonable explanation sought a scapegoat.
The Jews, as usual, became their selected target. The press was
inflammatory, the public were organizing pogroms, the police
were passive.

Peter Friesen, the liaison between the Mennonite Church and the
government, was living in Sevastopol. A historian and a politically
involved person, he followed the rising wave of anti-Semitism with
mounting concern. One morning he said to his wife, Susannah,
"During the night, I have realized that I must make public interces-
sion on behalf of the Jews." Susannah protested that he was still
in recovery from several weeks of serious illness and urged him to
consider the consequences of allying himself with the Jews. Peter
was adamant. They prayed together, and he left for the center of
town.

At the marketplace an angry crowd had gathered around a wagon that had been set up as a makeshift stage for speakers. Peter climbed into the driver's seat. Then this ethnic German, educated in Russian schools, spoke in fluent Ukrainian. He reminded them that they called themselves Christians. Christ was One who loved. Could they? Through his death we are one, and old walls are broken down. Surely no one present would want the blood of another soiling their hands and soul.

Standing beside the wagon was a burly Ukrainian dockworker, dusty with dirt and soot. Without warning, Peter pulled the man onto the wagon and kissed him, comrade style, on both cheeks. Then, with a firm voice, he sent them all home. And the crowd obeyed. That day in Sevastopol, not a single Jew was harmed (Dueck 2002, 72).

What is Authenticity?

These four accounts—of Shank, Cristano, Hofer, and Friesen—are authentic stories (true accounts) of authentic men (truthful people) giving authentic witness (being true to grace, mercy, and justice that was above and beyond themselves). Each was being authentic to himself, authentic to the moment, authentic to the persons he encountered, and authentic to something superior to the self, something we may even call eternal.

Authenticity is a remarkable word. It comes from the Greek word *authentikos*, meaning "original"—as an original oil painting is from the hand of the artist. So an authentic Rembrandt is from the hand of the master; an authentic piece by Mozart is as he played it; an authentic Chinese jade is true nephrite. To be authentic is to be true to essential humanness, to be true to one's nature. Rarely is the word used in this sense in contemporary speech.

Authenticity has come to mean being true to oneself, transparent with one's motives and intentions, genuine and sincere. Noble as these characteristics are, they miss the core meaning of authenticity. For one to be authentic there must be a model of personhood, an exemplar of wholeness and balance, a North Star of human existence, an original measure of humanness—of what is truly human—that is superior to simply being natural, unaffected, and simply oneself. Authenticity is being a self that expresses mature, complete, balanced, and fully human being. Christians stake their existence on the claim that Jesus Christ is the authentic model for authentic life as an authentic person in authentic relationships and authentic community (Kraus 1979, 16).

Authentic witness is given to this authentic model—Jesus Christ—when it is done in his own uniquely authentic way. We are free to choose how to go about sharing our faith with others, but our options and choices are never neutral. The methods we choose either embody or contradict the story we are seeking to share. Stories of Jesus are historical information. Beliefs about Jesus are personal conviction and opinion. Theologies of Jesus are thoughtful interpretations. But encounter with persons who embody Jesus's character—his compassion, concern, honesty, courage, selflessness, and above all, God-centeredness is more than encounter with story or belief or theology. It is authentic witness to the Jesus who is now among us.

When witness is offered with nothing to authenticate it, it is a matter of words, fitly spoken and full of content, yet not a part of the actual context. Witness to faith that emerges from the action of faithful presence, concern, and service is congruent when the content spoken and the context experienced validate each other. "Life and witness, method and message, nature and mission are one whole integrated experience" (Kraus 1979, 56).

Only an authentic witness (person) can give an authentic witness (proclamation). Personal authenticity is expressed in a particular kind of spirituality, a spirituality that is attached to the eternal roots (a radical attachment to an encountered God) and experienced consistently in how one lives out this attachment in the give and take of life (a radical obedience called discipleship). Such spirituality has content, not empty form. It is open-ended in relation to the future but grounded in past reality. It is not elusive, diffuse, mysteriously transcendent. It is tentative not dogmatic, humble not arrogant, mystic not mysterious, open not closed; it is confident not strident, firm not absolutistic, not set in concrete, yielded to all that is good and of God, not claiming to possess what is good or to be in control of what is God.

"Unless disciples are following the Great Commandment, it is fruitless to engage in the Great Commission," writes pastor and gadfly Brian McLaren. "Discipleship in this sense . . . means being called to learn a new way of living, a way of life characterized by love for God and one's neighbor and one's enemies. It positions one in the world as a servant, a doer of good works, and a friend to sinners, as was our Lord" (McLaren 2004, 5).

Elsewhere McLaren refers to those who seek to carry out the Great Commission without living the Great Commandment as producing only a Great Commotion. He is unabashedly calling for tripolar spirituality as essential to any trustworthy affirmations about Jesus. As McLaren comments, "If disciples don't love one another, according to Jesus, no one has much reason to believe their message. I suspect this is a fail-safe mechanism Jesus built into the gospel: the only messengers who should be trusted are those who exemplify the message" (McLaren 2004, 6). Witness that expresses a bipolar spirituality has a sale to make, a perspective to share, a set of beliefs to promote, a group of benefits to promise. But tripolar spirituality must be demonstrated, lived, known in actual encounter between persons. In Jesus's time one had to know a disciple to become one—truth was embodied not published; the good news was visible in changed people, not promised by impersonal media.

The practice of authentic witness grows from a tripolar spirituality that makes more claims about Christ than it does about itself, but seeks to model that Christ authentically in the details of life. Authentic witness is not pretentious perfectionism, but transparent vulnerability. It seeks not to change others, but to offer the story of its own need for change and discovery in a way that opens dialogue. John Drane offers pungent commentary on this point:

> Christians love to correct other people. But an appropriate prophetic attitude for a renewed and faithful church will begin with the recognition that we can only effectively challenge others to follow the way of Christ if we are continually hearing God's voice for ourselves, and allowing our own understandings to be changed in the process. We have something to share with others not because we

are different, but because we are no different, and we can become
credible witnesses not as we condemn others and dismiss what
we regard as their inadequate spiritualities, but as we constantly
listen to the gospel and appropriate its challenge in our own lives.
(Drane 2004, 99)

Leo Tolstoy wrote in his sharp critique of the institutional church
and its superficial—indeed, as he called it, fraudulent—religion:

> And the meaning of the fraud is merely that there are people who
> are beside themselves with desire to teach their religion to other
> people.
>   And why are they so anxious to teach their religion to other
> people? If they had a real religion they would know that religion
> is the understanding of life, the relation each man establishes to
> God, and that consequently you cannot teach a religion, but only
> a counterfeit of religion. (Tolstoy 1967, 273)

For Tolstoy no religion is valid that includes "those that make a
verbal expression of religion instead of its expression in the whole
of life—for religion cannot be expressed in words!" (175).

> The doctrine of Christ, which has entered into the consciousness of
> men, not by force or by the sword, as they say, but by non-resistance
> to evil, by humility, meekness, and the love of peace, can only be
> propagated among men by the example of peace, love, and concord
> given by its followers. (286)

Authentic embodiment, or authentic demonstration, is the basis
for any witness that has validity.

Søren Kierkegaard despaired of words and longed for "existential expression" of the imitation of Christ in the lives of those
who are witnesses to faith:

> If I try to think of [an apostle in our day] I think of him abstaining
> altogether from preaching in order, if possible, to draw attention
> to what it means to exist, preaching by giving self-denial existential
> expression, the imitation of Christ. And moreover how could he com-
> pete verbally with all these artists in rhetoric who now preach—and
> forget entirely about living?

A man is castrated in order to make him a singer who can take higher notes than any normal man can take: and so with these preachers: from a Christian point of view they are castrati, are deprived of their real manhood which is "the existential"—but they can take notes higher and more fascinating than any true Christian. (Kierkegaard 1938/1951, 424 [Item 1174])

What matters is not the height of rhetoric attained or the exaltation of stirring expression achieved. Rather, what matters is the integrity of a life lived in embodied witness.

Authentic Witness

What makes witness authentic is neither the charismatic personality of an individual nor the perfection of a particular life; it is the presence of a community of witnesses who verify, validate, and authenticate their life together. Witness is a shared task, not an independent one.

Authentic witness is the key factor in identifying the body of Christ in the world, in contrast to correct organization or clerical structure, perfection in lifestyle, or ecstatic experience of Holy Spirit power. The hallmark of the Jesus movement in history is authentic relationship—the reconciliation of the human family in Christ. The "true church" is the authentic community of witness. (Kraus 1979, 10–11)

In the practice of stubborn loyalty we call authentic community, we join in a collective demonstration of people living out an awareness of and allegiance to God. Such joint witness, when it is given in corporate life, makes both values and virtues visible. What is believed is lived; what is lived becomes believable to those who view it in the wider community. *We* live out our witness as a people; *we* find that a shared spirituality possesses a sociological authenticity not possible for an individual on a private journey; *we* become a community of co-questers, not a world where each is pursuing her or his own quest. Authentic witnesses live a common life of affirmation of all they value and invitation for others to join them in a life of shared virtues. This is a mutual process of serving one another while serving the wider, surrounding world.

An evangelical minister called on an Amish bishop in the community near Shipshewana, Indiana. New to the area, he wanted to meet fellow Christian leaders and perhaps arrive at some understanding of their faith in relation to his fundamentalist framework. At the end of several hours of conversation, thoroughly laced by quotations from and references to scripture by both men, the minister rose to leave, then paused to ask a final—and for him, the crucial—question.

"What I really want to know," he said, "Are you saved, truly born again through a personal faith in Christ?"

"You're asking the wrong person," the Amish bishop replied. "You do not ask that question of me. You ask my neighbors, you ask my people. Here, I will give you the names of people who have known me for years, of those who have been critical of me, or have real differences with me. Ask them. That is who you must ask if you want an answer to that question."

Contradictory Witness

In *Shantung Compound*, Langdon Gilkey wrote his reflections on three years in a Japanese internment camp during World War II. Trained at Harvard in the 1930s, he believed in the moral educability of humankind. Now he was interred with 1,500 European, Canadian, British, and American expatriates, most of whom were highly educated, socially sensitive missionaries. The American Red Cross at last succeeded in sending 2,100 food parcels into the compound. The authorities decreed that each prisoner receive one parcel and, since the shipment came from their country, that the three hundred Americans could share the remaining six hundred packets. Three parcels for each American, one parcel each for the rest. When this was announced, the Americans caucused and formally protested. They demanded that the three hundred Americans receive seven packets each and that the other 1,200 receive none. Fear and insecurity can turn even missionaries into raging survivalists (Gilkey 1966).

Tragically, too much of the witness offered by the church is not just inauthentic, it is contradictory. Think of the contrast between two kinds of evangelism: that done by conquerors and that done by servants.

Too often since the time of Constantine, Christians have tried to share the gospel as military conquerors rather than as servants. When the emperor Constantine became a Christian in the early fourth century, he baptized all his troops. That is power evangelism. But it is the power of the sword not the Spirit.

Since then Christians have dared to tell Muslims that Jesus is the only way to salvation even while they have launched vicious crusades and slaughtered hundreds of thousands of Muslims. Christians have invited Jews to accept their Messiah as they have tolerated anti-Semitic discrimination, pogroms, and the Nazi Holocaust.

British missionaries flooded into China right after the British government fought the Opium War with China to force the Chinese to allow Britain to sell opium to them!

North American Christians sent missionaries to the American Indians while their governments broke hundreds of treaties and almost wiped out the native peoples.

Spanish missionaries preached Christ to the indigenous people of South America while their relatives brutally conquered and massacred them.

Europeans even dared to tell Africans about Christianity while they forced them into slavery. One slave ship sent from Charleston was called the *Good Ship Jesus* (Sider 1999, 174).

The evangelism of marauding medieval crusaders, of settlers homesteading lands of native peoples, of conquering colonial armies, of current groups who settle newly won territory after military occupation has no integrity. "Servant evangelists who humbly, sacrificially minister to all the needs of people of other faiths do have integrity when they also invite them to accept the only Savior of the world." (Sider 1999, 175).

Witness in a Culture of Narcissism

The most common question or concern expressed when many Christians share their faith is, "What can Jesus do for you?" Persons being invited to consider following Christ are told that Jesus can make them happier, healthier, better adjusted, more satisfied, and more prosperous. Jesus is presented in attractive packaging and aggressively marketed to a consuming public. Videos, commercials, billboards, buttons, and bumper stickers advertise Jesus with persuasive selling propositions. Better than Coca Cola, Jesus is "the Real Thing." This Jesus will help us make it in the present order, not join with us in bringing in a new order.

> The gospel message has been molded to suit an increasingly narcissistic culture. Conversion is proclaimed as the road to self-realization. Whether through evangelical piety or liberal therapy, the role of religion is presented as a way to help us uncover our human potential—our potential for personal, social, and business success, that is. Modern conversion brings Jesus into our lives rather than bringing us into his. We are told Jesus is here to help us to do better that which we are already doing. Jesus doesn't change our lives, he improves them. Conversion is just for ourselves, not for the world. We ask how Jesus can fulfill our lives, not how we might serve his kingdom. (Wallis 1981, 28)

In an age of narcissism the past is irrelevant, and the future will have to take care of itself. What matters to the narcissist is me and my satisfaction, safety, and security here and now. In narcissistic spirituality, the questions are "What do I get out of it? What's in it for me?" A spirituality that is focused on self-fulfillment, self-actualization, even self-transcendence is focused on the self and on the realization of the self's capacity to claim the higher reaches of human experience. In the end, it's all about me.

This narcissism is evident in more than just occasional instances of immature spirituality. It is becoming the norm of both mainline and evangelical churches. The megachurch offers a cafeteria for individual selection. The media church allows a non-church-attending group to occasionally sing along with their favorite cathedral or studio audience. The traditional church with its long chancel allows people to be present without presence. The threat of meeting face-to-face is alleviated; the solitude of the worshiper is protected. Personal faith becomes individual faith. Spirituality is what one does with aloneness; religion is how one copes with solitude. In the end, it's finally about me.

In narcissistic faith, we focus on how God is meeting our needs and fulfilling our requests here and now. We no longer think of being part of God's purposes that stretch back into time and draw us toward his intentions for humanity. We lose our concern for the welfare of all humankind; we pray not for peace and justice in the world but for nice weather. Among individualists, witnessing is one climber telling another how to climb higher; an achiever telling of eternal achievements; one good person telling another to be good.

Authentic witness begins from a radically different starting point. A people who are living out discipleship—not as perfectionists who live perfectly but as strugglers who are seeking ways to be faithful day by day—form a circle around Jesus. In that circle they find acceptance, solidarity, meaning for their lives, healing for their woundedness, comfort in loss and sorrow. In witness they tell the story of life with Jesus as a community of believers, and they invite others to join them. "Come into the circle around Jesus," they say. "Join us in our seeking and finding." "Try it out, try our faith on; try it for yourself." "In community we find ourselves, we find our meaning, we find our hope."

Authentic Presence

In a concise summary of Christ's mission as the presentation of shalom, missiologist J. C. Hoekendijk notes three characteristics: (1) shalom is proclaimed, and the proclamation (the *kerygma*) makes it a present offer; (2) shalom is lived, and its embodiment in community (*koinonia*) makes it reality here and now; and (3) shalom is demonstrated, and the service (*diakonia*) makes it visible to others (Hoekendijk 1964, 25). James Metzler, who was in Vietnam as a Mennonite missionary during the U.S. war against that country, points out that Jesus's teaching is in the reverse order. The gospel must be seen and then felt before it is actually heard. He quotes Luke 10:8–9 (NRSV), where Jesus gives his commission to the disciples: "Whenever you enter a town and its people welcome you, eat what is set before you; cure the sick who are there and say to them, 'the kingdom of God has come near to you.'"

Note the order: "Eat," "heal," and "say." First, receive hospitality, identifying with others in solidarity and *koinonia*; then reach out in service, aid, and compassion where there is need in *agape*; and finally announce the meaning of this as God's loving reign by giving the *kerygma*. "The verbal witness is needed to explain and reinforce the living witness" (Metzler 1985, 115).

Metzler's message is congruent with the tradition of St. Francis, whose ministry—and that of his followers—was based on the same formula from Luke: Go, identify, serve, heal, and then speak. His most famous instruction was and is: "Preach the gospel at all times; if necessary, use words." Identification with others is the basis of understanding, and solidarity is the language of love; together they form the reality of embodied presence, incarnation of the gospel. They are the only way to authentic witness.

John V. Taylor, writing of Christian witness, concluded, "the Christian, whoever he may be, who stands in the world in the name of Christ, has nothing to offer unless he offers to be present, really and totally present, really and totally in the present" (Taylor 1963, 107).

> To become and to be a Christian is, therefore, to have the extraordinary freedom to share the burdens of the daily, common, ambiguous, transient, perishing existence of men, even to the point of actually taking the place of another, whether powerful or weak, in health or in sickness, clothed or naked, educated or illiterate, secure or persecuted, complacent or despondent, proud or forgotten, housed or homeless, fed or hungry, at liberty or in prison, young or old, white or Negro, rich or poor. (Stringfellow 1964, 32)

This is solidarity. Love embodied. Neighbor connected to neighbor in genuine fellow-feeling, not as a technique for making others see as we see, feel what we feel, believe what we believe, but as a way of life called solidarity. Solidarity with others in community is the basis of incarnational love, not its final result.

God has always stood with his people in solidarity—in prison, in the desert, in exile. The central truth, often explicit but sometimes implicit, is that "the Lord was with them there." In the Christ event, the solidarity of God with humanity becomes the central motif of this strange love story of God and creation. God is with us—in our struggles, our pain, our confusion. God's constant presence is the pattern for our relationships with each other and every other. If we will follow Christ, who came to join humanity in radical solidarity, then we must learn the same, give the same, live it out in the same way. Presence is the essential basis of all Christian discipleship.

> If we presume to approach [incarnation and presence] biblically, we are not free to choose or reject a theology of presence. Presence as incarnation is fundamental to all witness. All ministries of the church are rooted in "being present." . . . It is not enough to suggest that Christian presence is a kind of pre-evangelism but that it is not evangelism. It is not enough to see presence only as a first step in identification. Presence has an intrinsic value in itself. (Shenk 1983, 32–33)

As Clarence Jordan said in one of his Cotton Patch sermons:

> So far as I can determine, the only method of evangelization is that of incarnation. This is how God himself evangelized the world. . . . So the method of evangelization of the New Testament is to confront men with a visible word. . . . I don't think we have a right to bear witness to that which we do not experience. The incarnation, then is the announcement of the Good News as fact. . . .
>
> How can you go and say to people, "that which we would like to know—that declare we to you. That which is not a reality among us, we declare unto you—a brotherhood which we cannot practice." How *dare* we preach, how *dare* we evangelize, from any standpoint except that of incarnation! (Jordan 1972, 32–34)

The Real Commission

Not until the late eighteenth and early nineteenth centuries would Matthew 28:18–20 be called the Great Commission by the missionary movements. Prior to that these verses were read as the baptismal formula for all those who covenanted to follow Christ. The imperative "Go!" is not in the Greek original. Instead the original has a participle, "going," better translated "As you go." This is the mandate for authentic witness—as you live, as you go about your daily work, as you move to new settings for service, as you join or create new communities of discipleship, as you fulfill your vocation as a follower of Jesus—you shall be witnesses. This is not a sales strategy. This is not a mandate for mass media. This is not a justification for a state-church takeover of a people's religious affiliation. This is not a method for achieving church growth. This is a call to authentic, faithful witness in all of life.

The early Anabaptists frequently cited the words of instruction in Matthew 28:18–20, noting that the order is going, discipling, baptizing, teaching. In contrast to the Reformers, they held that every believer is commissioned to witness and called to offer a personal statement of their voluntary, mature commitment to discipleship even at the cost of arrest, imprisonment, or execution. In Anabaptism, both meanings of the Koine Greek word *martyria* were expressed: "witness" and "martyrdom." To confess one's faith was ultimately to be willing to die; to die for one's faith was the ultimate confession.

On the Other Hand

If we wait to speak until we deserve to speak, will we ever speak? Perhaps our lives are never good enough to bear adequate witness to the Christ. Does he not work in spite of us as well as through us? Since we always are flawed witnesses, and our faith is told in less than perfect ways, we can be grateful that the character of the messenger does not invalidate the truth of the message. So the story must be shared, even when the storytellers are broken people or come from an oppressive culture that belies the words they speak. Obviously the ambiguities of our personal lives and our social context, as well as the political map in which they unfold, render any witness suspect to those who are less advantaged or more oppressed than we are. But the truth is always greater than those who carry it.

As a form of practiced spirituality, authentic witness is prized by those who see embodiment as the true evidence of faith, who know that all ways of sharing the faith are not equally valid. Others believe that preaching the faith, marketing it, circulating it in print, selling it on TV, and profiting from its distribution are equally valid; they regard bearing witness as a task to be done more than a life to be lived, and they preach without regard for earning the right to address matters of the spirit. But authentic witnesses practice the way of humble and authentic service as embodiment, and in time they give their faith voice and name Jesus's name. The spiritual practice of authentic witness finds its center in the life lived more than the word given.

Authentic witness often casts a short shadow—the results may be slow in coming. The groups that stress the mandate "As you go, witness and teach" and seek to live faithfully and share the good news personally tend to be small circles. In an age of mass communication and global information, what kind of representation is this? Why go on seeking to create communities of faithful presence? Why think that the local and particular can model an authentic alternative? Does this become a way of withdrawing into the security and solidarity of like with like? Is the shadow of authentic witness reduced to the pursuit of little points of grace while believers forget the bigger picture? What kind of authenticity is that? Or in the end, is it the only kind?

Parable for Peditation

To meditate on Jesus's words on planting seeds of witness that grow into the full presence of the reign of God, you may copy the following on a bit of paper and walk to the parable in peditation.

(Rhythm—three syllables, rest, then next three syllables.)

Sower and Seeds

Sower goes
out to sow,
throws the seed
to and fro.

Some on rocks
where it dried;
some in weeds
where it died;

Some on path
for the birds;
some on soil,
mark my words,

It grew tall,
gave rich fruit.
See that you
follow suit!

(see Luke 8:4–15)

8

The Practice of—
Subversive Spirituality

Spirituality is celebrating the dawn. Discipleship sings in the
  dark.
Spirituality is sitting in awe by the seashore. Discipleship joins
  the dolphins.
Spirituality is dreaming of flying. Discipleship walks the distance.
Spirituality is loving the good neighbor. Discipleship loves the
  enemy.
Spirituality is knowing God's plan. Discipleship trusts when
  nothing makes sense.
Spirituality is turning life sunny side up. Discipleship turns the
  world down side up.
Spirituality is finding inner peace. Discipleship is making peace.
Spirituality is integrative. Discipleship is subversive.

Dissident Discipleship

In 1957 Gene Davenport, a college student in his teens, was as-
signed to pastor a small Methodist church in a then-segregated
community twenty-five miles outside Birmingham, Alabama.

189

One Sunday night, named Race Relations Sunday, Gene was preaching from Ezekiel's vision of a valley filled with dry bones when a procession of robed Klansmen entered the church and marched down the center aisle. Each dropped an offering on the communion table. The young preacher stepped over the communion rail and said, "We don't want your money." As the robed and hooded men continued their ritual without reply, the pastor scooped up their offering, held it above his head, and tore the bills to bits. They exited in formation, and he called after them, "I wish I had not torn your money up, I wish I had sent it to the NAACP."

Several days later, he answered a call in his college dorm.

"Are you Reverend Gene Davenport?"

"Yes, sir."

"Pastor of Pelham Methodist?"

"Yes, sir."

"Were you preaching last Sunday night when visitors made an offering?"

"A threat is not an offering," he replied. "But who are you? The joke is over."

It was not a joke. The caller was a U.S. Secret Service agent summoning him to the federal courthouse to be charged with defacing currency.

Although he was never indicted or tried, it was clear that defacing currency was a punishable crime, a violation of the Constitution. But mocking morality and profaning the church apparently were not.

Davenport's courage to witness authentically meant leaving the safety of the pulpit and stepping across the communion rail (condensed from Campbell 1988, 9–11).

—∞—

The hit man walked through a small flower garden to the door of a simple parsonage in Recife, Brazil. Pistol in hand, he knocked on the plain wooden door of Archbishop Dom Helder Camara, the spiritual leader of Brazil's northeast Roman Catholic province. A small, frail-looking man answered.

"I want to speak with Dom Helder Camara," he said.

"I am Dom Helder."

The assassin stared at the open, warm smile of the little man. "You are Dom Helder?"

"Yes, yes, come in my friend, what do you want? Do you need me for anything?" The archbishop gave him a chair and sat alongside. "How can I help you?" he asked.

"No, no," the assassin protested. "I don't want anything to do with you because I can see you are not one of those people that I kill."

"Kill? Why do you want to kill?"

"Because I was paid to kill you, but I can't."

"If you have been paid, why don't you kill me? I will go to the Lord."

"No," said the assassin. "You already belong to the Lord." He got up and went away (Kemper and Engle 1994, 209–10).

It is said that authentic disciples of Jesus, in following the way of the cross, are already dead, so no one can kill them; they are already citizens of a new regime, so the current regime does not control them.

Any disciple who, like Dom Helder, identifies with and advocates for the poor will upset the rich who live off those they deem beneath them. Discipleship has this disadvantage. It is inevitably dissident—dissenting from the status quo and especially challenging those systems where status is ranked, privileged, and rewarded—entitled to rise far above "quo."

—⁂—

Clarence Jordan, the founder of Koinonia Farm, the interracial commune outside Americus, Georgia, grew up in a prosperous family, received a traditional theological education (a Ph.D. in Greek New Testament from Southern Baptist Seminary in Louisville, Kentucky), and, known for his brilliance as a writer, was en route to becoming a professor.

Instead, he left seminary to establish an interracial community in segregated Georgia in the mid-1950s. Opposition was not unexpected, but it was led by his own people, the Southern Baptist congregation that eventually excommunicated the whole Koinonia Community. The charges leveled against them read: "Said members . . . have persisted in holding services where both white and colored attend together" (McClendon 1986, 96).

The excommunication was followed by vandalism, cross-burning, legal pressures, beatings, bombings, a comprehensive economic boycott, and shootings by snipers who aimed at any available target on the commune.

Clarence turned to his brother, attorney Robert Jordan, for legal counsel and asked him to become legal representative of the Koinonia Community.

Robert, who later served as a Georgia state senator and a justice of the Georgia State Supreme Court, declined.

"Clarence, I can't do that. You know my political aspirations. Why if I represented you, I might lose my job, my house, everything I've got."

"*We* might lose everything too, Bob."

"It's different for you."

"Why is it different? I remember, it seems to me, that you and I joined the church the same Sunday as boys. I expect when we came forward the preacher asked me about the same question he did you. He asked me, 'Do you accept Jesus as your Lord and Savior?' And I said, 'Yes.' What did you say?"

"I follow Jesus, Clarence, up to a point."

"Could that point by any chance be—the cross?"

"That's right. I follow him to the cross, but not on the cross. I'm not getting myself crucified."

"Then I don't believe you're a disciple. You're an admirer of Jesus, but not a disciple of his. I think you ought to go back to the church you belong to, and tell them you're an admirer not a disciple."

"Well now, if everyone who felt like I do did that, we wouldn't have a church, would we?"

"The question," Clarence said, "is do you have a church?" (McClendon 1986, 103).

Whose Life Project Will Endure?

"Who was Khrushchev?" a Russian child of the future asks his father in an oft-told Russian joke. The father replies, "A minor politician of the Solzhenitsyn and Sakharov period."

"Who were John Vorster and P. W. Botha?" a South African child may someday ask. "Inconsequential public figures in the time of Mandela and Tutu."

"Who was Pope Innocent II?" we may ask. An insignificant church functionary in the time of Francis of Assisi.

"Who was Lord Mountbatten?" A little-known British imperialist in the time of Gandhi.

"Who was Billy Graham?" A minor public preacher in the Dorothy Day period.

"Who was John Paul II?" A forgotten churchman in the time of Mother Teresa.

"Who was J. Edgar Hoover?" A paranoid government agent in the time of Martin Luther King Jr.

"Who was Robert Jordan?" Fifty years later the answer is, "He was the brother of radical Christian leader Clarence Jordan."

Those who seek to shape history, to control its movement forward toward their envisioned goal, succeed only for the moment. Raw power may sometimes be more effective in producing immediate change. But in the long view, truth has a way of surfacing, and enduring faithfulness ultimately cannot be hidden.

In time values change, things get turned upside down. Integrity will out. But even when a sacrifice is unnoticed, an act of moral courage goes unseen, or a risk is invisibly taken because it is the right thing to do, the act of faithfulness lives on in the memory of God. Those who live and act in faith may risk immediate failure, but they do so in the light of ultimate values. "Faith is not belief in spite of evidence, but a life in scorn of the consequences," Clarence Jordan wrote. Faith is living by values that possess the soul, not possessing values that validate self-image, esteem, or respect. Faith, judged by the values embraced by history, has it all backward in a world in which the ends justify the means, might makes right, haves lord over have-nots, and the powerful dominate those who are powerless.

Ambrose Bierce, in the classic *Devil's Dictionary*, wrote a satirical but prophetic definition of Christian practice:

> Christian, n. One who believes that the New Testament is a divinely inspired book admirably suited to the spiritual needs of his neighbor. One who follows the teachings of Christ in so far as they are not inconsistent with a life of sin. (Bierce 1987, 248)

Leader as Lion? Or as Lamb?

Dissident discipleship is the practice of reverse theology—not the worship of sovereignty, lordship, almighty power, total dominance, or utter and final control, but worship of its opposites. It begins by noting that the Master is anything *but* master in the earthly realm.

When the wise men looked for a king born of royalty, they found a baby swathed in torn cloth in a cattle stable—indeed, in a manger—with a peasant girl for his mother.

As the documents set forth his growth and development, he was first a refugee in an enemy country, then a child in a nondescript village, then a laborer in the trade of itinerant craftsmen; in sum, he was a nobody in a small, subdued country at the farther reaches of the Roman Empire. When Jesus appeared before the most authoritative Jewish prophet of his century, John the Baptist, he claimed no role as successor but humbly requested baptism.

When he announced the prophetic reality of jubilee and the radical program of social revolution that it entails (Luke 4), he did not claim political position or seek influence with authorities; instead he associated with the weak, the oppressed, even the outcast. When rejected by the Samaritans, he did not abuse them in return as his disciples requested. When criticized and condemned by religious leaders, he simply cited his actions as evidence of his identity. When confronted with injustice, he was angry for the sake of others, not for his own sake.

When marching at last on Jerusalem, he chose a crowd of pilgrims, not an army of revolutionaries, and he rode the symbol of the poor—a donkey—not the white horse of a conqueror.

When seated at his inaugural dinner, he did the servants' work—or women's work—of foot washing. When arrested, he did not resist; when tried, he did not defend himself; when abused, he did not return his abusers' invectives; when condemned to death, he did not protest; when executed, he remained true to his way of steadfast love.

Perhaps the perfect metaphor for this inversion of all that humankind values is found in John's book of Revelation. In the great pivotal moment of the drama (Rev. 5:4–6), John turns to look for the announced lion who can open the scroll of history and break its seven seals, but on turning he sees not a lion but a lamb. This is the face of the King of kings.

These contrasts and contradictions have often been perceived as a graceful frame for the master story that provides the true picture of the almighty, absolute, ultimately sovereign Lord of time and eternity, the King who epitomizes, exceeds, excels, and eclipses all human kings. But this misses the point. The image of lamb, servant, peasant, and prophet is not a frame for the soon-to-be-revealed divine, leonine sovereign; indeed, it negates any such power-oriented picture. The astounding truth of Jesus is his stubborn belief that he was showing us what God is actually like. To see him was and is to see his Father. This reversal is not a matter of a human mask hiding the infinite power and unapproachable distance of a terribly other deity; it is not a mere frame but the picture itself. Jesus is the face of God.

This truth is not what we naturally want. We want a god from central casting, a god worth his heavenly salt, a god who acts like our dreams of utter and ultimate power—the sort of god we would be if only we could be a god.

Inversion, Not Conversion

In one of the finest studies on discipleship, *The Upside-Down Kingdom*, Don Kraybill offers a radical—going to the roots—return to envisioning Christ's mission and original call to discipleship. It begins with the words of a humble village girl, Mary of Nazareth. She announces a spirituality of inversion, not conversion—the high brought low, the low now high, the proud humbled, the humble exalted, the mighty reduced, the weak empowered, the rich empty, the hungry filled. Mary's song, the Magnificat, is a song predicting an upside-down kingdom, a song full of surprises and subversive predictions. It is the perfect introduction to the revolutionary work of her son, Jesus.

At the outset of his ministry Jesus faced a tempting set of four possible paths—three that promised escape from danger and a fourth that demanded unparalleled courage. He could have seized political power over all the kingdoms he could see from the mountaintop; proclaimed religious imperialism and enjoyed acclaim as he allied himself with the temple; or offered economic leveling to all, winning popularity by providing food reserves for the wide population (Matt. 4:1–11; Luke 4:1–13).

Instead he chose alternatives to each of these temptations. He proclaimed a politics of nonviolent, revolutionary love; a religious experience of nonhierarchical equality in mutual service; and a jubilee economics of voluntary distributive justice. This fourth path is the upside-down politics of compassion not coercion. He chose love, not coercive power; suffering, not vindictive triumph; mutual service, not mastery and domination. He offered an upside-down religion—not a building, not a program, not a clergy elite. He stood for an upside-down economics that leads to lateral sharing, not the trickling down of leftovers from the greedy to the needy.

Jesus's alternative of an upside-down kingdom taught a new order of:

- *free slaves*: a jubilee vision of setting slaves free, linking spirituality and economic justice, subversively sharing world resources;
- *luxurious poverty*: a call to continuously search for transforming justice, redistributive policies, open opportunities to live;
- *impious piety*: a new understanding of religion as a life of agape that punctures pompous piety, superior sainthood, and exclusive holy structures and clubs;

- *lovable enemies*: a new way of responding to enmity and violence by breaking the cycle of retaliation and revenge through love and forgiveness;
- *inside outsiders*: an upside-down revolution of traditional gender, social, and occupational status and other determiners of old "inside circle" position;
- *inverted values*: an inversion of all social levels, ladders, privileges, entitlements, and pleadings of specialness. Low is high, high is low, and failure is success;
- *countercultural community*: a new way of life characterized by service and ministry in which believers lose life to gain it in a new community of compassion.

The upside-down kingdom offers a radically inverted mandate for living. It calls us to question the values of our society, community, and age. But most of all it calls us to question our own values, our claims to faith and discipleship. It demands that we grapple with these questions that Kraybill poses:

- How do we refuse to participate in systems that enslave? How can our economics be part of jubilee economics? How can our spirituality and visions of economic justice become one?
- How can we hear Jesus's six warnings about wealth clearly? (He warns that wealth is a strangler—choking out maturation [Luke 8:14]; that wealth is a worrier—controlling our anxiety and concern [Luke 12:22–34]; wealth is a blinder—preventing us from seeing real human need [Luke 16:19–23]; that wealth is a damner—leading us away from God [Luke 12:13–21]; and that wealth can be a curse [Luke 6:20, 24].)
- How can we catch the irreverent spirit of Jesus in challenging sacred cows while prizing all that is truly holy? Can we recognize that the old structures that serve us will need to die, that old systems that we have shared will need to be broken open?
- How can we be a neighbor to others—not merely asking, Who is my neighbor? How can we learn the art of nonviolent love

in all relationships? How can we repent of our reliance on and participation in beliefs that support military answers to human differences?

- What is the value of hospitality—of welcoming the stranger—and how can we practice it? How can we repudiate prejudice, refuse to participate in the games of social stigma, turn from excluding "outsiders"?

- What entitlement, what social stratification, what ladders of respect do we assume, defend, or enjoy? How can we refuse, reject, rebalance power differentials in all our relationships?

- What would it mean if we were willing to lose—not save—our lives in the decisions we make about success, about our life contribution, about security in older years, about our decisions in career and service right now? (Kraybill 1978/1990)

As Jesus announced this social overturn or turnover, he spoke a resounding yes to the prophets of the Hebrew scriptures, who had called for the practice of jubilee, and he said no to competing interpretations taught by many other groups in his time and culture. The cultural options that Jesus refused are clear: The Essene ascetics saw God's reign in a heavenly court; Jesus was down to earth. The Pharisees saw God's reign resulting from love for and faithfulness to Torah, text, and truth; Jesus taught the law lived in love of God and neighbor. Hellenists believed God's reign could be seen in philosophical cosmic sovereignty and providence; Jesus believed it was visible in including the outcast, touching the leper, welcoming the adulterer. Zealots demanded military thinking, violent revolutionary victory, and they practiced guerilla banditry; Jesus taught nonviolence, lived nonresistance, proclaimed an alternative political revolution.

The framing metaphor of Jesus's teaching is, "Human exile ends in a new reign of God. Welcome home from exile!" "Come back from your wandering!" The long human exile in alienation and oppression is over; a new reign of justice and peace is come. The old walls of imprisonment are coming down; a new community of reconciliation has begun. God now reigns. All other powers are provisional, temporary, heuristic, their leaders imposters, frauds, antihuman captors and oppressors.

Jesus reframed the central metaphor of Jewish identity in subversive ways. God's reign had not returned to Israel; the restoration promises of Isaiah and Zechariah had not been fulfilled; Torah was not yet ruling; Yahweh's glory was not the spiritual center; the guilt, alienation, and culpability for the long exile was obviously not forgiven; the national sense of failure was oppressive and depressive. And Jesus announced, "The reign is now; jubilee is come; Torah is fully realized; Yahweh is present; sin is forgiven; depression is over; the exile has ended. Welcome home. Rejoice!"

The Movement Downward

Gordon Cosby, of the Church of the Savior, Washington, D.C., describes the downward pilgrimage of discipleship:

> Part of the scandal of the gospel is that when you meet the abandoned, crucified Messiah, he grabs you and you belong to him. Wherever you are in privilege and power and status and opportunity, you start the movement down, not up. And you go down and down and down until you are powerless, except for his power; you go down until you find yourself with the riffraff. The evangelists I listened to in my youth didn't make that clear. But the evangelists in the New Testament make that devastatingly clear. One keeps going down and down until one is identified with the victimized poor wherever they are scattered throughout the earth. Wherever you see them and hear about them, you know that your lot is cast with them, that they are your people. (Cosby in Wallis 1976, 96–97)

This downward movement runs counter to the escalators built into our social order. We assume that the journey through life is meant to be upward, onward in a lifelong advance toward increases in power, success, and influence. But discipleship is headed in the opposite direction.

This movement downward is a big step away from standard spiritualities of comfort, support, self-validation, and optimism. It is a step toward a spirituality that subverts comfort at the expense of conscience, subverts the social support that costs us our integrity, subverts any easy validation of our entitlement to personal advantage or privilege. It may even subvert the safety and security of our life in the institutional church, which has defined the status quo and defends it against all challenge.

Jim Wallis tells of a conference in New York City where theologians, pastors, priests, nuns, and lay leaders gathered to discuss social justice. A Native American stood, faced the largely white audience and said:

> Regardless of what the New Testament says, most Christians are materialists with no experience of the Spirit.
>
> Regardless of what the New Testament says, most Christians are individualists with no real experience of community.
>
> Let's pretend that you were all Christians. If you were Christians, you would no longer accumulate. You would share everything you had. You would actually love one another. And you would treat each other as if you were family. Why don't you do that? Why don't you love that way?

In that room full of believers in Jesus, Wallis concludes, it was not easy to find commitment to radical discipleship (Wallis 1981, 18).

If a tripolar spiritual transformation were to take place, as it keeps threatening to do in many traditions and in many nontraditional groups, a disturbing discovery would be made. At the very heart of Christian faith, the gospel is a message of complacency being replaced with joy in seeing justice done.

As far back as 1967, Will Campbell, a southern Christian leader who is known as one of the radical prophets of our generation, wrote in the theological journal of the Fellowship of Southern Churchmen a landmark article, "Footwashing or the New Hermeneutics?" He questioned whether faithful discipleship is possible in a Christianity that has so accommodated itself to popular culture that it has lost its Jesus-like uniqueness, and argued that the time was ripe for groups to break out and risk radical discipleship by "thinking sect." He used Jesus's words to the rich young ruler as the key to the situation of the church, "Go, sell, give to the poor. Then come follow me." To truly swallow that truth could kill the structures that we now inhabit, he said, but it would free us to live out a truthful discipleship. Here is the conclusion of his argument.

> *Think Sect* means carrying a cyanide capsule in your navel against the day the enemy is so strong against you that the only way you can preserve that with which you have been entrusted is to kill yourself. The enemy is now that strong against us. The enemy has made us rich, powerful and good, knowing that when there is a racial crisis or a Vietnam war, the best we would risk would be debates and resolutions and petitions. The cyanide capsule tucked in our navel is Matthew 19 ["Go, sell, give to the poor. Then come follow me"]. Let us now swallow it with a joyful gulp. Sell the steeples, the organs, the gold cups, the silver hats, the mahogany pews and the valuable downtown property and give the money away . . . to the poor who happen to be nigh. And Think Sect. Then shout Hallelujah! Then sing the Psalms. Then follow! (Campbell 1967)

People who would follow Campbell's challenge would allow their institutional security, their established place in society, to die, and the voluntary believers could then be born again as groups of disciples who spend less time conserving their power, place, and prestige.

An Upside-Down Spirituality

If an upside-down pattern of spirituality leads us to embrace Jesus's way—with humility in self-valuation, stubborn solidarity with co-travelers, commitment to service as a life goal, enjoyment of serenity as surrender to a higher call, pursuit of nonviolence as a way of caring, witness borne in lived integrity—then we must "get down." These downward trajectories offer an alternative way of actively loving and serving God and neighbor in a spirituality that turns the downside up. We turn the current spiritualities of self-fulfillment on their heads, we invert the idea that the goal of spirituality is to meet our individual needs. We open eyes, souls, and lives to caring equally or perhaps even primarily about the needs of others; and we subvert the spiritualities of nationalism, ethnic superiority, and religious hegemony to get a little closer to what Jesus was calling discipleship.

If upside-down discipleship caught on among followers of Jesus we would meet to plan how to do our investing in people's outer as well as inner lives. Although virtually all Christians hold to the idea of being disciples, most prefer a sort of loose association with Christ, the center of their faith, rather than the hard alternative of a demanding attachment to Jesus in discipleship. J. Lawrence Burkholder, confronting our contemporary practices of reducing Jesus to the acceptable model of common wisdom and of redefining discipleship according to "normal behavior," wrote tersely:

> What I resist is "sliding scale" discipleship—that is, discipleship redefined to reduce or remove the tension between the perfectionist ideal and contemporary reality. Jesus "cannot be dysfunctional," it is claimed. Therefore, Jesus must have meant what makes sense to us. (Burkholder 1993, 41)

Standard Christian spirituality interprets the Jesus story in the light of the believer's own story and social history. Subversive spirituality interprets the believer's story and history in the light of his! Standard spirituality takes Jesus as the picture of what is mature, functional, mentally healthy, socially approved, relationally harmonious, and truly good and nice. (Some of this is wonderfully true, but it is not the point). Subversive spirituality faces the jarring reality of his demand that we love others as unconditionally as is possible for each of us, serving others as selflessly as we are able whether this fits into the socially approved ways of behaving or not.

Spirituality of the standard sort interprets the meaning of life and its struggles from the starting point of socially acceptable conventions and beliefs. (This is useful, but it sells us short). Subversive spirituality responds to compelling counterconventional, countercultural beliefs that invert the meaning of life from hedonism or the pursuit of happiness to caring passionately about real goodness (God) and real relationships (others).

Spirituality of conventional wisdom offers the believer a breath of hope in a congested world, a bit of courage to face the complexities of a confusing environment, sustaining support in the midst of trying and frustrating times. (All of these are great, but they are not enough.) Subversive spirituality calls for active resistance to the prevailing disorder of the world.

Standard forms of spirituality use personal experience to validate beliefs and employ current thought to determine what is relevant to contemporary issues and emphases. (This is good when it opens our eyes to see the spiritual side of every day life, but we need more). Subversive spirituality validates our experience by critiquing it from the perspective of the love, truth, compassion, and justice revealed in all those moments in history when God has overcome our alienation.

Since Jesus is our window to divinity and the mirror of our humanity, Christian spirituality is truly Christian only when we are seeing *through Christ* who God is and seeing *in Christ* who we are. Christian spirituality welcomes a wide range of experience, consciousness, and practice. But because Jesus refused all splitting between love of God and love of neighbor (whether the neighbor is friendly or unfriendly), Christian spirituality is truly Christian only when positive response to God is inseparable from positive response to enemy or friend. Jesus did not offer a cut-rate spirituality that can be reduced to the single pole of self or the two poles of self and God. Radical tripolar discipleship, as Jesus defined it, is intense love of God and inclusive love of neighbor, which refuses any prioritizing, splitting, or devaluing of one of these in preference to the other. Indeed, love of God is made visible in love of neighbor, and love of neighbor is the means by which love for God is expressed. The two are aspects of the same radical vision of grace becoming graciousness, saving love becoming serving love.

Three radical ideas combine here. One, Jesus expands the definition of neighbor to include all persons. By inverting the question "Who is my neighbor?" Jesus asks "Are you willing to be a neighbor—to the stranger, the alien, the enemy?" (Luke 10:25–37). Two, Jesus shows respect for the neighbor's dignity by respecting the neighbor's right to define his or her own needs. When

Jesus asks the question, "What do you want me to do for you?" he refuses control, rejects paternalism, and restores responsible agency (Mark 10:46–52; John 5:1–15). Three, Jesus sees love of neighbor and love of self as two aspects of one and the same love. To love the neighbor is an act of solidarity: "You shall love your neighbor for he is as yourself," or "he is like you." "You shall love your neighbour as a man like yourself" (Lev. 19:18 NEB; compare with Mark 12:28–34).

In loving your neighbor rightly, you come to know yourself with integrity. But in narcissistic self-love that ignores the neighbor, you are loving neither yourself nor your neighbor since self-absorption is the antithesis of self-love, which delights in giving, serving, and reaching out from its inner core of compassion. To give up self-absorption seems at first blush like a sacrifice of selfhood, but it is a part of selfhood that one does well to surrender. It is in letting go, stepping down, and opening outward that we discover the capacity to give and receive love.

What Has Faith to Do with Politics?

> What matters most today is whether one is a supporter of establishment Christianity or a practitioner of biblical faith. Establishment Christianity has made its peace with the established order. It no longer feels itself to be in conflict with the pretensions of the state, with the designs of economic and political power, or with the values and style of life enshrined in the national culture. Establishment Christianity is a religion of accommodation and conformity, which values realism and success more than faithfulness and obedience. (Wallis 1976, 1)

The confession "Jesus is Lord" is a radical political statement. It means that no one and no thing can supplant him as the arbiter of ultimate values. John Howard Yoder stated this with incisive clarity.

> To participate in the military requires a willingness to take the life of another when so commanded in the name of Caesar—whoever and in whatever age the political Caesar may rule—and this is, in

actuality, confessing Caesar as Lord. This is not what is classically called heresy. Instead, to confess that Caesar is Lord by granting him the authority to command your ultimate decisions (to take another's life into your hands) is what is classically called apostasy. It is painful to recognize the implications of this incontrovertible, though obviously compromisable proposition. By definition, a Christian is one who confesses that Jesus alone is Lord. Any action that yields this lordship to any Caesar, even though the person claims a pietistic, mystic, liturgical or experiential faith in Jesus while serving Caesar, is tragically, and we say it with sadness, apostasy. (Yoder 1960, 1)

Martin Niemoeller, a German Lutheran pastor during the Nazi period who was finally imprisoned for his stand against the policies of the Third Reich, wrote of the danger of splitting faith from political actions.

Bismarck was a good Christian. Not only did he want to *appear* to be one, but he sincerely wanted to *be* one. But on his office door, the same office in which I met Hitler in 1934, one could read an invisible sign: "Jesus Christ not allowed to enter here." That's what Bismarck's mentality said. Anyone could approach Hitler and Bismarck and all the figures in authority, but you had to leave Jesus Christ outside. (Niemoeller in Wallis and Hollyday 1994, 271)

Those who refuse to split faith in Jesus Christ from moral concern for a just human community (what we often call politics) become dissidents. It is dissident in a greed-based world to refuse to support organized greed; it is subversive in an unjust world to opt out of unjust systems; it is radical to absent oneself from any and all uses of violence, even justified violence.

If one refuses splitting as a solution to the complex contradictions of living in the twenty-first century, then faith and politics, values and economics, morality and concern for the neighbor become one. They cannot be divided, prioritized, delegated, ignored.

As Martin Niemoeller asked, "What do I do when the state tells me something different than what Jesus Christ, or my Christian conscience, tells me is just?" He answered,

To whom am I ultimately accountable? As a Christian, to Christ; as an idealist, to my ideal. Everyone has some higher authority. It is a grave mistake today to think one can attain true ends without a true authority. Today, that is the ultimate question. I have always said that a pious Christian can be essentially atheist in ultimate commitment. The decisive factor is whether I love the consequences of my faith. Is God my authority? Which God?

Clarifying his central beliefs, Niemoller added,

> As a Christian, I can say that God comes to me in Jesus Christ and in the spirit of love. That is the essence of the doctrine of the Trinity. I cannot know God at all; rather, I have some idea or other about God. But when I know Jesus, I no longer flounder with ideas about God, but I ask Jesus—who tells me I can say "My Father," or "Our Father" to God—I ask how Jesus relates to this Father and how I can know the Father through Jesus. For me, the authority of the living God is expressed in Jesus' teaching us to pray "Our Father." If I live in this authority, I live in the Holy Spirit. (Niemoeller in Wallis and Hollyday 1994, 271–72)

For the early Christians the confession "Jesus is Lord" meant "Jesus is supreme, not Caesar." For the disciple, Jesus is supra-emperor, beyond any president, above any judge or general. There is no way to avoid participation in the political life of our world, just as we cannot refuse to be a part of the economic, social, educational, or professional life of a society in the twenty-first century. We dare not split our commitment to following Christ from the decisions we make in any or all of these aspects of our lives. No splitting is permitted if we seek to be salt and light, a presence that embodies the way of Christ and the way of the cross. The most insistent form of splitting is the clear cut made between personal faith in action and political beliefs and allegiances: sin becomes personal and not social; evil is individual and not political; one's faith is private and not a public confession of allegiance.

Tripolar spirituality sees love of others as the primary way we go about loving God, so that where we stand socially and politically is also where we stand religiously and spiritually. Concern for the welfare of all humanity is not separable and detachable; it is all of a piece.

Decades ago, Mohandas Gandhi warned against what he called the seven social sins: politics without principle, wealth without work, commerce without morality, pleasure without conscience, education without character, science without humanity, worship without sacrifice (Wallis 1994, xv, 257). We may, with no irreverence to Gandhi's words, name seven political sins: enrich the wealthy, tax the poor; aid the health industry, ignore the uninsured; honor the greedy, disregard the hungry; exploit the earth, pollute the environment; peddle armaments, consume their buyers' resources; condemn poor tyrants, support rich despots; call their violence terror, our violence deterrence. (How I pray that this list will soon be out of date and that readers in future years will laugh about the fact that anyone needed to mention such things because they are no longer the besetting sins of persons, communities, and nations.)

Dissident Discipleship

"Those who would serve their generation must betray it," Irish singer Bono said in his commencement address to the 2003 graduates of the University of Pennsylvania. "We must betray the self-serving, racist, nationalist, consumer-oriented values of the age and live as though all people mattered equally—the one-third of Africa suffering infection with the HIV virus are as important equally as are we ourselves and our kind of people." In his call for the graduates to be dissidents, he said, "Go out and break the laws—the laws of trickle-down economics that do not flow down to the poorer, the laws of northern hemisphere dominance over the economies of the southern hemisphere, the laws of racism that suggest that a person dying of AIDS in Africa is of less value than any ill person in our own community." As he continued to cite laws of injustice, exploitation, and human indifference, my ability to take notes was limited by the need to stop and applaud with the thousands of young people in the stadium cheering Bono on for his truly subversive words.

Dissident discipleship is not a political movement, but it takes politics seriously; it is not optimistic about the power of political change, but it is concerned about calling for justice, equality, and sensitivity to human need, and it is committed to seeking solutions that do not cost lives and that take into account the needs of all people.

Politics, "the organized assertion of human cunning and power upon the social dynamic," is not the Christian's first concern; nor is it the church's central mission. When we pray, "thy kingdom come, thy will be done on earth as it is in heaven," we mean something much more radical, more revolutionary, more life- and culture-changing than politics (Williamson 1986, 73). But radical spirituality cares about injustice, about persons, about poverty, about forgotten peoples, so it takes the social dynamics that cause pain and deprivation very seriously. It neither participates in legitimating the wretched policies that exploit the world nor withdraws from politics in pious flight. It seizes opportunities for prophetic witness in actions that model change as well as in words that point to it. It creates islands of change that model a new justice as well as writing, speaking, and arguing to persuade others that justice is possible.

Spirituality cannot be found at the end of a search for self-fulfillment. Spirituality does not lie at the end of the drive for gratified greed. Spirituality does not associate itself with the lifelong quest for power and dominance.

Subversive spirituality may lead to hard choices, major decisions, and courageous positions that challenge a society, a nation, the world. But its authenticity is seen most clearly in the little things, the local situation, the daily actions of simple faithfulness to the compassionate way.

The dissenting disciple has eyes that are open to the poor, who cannot be invisible to any follower of Jesus, and is seeking to change the system that ignores them.

The dissenting disciple sees the connections between the cover-up of poverty and the anger, desperation, and violence in poor neighborhoods on the one hand, and the exploitive systems that ensure privilege for the affluent and absence of opportunity for the poor on the other.

The dissenting disciple sees the signs of racism in society's history, its present systems, its community educational, justice, and police systems and speaks out on, intercedes about, and acts to help dismantle it. The dissenting disciple refuses to join in the pitched battles over abortion, "family values," and rights for those who are either straight or gay, recognizing that these battles are pernicious, exaggerated in rhetoric, and reductionistic in their simplified positions, and that they end in denying the humanity, worth, and preciousness of those viewed as the opponents. The dissenting disciple knows that there are legitimate concerns on both sides that must be listened to, respected, confronted, honored.

The dissenting disciple sees the inequalities that continue between women and men and refuses to be silent or defensive, to yield to them or to benefit from them, to be disenfranchised or to be entitled. Both genders must take full responsibility for equality and justice, for healing and integrity. The dissenting disciple will not settle for a spirituality of personal growth or a religious experience of individual salvation and goodness. Concern for others, love for God, discovery of one's caring vocation and calling are all bound up in one another in the daily practice of following Jesus and shouldering the cross when it falls in our path.

A minister was showing his new church to Clarence Jordan, the theologian in overalls who founded the interracially reconciled Koinonia Community near Americus, Georgia. He pointed out the architect's distinctive touches, the imported pews and stained glass. As they stepped outside, a spotlight illuminated the large cross on top of the steeple. The pastor couldn't keep from saying, "That cross alone cost us ten thousand dollars."

"You got cheated," Clarence said. "Time was when Christians could get them for free" (Wallis and Hollyday 1994, 69).

A cross may be free, but discipleship was and always will be costly. As Dietrich Bonhoeffer said, in words that have become virtually scripture in any conversation about discipleship:

> "Cheap grace is the preaching of . . .
>   forgiveness without requiring repentance,
>   baptism without church discipline,

communion without confession,
absolution without personal confession.
Cheap grace is . . .
grace without discipleship,
grace without the cross,
grace without Jesus Christ living and incarnate.
Costly grace is . . .
the gospel which must be *sought* again and again,
the gift which must be *asked* for,
the door at which one must *knock*,
Such grace is *costly*
because it calls us to follow *Jesus Christ*.
It is costly because it costs us our lives.
It is grace because it gives us the only true life.

(Bonhoeffer 1963, 46–47, rephrased for gender inclusivity)

On the Other Hand

Why all this talk about dissidence and subversion? Jesus said that his kingdom is not of this world and it is to his kingdom that the disciple belongs. Doesn't that mean refusing involvement in the way this world is run? St. Paul called us to be resident aliens in this world. Doesn't that mean separating ourselves from the concerns of society, state, and global politics? John of Revelation addressed us as persons who follow the Lamb, not the lion. Shall we not ignore the lions of this world and set our hearts on other things?

But if we pursue a tripolar spirituality that takes God and neighbor with equal seriousness, will we not inevitably be heard giving voice to subversive protest against the status quo, be seen in stubborn service that is not motivated by personal gain, be known for dissident discipleship that constantly points to another reign, that of our Lord? As members of another kingdom, aliens with citizenship in heaven, disciples of the One who confronted this world head on, how can we not live our faith, speak our hope, and act in his love for all, from the poorest and weakest to the most comfortable and satisfied?

On the other hand. . . . Perhaps, in the long view, there is no other hand?

Parables for Peditation

For meditation on the call to break free and follow, copy the following on a bit of paper, and walk to one of these parables in peditation.

(Rhythm—three syllables, rest, then next three syllables.)

The Buried Treasure

Farmer finds
buried wealth,
shrewdly hides
it in stealth.

Goes, sells all
to buy field
with the gold
it concealed.

So God's reign
costs no less.
All you have,
recklessness.

(see Matt. 13:44)

The Priceless Pearl

Like a man
seeking art,
perfect pearl
wins his heart.

It will cost
everything,
all he owns,
venturing.

Does not flinch,
sells all, buys
perfect pearl.
Seize the prize!

So God's reign,
costs your soul.
Risk it all
like a fool.

(see Matt 13:45–46)

Appendix One

Anabaptist Core Convictions

(a confession of tripolar spirituality)

God alone is God.

> God who is love, light, and life
> creates, precedes, enables, sustains all.
> (There is a God. It is neither me
> nor my culture, state, science, sports,
> sex, success, security, or survival.)
> Our love for God takes precedence over all else.
> What we do to neighbor or enemy, we do to God.

Jesus Christ is Lord.

> Jesus who embodied God's radical love
> transforms all things in heaven and earth.
> (There is one Lord. It is neither Caesar
> nor the military, the dollar, the president, or the pope;
> nor what is rational, functional, or mentally healthy.)
> Our love for Christ takes precedence over all else.
> What we do to the least of others, we do to Christ.

God is sacred Spirit.

God is Spirit, the Third present when any two disciples meet,
at work at large in the world,
yearning for and drawing all people.
(There is one Spirit. She is not the secret of prosperity,
the guarantor of success, the swell of good feelings.
She is not mood, magic, means, or group excitement.)
The ever-present Spirit reveals Jesus, who shows us God.
In loving God and neighbor as self,
we love and serve God's Spirit.

We, as humans, are alienating and alienated.

Alienated from God, in our natural state,
we alienate each other.
We fragment into power blocks, dominate and exploit.
We spoil and abuse creation, exalt self-sufficiency, play god.
In Jesus Christ these sins are removed,
these walls are broken down,
and we are reunited in a community of the Spirit.

Jesus's way—love even unto death—is to be our way.

His living, dying, and rising redeemed the world,
challenged and confronted its powers,
revealed true humanness.
He is our model, means, and end.
In imitation of Christ, we renounce violence,
return good for evil, seek transforming justice,
refuse domination, conciliate differences,
restore relationships, share shalom,
suffer patiently, sacrifice willingly.
No one for whom Christ died can be our enemy.

The church is our primary social location.

We join by choice, are baptized into the circle around Jesus,
where we meet in love, sing with joy, pray in attachment,
live in openness, share bread and wine in celebration,
hear the Word and discern the way in mutual accountability,
following Christ in stubborn loyalty to him and to each other.
We join in the community of the Spirit,
where God constantly woos us with grace,
nudges us toward faith,

calls us to discipleship, draws us toward wholeness,
creates community, levels walls, leaps barriers,
offers power to love neighbor, enemy, and stranger.

Service is our vocation; caring is our calling.
We love the world, care for creation, live simply,
serve human need, offer concrete aid,
embody Christ's way in authentic witness,
welcome all into the circle around Jesus,
and constantly sing our faith as a way
of weaving communal bonds, giving voice to hope,
acclaiming the lordship of Jesus the Christ.

David Augsburger, 2005

Appendix Two

The Politics of Jesus

John Howard Yoder, one of the most influential voices in the twentieth century for a theology of faithful dissident discipleship, called for a radical return to the Jesus of the Gospels.

The reign of God is not an a-political spiritual concept, he argued, instead it is a life commanding, commitment demanding social and political reality that calls the believer/follower to reorder life, loyalties and ultimate allegiance in faithful obedience.

Here is a brief summary of his Anabaptist theology of revolutionary Christology, called "The Politics of Jesus":

Jesus of Nazareth, the prophet from Galilee
led the only truly new, original revolution
of justice and peace. His unprecedented life
offers a new possibility for human social and
political relationships.

In his life and teaching, Jesus:

- announced the reign of God,
- stood with the oppressed and the poor,
- cared for the needy and sick,
- refused coercive power,

- confronted the "powers" of political oppression,
- faced aggression with nonviolence, and
- revealed a God of steadfast, suffering love.

He is our exclusive and final model for the practices of service, justice, mercy, and peacemaking.

The Bible, the record of God's intention, intervention, and presence in our world, is interpreted through Jesus, who is the final word.

- Hebrew scriptures are read through the Hebrew prophets with their radical allegiance to God and their condemnation of social injustice, dominance, and empire building.
- Christian scriptures are read through the Gospel narratives with their call to radical obedience to Jesus as Lord.
- The whole is read through the self-giving nonviolent teaching, life, death, and resurrection of Jesus.

Jesus's revolutionary life is the definitive exemplar for Christian social and political ethics. No other source of moral guidance should set aside or negate the claims of Jesus, which we shall call POJ for "the politics of Jesus."

- POJ is grounded in a revolution of stubborn, steadfast love, fully convinced that Jesus's social and political stance of nonviolent, suffering love goes with the grain of the universe, indeed moves with the orbits and destinies of the galaxies, so nothing else can create just, merciful, human community.
- POJ confronts and engages the "powers" of human domination systems, commonly known as political structures, systems, and institutions, and calls them to act justly in distribution, retribution, and sustenance of community.
- POJ works to transform the inequalities of marriage, family, and community by noncoercive change from within the roles, undermining what is unequal, transforming what is unjust. In any society or time the follower of Jesus can be faithful to his radical call to servanthood.

- POJ is central to the claims of Jesus. Confessing that "Jesus is Lord" and denying that "Caesar is Lord" is radical obedience that distinguishes clearly between those who follow the way of Jesus and those who do not.
- POJ clarifies the basic distinction between the community of those who follow Jesus (the church), and those who follow Caesar in trusting in power, sword, and security through dominance (the world).
- POJ sees the state as part of God's ordering function in the world, but the church, not the state, as the center of God's purposes in history.
- POJ offers constructive social leadership and is constantly socially responsible, but not through the state and its domination functions as definer and censor, nor through the state's methods of managing society with coercive power.
- POJ leads through prophetic witness to the state (witness is the most powerful lateral influence), by invitation (invitation is the most powerful social communication), and by demonstrated embodiment in community (embodiment is undeniable witness, being and telling truth in the social order).
- POJ, in embodying dialogue and discernment, begins from the other's point of view, addresses issues in the other's categories, starts from the other side while steadfastly remaining true to its core commitments. It does not begin from its own "correct position" or its claims to moral high ground.
- POJ remains true to the moral claims of Jesus while fully engaging with a pluralistic social world, honestly respecting pluralism and its concomitant relativism but without compromising or modifying Jesus.
- POJ lives in unshakable hope in the God of history, in trust of this God's redemptive actions that transcend our best and most brilliant, heroic, sacrificial, or systematized social or political struggles and strategies, ultimately wagering all on the resurrection.

John Howard Yoder (1972), summary by David Augsburger

Appendix Three

The Sermon on the Mount for Peditation

Couplets for Peditation

Peditation is meditation and reflection while walking. Walking and following are Jesus's metaphors for discipleship. As a spiritual exercise, walk the Sermon on the Mount in meditation. Follow the rhythm of a couplet until you have thoroughly absorbed its meanings for you in your walk with Jesus as it speaks to the issues of this particular day. When you feel finished with each couplet, move on to the next. Do not skip couplets. Let the lines lead you back to the original words of the Sermon on the Mount for further study and the discovery of many alternate interpretations to the ones these couplets offer. (Walking rhythm: 1–2–3–4–5 rest-rest-rest 1–2–3–4–5 rest-rest-rest, etc.)

Matthew 5

5:3   Bless you, poor, down-trod.
Claim the reign of God.
(God sees things reversed.
The last will be first.)

5:4   Bless you, friends in grief.
        You shall find relief.
        (Now your sorrow's deep.
        You shall dance and leap.)
5:5   Bless you, meek. In truth,
        you'll inherit earth.
        (Meek folks scorned in mirth
        will possess the earth.)
5:6   Bless you, all who thirst
        for what's true and just.
        (Hunger for what's right,
        thirst for truth and light.)
5:7   Bless you, merciful,
        You'll be paid in full.
        (Mercy has this knack.
        Give, and you get back.)
5:8   Bless you, truly good,
        for you shall see God.
        (All those pure in heart,
        are God's work of art.)
5:9   Bless you, go-between.
        You're God's special kin.
        (Peacemakers, stand tall;
        you're God's children, all.)
5:10   Bless you, when reviled.
        You are heaven's child.
5:11   (Stand firm, resolute,
        when some persecute.)
5:12   Sufferer, do not fret.
        God will not forget.
        (Laugh at pain, dear folk,
        you have got the joke.)
5:13   You are the earth's salts.
        Cleanse and heal its faults.
        (Like dung spread on field,
        go increase the yield.)
5:14   When the world is black,
        be the light we lack.

5:15	Like a candle lit, do your humble bit.
5:16	Let the good you do point to God, not you.
5:17	Learn the wisdom of law transformed by love.
5:18	Heav'n and earth may fall; truth will outlast all.
5:19	Those who are great souls live above the rules.
5:20	Let your justice show God reigns here and now.
5:21	"Do not kill," law said, I say, "Don't wish dead."
5:22	Anger hurts the most those who are its host. (View none with contempt. No one is exempt.)
5:23	Come to worship riled? First be reconciled.
5:24	First make peace when miffed, then offer your gift.
5:25–26	Take no one to court. You'll lose your last cent.
5:27	Law says, "Do not stray." "Keep thoughts pure," I say.
5:28	Use no one in lust. Love is true and just.
5:29	Guard your heart and mind, more than eye or hand.
5:31–32	Law says, "Divorce well." I say, "Not at all."
5:33	Law says, "Keep your oath." I say, "Be the truth."
5:34	Do not swear an oath by heav'n, earth, or both,
5:35–36	Don't presume to swear. You can't change a hair.

5:37   Speak with truthfulness.
        Let your yes be yes.
5:38   "Eye for eye," law said.
        I say, "Love instead."
5:39   If you're struck don't speak;
        turn the other cheek.
5:40   Sued for coat you wear,
        give your shirt, go bare.
5:41   Though men treat you vile,
        Go the second mile.
5:42   Give the needy aid,
        though you're not repaid.
5:43   Law says, "Love your friend."
        I say, "Foe or fiend."
5:44   Show true charity
        to your enemy.
5:45   Pray when you're downtrod,
        be children of God.
        Sun and rain are signs,
        God's love draws no lines.
5:46   Love those who love you?
        Crooks and thugs do too.
5:47   Greet only your kind?
        What a narrow mind!
5:48   God our Drive and Lure
        draws us to mature.

Matthew 6

6:1   What you do for show
        gets God's sure veto.
6:2   Great and grand displays
        win just public praise.
6:3   Left from right hand hide;
        do not clap in pride.
6:4   For respect on high
        do good on the sly.
6:5   God loves secret prayers;
        all else put on airs.

6:6	In a private place
	claim the Father's grace.
6:7	Let your prayers be short;
	do not pray for sport.
6:8	Do not beg or plead;
	God knows what you need.
6:9	This is what to say
	as you daily pray:

Abba Father God,
bless your holy name.

6:10	Let your reign now come;
	let your will be done.
	Bring your peace to birth
	as in heav'n, so earth.
6:11–12	Give us bread daily;
	free us, as we free.
6:13	When the way is hard,
	be our guide and guard.
6:14	Forgive those in need;
	be forgiv'n indeed.
6:15	When we don't forgive,
	then God won't forgive.
6:16	Unless you can smile,
	fasting is futile.
6:17	Make no pious show;
	God alone should know.
6:18	Secret sacrifice?
	God will bless it twice.
6:19	Gold laid up on earth
	has no lasting worth.
6:20	Prize only virtues
	you can never lose.
6:21	Where your treasure hides,
	there your heart resides.
6:22	Open your soul wide;
	let light pour inside.
6:23	If your heart is dark,
	every part is dark.

6:24	God and gold conflict;
	two kings contradict.
6:25	Why obsess on stuff?
	Enough is enough.
6:26	Control is absurd;
	be free as a bird.
6:27	Fret and worry much?
	Can you grow an inch?
6:28	Stop, look, smell the flow'rs.
	Do not waste your hours.
6:29–30	Good fortune is ours;
	God clothes weeds with flow'rs.
6:31–32	You lack food and clothes?
	Wait, your Father knows.
6:33	First, God's reign possess;
	seek his righteousness.
6:34	Let tomorrow wait;
	keep days separate.

Matthew 7

7:1–2	Judge not those who lack.
	What you judge comes back.
7:3	Spite of beam, I note,
	you've a nasty mote!
7:4	Faults I hate in you
	show they're my fault too.
7:5	First, do own eye-check,
	then seek neighbor's speck.
7:6	Serve the Roman hogs?
	Sell your soul to dogs!
	(Their teeth tear and rend.
	You lose in the end.)
7:7–8	Prayer is strong, not weak.
	Knock and ask and seek.
7:9	Your child asks for bread;
	you give stone instead?
7:10	Your child asks for fish;
	you slip snake in dish?

7:11	As you love your child,
	God gives grace gone wild.
7:12	Do to everyone
	as you would be done.
7:13	Choose the narrow way
	or there's hell to pay.
7:14	When the way is hard,
	so few press onward.
	(God has done the math;
	few will find the path.)
7:15	Don't be made a fool
	by wolves wearing wool.
7:16	Beware priestly prigs;
	thorns do not grow figs.
7:17	Bad trees bear bad fruit;
	good give their good fruit.
7:18	Don't expect to see
	good fruit from bad tree.
7:19	Trees that are no good
	end as firewood.
7:20	Watch what leaders do;
	character's the clue.
7:21	Make no sweeping claim;
	simply join God's reign.
7:22	Many do great deeds
	that serve their own needs.
	("Lord, Lord," they may say,
	yet take their own way.)
7:23	Though you win great fame,
	will God know your name?
7:24	Listen, practice, act.
	Don't hear yet hold back.
7:25	A house built on rock
	withstands any shock.
7:26–27	Build your life on sand;
	it will never stand.

The Disciple's Prayer

Abba Father God,
Bless your holy name.
Let your reign now come,
Let your will be done.
Bring your peace to birth,
As in heav'n, so earth.
Give us bread, daily;
Free us, as we free.
When the way is hard,
Be our guide and guard.
Your rule, power, and praise
Reign supreme, always.

Appendix Four

The Jesus Prayer for Peditation

This disciple prayer is for a meditative walk called peditation. One's walk is a biblical metaphor for a spiritual and moral life encompassing the whole of one's daily experience. *Peditation* on the life of Christ is a meditative exercise that reviews the metastory, the foundational narrative of the disciple's life. You can reexperience the story of Jesus's life as you pray these couplets, matching the "feet of the line" to your feet, repeating each couplet at least three times in peditation, or as often as you need to to allow yourself to fully encounter that part of the gospel story. (Try walking to the rhythm of the couplet, as if singing a hymn with syllables of: 1–2–3–4–5 rest-rest-rest 1–2–3–4–5 rest-rest-rest, etc.)

	The Disciple Prayer
Imitation	Lord we seek love's depths;
(Discipleship)	Follow in your steps.
Incarnation	Be present, we pray,
(Embodiment)	Walk with us this day.
Youth	Lord may we be whole:
(Growth)	Heart, mind, body, soul.
Baptism	Like pure water poured,
(Commitment)	Fill my soul, O Lord.

Wilderness	Lord open my eyes
(Temptation)	to evil's disguise.
Preaching	Turn, my soul, draw near!
(Invitation)	God's new reign is here.
Compassion	Your compassion leads
(Caring)	us to human needs.
Prophecy	Let justice be done;
(Call to Justice)	Let mercy be shown.
Service	Teach us how to serve
(Action)	without self-reserve.
Communion	In all bread and wine,
(Covenanting)	O Lord, we are thine.
Gethsemane	When in crisis hours
(Crisis)	not my will but yours.
Persecution	May we facing hate
(Nonviolence)	not reciprocate.
Cross	Jesus when you died
(Sacrifice)	God was crucified.
Triumph	By your wrongful death,
(Transformation)	You transform our life.
Resurrection	When we thought you dead:
(Emmaus)	You came breaking bread.
Commission	We teach as we go.
("As you go")	The whole earth will know.
Pentecost	Beneath tongues of flame
(Presence)	We shout out your name.
Discipleship	Lord we seek love's depths:
(Following Christ)	Follow in your steps.

Appendix Five

Anabaptist Order of Communion

Balthasar Hubmaier, 1537

Balthazar Hubmaier (1480/85–1528) was an early Anabaptist leader. He was burned at the stake on March 10, 1528, in Vienna, Austria. This order of communion is the first truly tripolar liturgy for covenanting love of God, love of Christ, love of neighbor.

> Leader: Sisters and Brothers, I now announce, Jesus Christ is in our midst. In the presence of our Lord we gather to share bread and wine in celebration of his Holy Supper. Let us confess our need of his grace:
>
> People: **O God, loving Father to whom we return, we have sinned against heaven and against you. We are not worthy to be called your children, but speak the consoling word and we shall be healed.**
>
> Leader: May the eternal, merciful, and loving God have compassion on us and forgive all our sins.
>
> People: **Thanks be to God our loving Father who runs to welcome us and bids us come and join him at his table.**

Leader: Sisters and Brothers, before we take bread and cup, Will you join in the renewal of our covenant? If so, let each say:

People: (each says) **I WILL.** (all together say) **WE WILL.**

Leader: Do you will, in the power of the Spirit, to love God in and above all things, to serve, honor, and worship God alone, to hallow God's name, to subject your will to the divine will in life and death? If so, let each say:

People: (each says) **I WILL.** (all together say) **WE WILL.**

Leader: Do you will to love your neighbor, to serve one another in love, to offer your flesh and shed your blood for the other, doing this in the power of the Lord Jesus Christ, who also offered his flesh and shed his blood for us? If so, let each say:

People: (each says) **I WILL.** (all together say) **WE WILL.**

Leader: Do you will to foster peace and unity with your sisters and brothers, to reconcile yourself with all those whom you have offended, to renounce all envy, hatred, and ill will toward anyone, to love even your enemies and to do them good? If so, let each say:

People: (each says) **I WILL.** (all together say) **WE WILL.**

Leader: Do you desire, by eating and drinking the bread and wine of the supper of Christ, to confirm and attest publicly before the Church the pledge of love which you have just spoken in the living memory of the suffering and death of Jesus Christ our Lord? If so, let each say:

People: (each says) **I WILL.** (all together say) **WE WILL.**

Leader: The Lord Jesus, on the night he was arrested, took bread, gave thanks to God, broke it, and said, "This is my body broken for you. Take, eat, and think on me."

People: **Lord Jesus, we remember. You are in our midst.**

Leader: In the same way he took the cup and said, "This cup seals the new covenant with my blood. Drink and think on me."

Leader: **Lord Jesus, we remember. You are in our midst.**

All: (Pray together the prayer our Lord taught in the Sermon on the Mount.)

Translated and adapted by Marlin E. Miller

Appendix Six

The Discipleship Prayer

Lord Jesus Christ,
    Most gentle example,
    Most perfect model,
    Most patient guide,
    Most beautiful image,
    Faultless standard of faithfulness,
    Unspotted mirror of virtue,
    Sure plumb line of righteousness
Grant that I
    May so know you,
    So love you,
    So walk in your steps
    That you walk in mine.

Compassionate master,
Patient long-suffering Lord,
    Forgive my sins,
    Cover my faults,
    Cleanse my heart,
    Plant your humility,
    Pull up weeds of pride,
    Root out vengeance,
    Cultivate your love.

Jewel of highest virtue,
My honor, my treasure,
   Beautify my heart
   With your pure faith,
   With your holy devotion,
   With your living hope,
   With your fervent love,
   With your simple trust,
   With your childlike awe.

Oh perfect Image of God,
   Renew me after your likeness
      Until I am complete.
   May your virtuous life
      Be also my life.
   May your noble soul
      Be also within me.
   May I be one spirit with you
      That I may live in you.
   May you, not I, live in me.

You, Eternal Way, lead me!
You, Eternal Truth, teach me!
You, Eternal Life, enliven me!

If you are my light,
   Then shine in me.
If you are my life,
   Then live in me.
If you are my joy,
   Then rejoice in me.
If I am your dwelling place,
   Then take possession of me.
If I am your instrument,
   Then make me wholly holy.
If you are my jewel,
   Then adorn me with your beauty.

Let me be crucified with you,
   That I may stand with you.
Let me die to the world,
   That I may live unto you.

> Let me rise with you,
>> That I may join you in heaven.
> Let me enter your glory,
>> That I may dwell with you.

Die Ernsthafte Christenpflict, (1708/1994) translated from
German and set in verse by David Augsburger

Bibliography

Ahlgrim, Ryan. 1995. "Laughing our Way to Humility." *Gospel Herald* 88 (10): 1–3.

Arnett, Ron. 1986. *Communication and Community: Implications of Martin Buber's Dialogue.* Carbondale: Southern Illinois University Press.

Barringer, Terry. 2004. "Vocation in a Post-vocational World." In *The Bible and the Business of Life*, ed. Simon Holt and Gordon Preece. Adelaide, Australia: ATF Press.

Bauman, Clarence, ed. and trans. 1991. *The Spiritual Legacy of Hans Denck.* New York: E. J. Brill.

Bellah, Robert, et al. 1985. *Habits of the Heart: Individualism and Commitment in American Life.* Berkley: University of California Press.

Bergson, Henri. 1911. *Laughter: An Essay on the Meaning of the Comic.* London: Macmillan.

Berry, Wendell. 2000. *Jayber Crow.* New York: Counterpoint.

Bierce, Ambrose. 1987. *The Devil's Advocate: An Ambrose Bierce Reader.* San Francisco: Chronicle.

Bonhoeffer, Dietrich. 1952. *Life Together.* New York: Harper and Row.

———. 1955. *Ethics.* London: SCM Press.

———. 1963. *The Cost of Discipleship.* New York: Macmillan.

Bregman, Lucy. 2004. "Defining Spirituality: Multiple Uses and Murky Meanings." *Journal of Pastoral Care and Counseling.* Fall, vol. 58, no. 3.

Brueggemann, Walter. 1995. *The Psalms and the Life of Faith.* Minneapolis: Fortress.

Buber, Martin. 1965. *Between Man and Man.* New York: Macmillan.

Buechner, Frederick. 1973. *Wishful Thinking.* New York: Harper and Row.

Burkholder, J. Lawrence. 1993. "Autobiographical Reflections." In *The Limits of Perfection*, ed. Rodney J. Sawatsky and Scott Holland. Kitchener, ON: Pandora Press.

Burkholder, John Richard. 2000. "Leitourgia Beyond Altar and Sacrifice." In *Anabaptists and Postmodernity*, ed. Susan Biesecker-Mast, et al. Scottdale, PA: Herald Press.

Burrows, Ruth. 1981. *Before the Living God.* Denville, NJ: Dimension Books.

Butigan, Ken. 2002. *From Violence to Wholeness.* Las Vegas: Pace e Bene.

Campbell, Will. 1967. *Brother to a Dragonfly.* New York: Continuum.

———. 1988. Foreword to *Into the Darkness: Discipleship in the Sermon on the Mount*, by Gene L. Davenport. Nashville: Abingdon.

Castells, Manuel. 2000. *Information Age: The Network Society.* Oxford: Blackwell.

Clapp, Rodney. 1998. *The Consuming Passion: Christianity and the Consumer Culture.* Downers Grove, IL: InterVarsity Press.

———. 2004. *Tortured Wonders.* Grand Rapids: Brazos.

Claypool, John R. 1983. *Opening Blind Eyes.* Nashville: Abingdon.

Cone, James. 1975. *God of the Oppressed.* New York: Seabury.

Cox, Harvey. 1978. *The Secular City.* New York: Macmillan.

Davenport, Gene L. 1989. *Into the Darkness.* Nashville, Abingdon.

Dear, John. 1987. *Disarming the Heart.* Mahwah, NJ: Paulist Press.

———. 1990. *Our God Is Nonviolent.* New York: Pilgrim.

De Wolf, L. Harold. 1971. *Responsible Freedom.* New York: Harper and Row.

Dodd, C. H. 1958. *About the Gospels.* Cambridge: Cambridge University Press.

Douglass, James W. 1991. *The Nonviolent Coming of God.* Maryknoll, NY: Orbis.

Drane, John. 2004. "Community, Mystery and the Future of the Church." In *The Bible and the Business of Life,* ed. Simon Holt and Gordon Preece. Adelaide, Australia: ATF Press.

Dueck, Alvin. 2002. Installation Address, Fuller Theological Seminary, Pasadena, CA.

Duke, David N. 1983. "Christians, Enemies and Nuclear Weapons." *Christian Century* (Nov. 2), 986–89.

Dyck, Cornelius J. 1996. *Spiritual Life in Anabaptism.* Scottdale, PA: Herald Press.

Dyck, Peter J. 1968. "When Is Service Christian?" Akron, PA: MCC News Service, May 24.

Erasmus. 1518/1941. *The Praise of Folly,* trans. Hoyt Hopewell Hudson. Princeton: Princeton University Press.

Erb, Peter. 2000. "Anabaptist Spirituality." In *Protestant Spiritual Traditions,* ed. Frank C. Senn. Eugene, OR: Wipf and Stock.

Fodor, Jim. 2000. "Christian Discipleship as Participative Imitation." In William Swartley, *Violence Renounced.* Scottdale, PA: Herald Press.

Gandhi, Mohandas K. 1944. *Non-Violence in Peace and War.* Ahmedabad, India: Navajevan Press.

———. 1986. *Seeds of Peace: A Catalogue of Quotations,* comp. Jeanne Larson and Madge Micheels-Cyrus. Philadelphia: New Society Publishers.

George, Timothy. 1988. "Early Anabaptist Spirituality in the Low Countries." *Mennonite Quarterly Review* 62, no. 3: 257–75.

Gilkey, Langdon. 1966. *Shantung Compound.* New York: Harper and Row.

Gill, Athol. 1989. *Life on the Road: The Gospel Basis for a Messianic Lifestyle.* Homebush West, Australia: Anzea Publishers.

Goertz, Hans-Jurgen. 1971. *Die Mennoniten.* Stuttgart: Evangelisches Verlagswerk.

Häring, Bernhard. 1970. *A Theology of Protest.* New York: Farrar, Straus & Giroux.

———. 1986. *The Healing Power of Peace and Nonviolence.* New York: Paulist Press.

Hauerwas, Stanley. 1992. *Against the Nations: War and Survival in a Liberal Society.* Notre Dame, IN: University of Notre Dame Press.

Hauerwas, Stanley, and William H. Willimon. 1989. *Resident Aliens.* Nashville: Abingdon.

Hershberger, Michele. 1999. *A Christian View of Spirituality: Expecting Surprise.* Scottdale, PA: Herald Press.

Hoekendijk, J. C. 1964. *The Church Inside Out*, trans. Isaac C. Rottenberg. Philadelphia: Westminster.

Homer. 1962. *Iliad*, trans. Richard Lattimore. Chicago: University of Chicago Press.

Huebner, Harry, and David Schroeder. 1993. *The Church as Parable.* Winnepeg: CMBC Publications.

Inge, William Ralph. 1899. *Christian Mysticism.* New York: Scribner's.

Jones, E. Stanley. 1972. *The Unshakable Kingdom.* Nashville: Abingdon.

Jordan, Clarence. 1952. *Sermon on the Mount.* Valley Forge, PA: Judson.

———. 1972. *The Substance of Faith and Other Cotton Patch Sermons*, ed. Dallas Lee. New York: Association Press.

Kaplan, Robert D. 1994. "The Coming Anarchy." *Atlantic Monthly* 273, no. 2: 44–76.

Kavanaugh, John. 1992. *Following Christ in a Consumer Society.* Maryknoll, NY: Orbis.

Kegan, Robert. 1982. *The Evolving Self: Problem and Process in Human Development.* Cambridge, MA: Harvard University Press.

Kemper, Vickie, and Larry Engle. 1994. "Dom Helder Camara: Hope against Hope." In *Cloud of Witnesses*, ed. Jim Wallis and Joyce Hollyday. Maryknoll, NY: Orbis.

Kierkegaard, Søren. 1938/1951. *The Journals of Søren Kierke-gaard.* Princeton, NJ: Princeton University Press.

———. 1962. *Works of Love.* New York: Harper and Row.

Kilpatrick, Lee A. 1998. "God as a Substitute Attachment Figure: A Longitudinal Study of Adult Attachment Style and Religious Change in College Students." *Personality and Social Psychology Bulletin* 24:961–73.

King, Martin Luther, Jr., 1963. *Strength to Love.* New York: Harper and Row.

Koontz, Ted, ed. 1996. *Godward: Personal Stories of Grace.* Scottdale, PA: Herald Press.

Kraus, C. Norman. 1975. *The Community of the Spirit.* Grand Rapids: Eerdmans.

———. 1979. *The Authentic Witness.* Grand Rapids: Eerdmans.

———. 1987. *Jesus Christ Our Lord.* Scottdale, PA: Herald Press.

———. 1994. *God Our Savior.* Scottdale, PA: Herald Press.

Kraybill, Donald. 1978/1990. *The Upside-Down Kingdom.* Scottdale, PA: Herald Press.

———. 1989. *The Riddle of Amish Culture.* Baltimore: Johns Hopkins University Press.

Legge, James, trans. 1861. *Confucian Analects.* Vol. 1 of *The Chinese Classics.* London: Trübner.

———. 1861. *Works of Mencius.* Vol. 2 of *The Chinese Classics.* London: Trübner.

L'Engle, Madeleine. 1972. *The Circle of Quiet.* San Francisco: Harper and Row.

Lewis, C. S. 1946. *The Great Divorce.* New York: Collier.

———. 1960. *The Four Loves.* London: Geoffrey Bles.

MacIntyre, Alasdair. 1981. *After Virtue.* Notre Dame, IN: University of Notre Dame Press.

Marcel, Gabriel. 1949a. *Being and Having.* Paris: Dacre Press.

———. 1949b. *The Philosophy of Existence.* New York: Philosophical Library.

McClendon, James William. 1986. *Systematic Theology.* Vol. 1: *Ethics.* Nashville: Abingdon.

McGinn, Bernard, and John Meyendorff, eds. 1986. *Christian Spirituality: Origins to the Twelfth Century.* World Spirituality 16. London: Routledge & Kegan Paul.

McGinnis, Daniel, ed. 1984. *For Swords into Plowshares, the Hammer Has to Fall.* Piscataway, NJ: Plowshares Press.

McIntosh, Mark A. 1998. *Mystical Theology.* Malden, MA: Blackwell.

McLaren, Brian. 2004. "A Radical Rethinking of Our Evangelistic Strategy." *Theology News and Notes* (Fall), Fuller Seminary, Pasadena, CA.

Metzler, James. 1985. *From Saigon to Shalom.* Scottdale, PA: Herald.

Milbank, John. 1990. *Theology and Social Theory.* Oxford: Basil Blackwell.

———. 1999. *Radical Orthodoxy: A New Theology.* London: Routledge.

Moltmann, Jürgen. 1973. *The Crucified God.* London: SCM Press.

———. 1997. *The Source of Life: The Holy Spirit and the Theology of Life.* Minneapolis: Fortress.

Morreall, John. 1983. *Taking Laughter Seriously.* Albany: State University of New York.

Myers, Ched. 1994. *Who Will Roll Away the Stone.* Maryknoll, NY: Orbis.

Niebuhr, Reinhold. 1969. *Essays on Religion in the Comic Perspective.* New York: Seabury.

Nietzsche, Friedrich. 1911. *The Twilight of the Idols.* Vol. 16 of *The Complete Works of Friedrich Nietzsche*, ed. Oscar Levy. New York: Gordon Press, 1974.

Nouwen, Henri. 1994. *Here and Now, Living in the Spirit.* New York: Crossroads.

Origen of Alexandria. 1953. *Contra Celsum*, trans. Henry Chadwick. Cambridge: Cambridge University Press.

Palmer, Parker. 1977. *A Place Called Community.* Philadelphia: Pendle Hill.

Peachey, Titus, and Linda Gehman Peachey. 1984. *Seeking Peace.* Intercourse, PA: Good Books.

Pokrifka-Joe, Todd. 2001. "May God Forgive?" In Alistair Mcfadyen and Marcel Sarot. *Forgiveness and Truth*. New York: T & T Clark.

Raines, John, et al. 1986. *Modern Work and Human Meaning*. Philadelphia: Westminster.

Richards, Norvin. 1992. *Humility*. Philadelphia: Temple University Press.

Roth, Jonathan. 2002. *Choosing against War*. Intercourse, PA: Good Books.

Sayers, Dorothy L. 1946. *Unpopular Opinions*. London: Victor Gollancz.

Schipani, Daniel, and Anton Wessels, eds. 2002. *The Promise of Hope*. Elkhart, IN: Institute of Mennonite Studies.

Schore, Allan H. 1994. *Affect Regulation and the Origin of the Self*. Hillsdale, NJ: Laurence Erlbaum.

Shank, David A. 1969. *Who Will Answer?* Scottdale, PA: Herald.

Sheldon, Charles M. 1993. *In His Steps*. New York: Revell.

Shenk, Calvin. 1983. *A Relevant Theology of Presence*. Valley Center, CA: MBM Books.

Sider, Ronald J. 1999. *Living Like Jesus*. Grand Rapids: Baker.

Snyder, Arnold. 1995. *Anabaptist History and Theology*. Kitchener, ON: Pandora Press.

Spohn, William. 2000. *Go and Do Likewise*. New York: Continuum.

Stringfellow, William. 1964. *My People Is the Enemy*. New York: Holt, Rinehart & Winston.

———. 1976. *Instead of Jesus*. New York: Seabury.

———. 1984. *The Politics of Spirituality*. Philadelphia: Westminster.

Swartley, Willard, ed. 2000. *Violence Renounced: René Girard, Biblical Studies, and Peacemaking*. Scottdale, PA: Herald.

Taylor, John V. 1963. *The Primal Vision*. New York: Oxford University Press.

Thurber, Jon. 2004. "D-Day Troop's Chaplain." *Los Angeles Times* (Sunday, December 26).

Tinsley, E. J. 1960. *The Imitation of God in Christ*. Philadelphia: Westminster.

Tolstoy, Leo. 1967. "Church and State." In *Tolstoy's Writings on Civil Disobedience and Nonviolence*. New York: Bergman.

Trueblood, D. Elton. 1964. *The Humor of Christ*. New York: Harper.

Vaage, Leif E. 1997. *Subversive Scriptures*. Valley Forge, PA: Trinity.

Van Braght, Thieleman. 1660/1985. *The Martyr's Mirror: The Story of Seventeen Centuries of Christian Martyrdom*. Scottdale, PA: Herald.

Volf, Miroslav, and Dorothy C. Bass, eds. 2002. *Practicing Theology: Beliefs and Practices in Christian Life*. Grand Rapids: Eerdmans.

Wallis, Jim. 1976. *Agenda for a Biblical People*. New York: Harper and Row.

———. 1981. *The Call to Conversion*. San Francisco: Harper and Row.

———. 1994. *The Soul of Politics*. New York: The New Press/Orbis.

———. 1996. *Who Speaks for God?* New York: Delacorte.

Wallis, Jim, and Joyce Hollyday, eds. 1994. *Cloud of Witnesses*. Maryknoll, NY: Orbis.

Warren, Michael. 1992. "Imitating Jesus in a Time of Imitation." In *Schooling Christians: "Holy Experiments" in American Education*, ed. Stanley Hauerwas and John M. Westerhoff. Grand Rapids: Eerdmans.

Weil, Simone. 1959. *Waiting on God*. London: Fontana.

Wenger, John C., trans. 1956. *The Complete Writings of Menno Simons*. Scottdale, PA: Herald.

Wengst, Klaus. 1988. *Humility: Solidarity of the Humiliated*. Philadelphia: Fortress.

Willeford, William. 1969. *The Fool and His Scepter: A Study in Clowns and Jesters and Their Audience*. Evanston, IL: Northwestern University Press.

Williams, Harry Abbott. 1979. *The Joy of God*. Springfield, IL: Templegate Publishing.

———. 1982. *Tensions*. Springfield, IL: Templegate Publishing.

Williams, Linda K. 2002. "On Earth Peace." Available at www.brethren.org/oepa.

Williamson, George. 1986. "Religion and the Second Crisis." In *Communities of Faith and Radical Discipleship*, ed. G. McLeod Bryan. Macon, GA: Mercer University Press.

Wink, Walter. 1992. *Engaging the Powers: Discernment and Resistance in a World of Domination*. Minneapolis: Fortress.

Yalom, Irving. 1989. *Love's Executioner*. New York: Basic Books.

Yoder, John H. 1960. "Jesus Is Lord—Its Meaning for the Disciple." Address given at intercollegiate peace conference, Goshen College, Goshen, Indiana, April 1960 (author's notes).

———. 1971a. *Nevertheless: Varieties of Christian Pacifism*. Scottdale, PA: Herald.

———. 1971b. *The Original Revolution*. Scottdale, PA: Herald.

———. 1971c. "Sendung und Auftrag der Gemeinde." In *Die Mennoniten*, ed. Hans-Jürgen Goertz. Stuttgart: Evangelisches Verlagswerk.

———. 1972. *The Politics of Jesus: Vicit Agnus Noster*. Grand Rapids: Eerdmans.

———. 1994. *The Royal Priesthood*. Grand Rapids: Eerdmans.